# COMPETENCE

# COMPETENCE
## Theoretical Frameworks

## Roberta R. Greene
## and Nancy P. Kropf

Routledge
Taylor & Francis Group

LONDON AND NEW YORK

First published 2011 by Transaction Publishers

2 Park Square, Milton Park, Abingdon, Oxfordshire OX14 4RN
711 Third Avenue, New York, NY 10017

*Routledge is an imprint of the Taylor & Francis Group, an informa business*

First issued in paperback 2017

Copyright © 2011 Taylor & Francis

Library of Congress Catalog Number: 2011003511

Library of Congress Cataloging-in-Publication Data

Greene, Roberta R. (Roberta Rubin), 1940-
    Competence : theoretical frameworks / Roberta R. Greene and Nancy P. Kropf.
      p. cm.
  ISBN 978-1-4128-4212-9
  1. Performance. 2. Social service. 3. Social work with older people.
I. Kropf, Nancy P. II. Title.
  HV40.G744 2011
  361.3—dc22
                    2011003511

ISBN 13: 978-1-4128-4212-9 (hbk)
ISBN 13: 978-1-138-50835-4 (pbk)

# Contents

# List of Tables and Figures

# 1

# Social Work's Mission: Fostering Competence

*The purpose of the social work profession is to promote human and community well-being. Guided by a person and environment construct, a global perspective, respect for human diversity, and knowledge based on scientific inquiry, social work's purpose is actualized through its quest for social and economic justice, the prevention of conditions that limit human rights, the elimination of poverty, and the enhancement of the quality of life for all persons.*
*—Council on Social Work Education (2008, 1)*

This text focuses on the lifelong process of achieving competence in social functioning as an individual and in families, groups, and communities. The chapters address theories relevant to select life course transitions and to the concept of person-in-environment. They apply the competency-based approach to social work education recently adopted by Council on Social Work Education (CSWE). Each chapter in this text addresses various practice behaviors that will help guide students in understanding how content contributes to their knowledge and skills for effective social work practice. In addition, Appendix A provides a summary of various practice behaviors that are associated with each chapter of the book. In this way, students will have a summary of how the various theories fit with the knowledge and skills of social work practice.

## Competency-Based Education

*Social work is a profession devoted to helping people function as well as they can within their social environments and to changing their environments to make that possible.... In order to be a responsible professional, the social worker must understand and function within the professions' accepted area of expertise.*
*— Sheafor and Horejsi (2008, 1)*

## Ten Core Social Work Competencies

Competency-based education "is an outcome performance approach to curriculum design" (CSWE 2008, 3). In this approach, you are expected to demonstrate upon graduation that you have mastered the following ten core competencies expressed as "measurable practice behaviors that are comprised of knowledge, values, and skills" (3):

Educational Policy 2.1.1—Identify as a professional social worker and conduct oneself accordingly.

Educational Policy 2.1.2—Apply social work ethical principles to guide professional practice.

Educational Policy 2.1.3—Apply critical thinking to inform and communicate professional judgments.

Educational Policy 2.1.4—Engage diversity and difference in practice.

Educational Policy 2.1.5—Advance human rights and social and economic justice.

Educational Policy 2.1.6—Engage in research-informed practice and practice-informed research.

Educational Policy 2.1.7—Apply knowledge of human behavior and the social environment.

Educational Policy 2.1.8—Engage in policy practice to advance social and economic well-being and to deliver effective social work services.

Educational Policy 2.1.9—Respond to contexts that shape practice.

Educational Policy 2.1.10(a)–(d)—Engage, assess, intervene, and evaluate with individuals, families, groups, organizations, and communities.

## Human Behavior and the Social Environment

Although this text discusses all ten of these curriculum competencies, it emphasizes those related to human behavior in the social environment. In that arena, social workers are expected to be "knowledgeable about human behavior across the life course; the range of social systems in which people live; and the ways social systems promote or deter people in maintaining or achieving health and well-being" (CSWE 2008, 6).

Human behavior theory is an integral part of the multifaceted social work curriculum. It attempts to explain people's actions and enables practitioners and their clients to make sense of and more readily assess and resolve difficult situations. The purpose of this text is to provide future social workers with such practice-enhancing theory (Greene 2008b; Longres 2000; Schriver 2003).

*Competent Human Functioning*

At the core of every human behavior theory is an explanation of how people can be helped to function better in society and what needs to be done to remediate their difficulties. That is, what makes people more competent, better functioning individuals at any time in their life course? This text explores the concept of *competence* and how it is expressed in various theoretical frameworks, including traditional models and emerging theoretical approaches. It brings a strengths perspective to viewing the social worker's professional role.

The various theories presented and discussed in this text provide different definitions of competence. For example, a practitioner taking a cognitive approach might relate competence to processes and structures that help resolve cognitive dissonance, whereas a practitioner concerned with community organization would emphasize supporting community efficacy. Thus, practitioners' underlying theories and intervention strategies flow from clients' strengths and resources; both help clients perceive choices (Saleebey 2008).

To demonstrate that you have mastered course content, you should be able to answer the following questions:

1. What do various theorists believe is competent human functioning? What are the norms of social functioning in a given person's historical time and place? What are the theorist's views of "the person" and "the environment"?
2. What does the theorist say supports, enhances, and promotes client (systems) competence?
3. What interventions follow from this line of reasoning?

*Text Outcomes*

This book examines the concept of competence from a variety of theoretical perspectives. Upon completion of the course, you should be able to assess client competence from several perspectives and within multiple systems, including individuals, families, groups, and communities. Thus, you will be able to examine how these theories factor into assessment and practice protocols.

Each chapter presents theoretical content, provides a critique from a multicultural perspective, and applies the theory in question to a case situation. In addition, reflection questions are included at the conclusion of each chapter for analysis and discussion of the content and issues present. Chapter 2 emphasizes attachment theory, focusing on how the caregiver–infant bond and Erikson's concept of trust establishes the foundation for positive adult functioning. Chapter 3 uses Eriksonian theory to explore autonomy, initiative, and identity formation as components of a competent self. In addition, it presents contemporary research on identity formation to critique Erikson's earlier work.

Chapter 4 describes the various social systems in which people interact, including the family and the workplace. It explores various forms of families and uses systems theory to examine the basis for the functionality of systems. The concept of crisis competence is also explored. Chapter 4 takes a humanistic and postmodern stance to competence formation. It presents the concept of meaning-making that is used as a prism to discover personal affirmation. It also discusses how competence is viewed through the lens of local cultures and interaction.

Chapter 5 presents theories that deal with meaning-making involving self-affirmation and transcendence. Chapter 6 uses cognitive–behavioral theory to explore what constitutes competent behavior that involves the ability to problem solve and to assess one's own reality. In Chapter 7, Lazarus and Folkman's concept of environmental press is used to explore older adults' functional capacity and their ability to live independently in the community. This is contrasted with relational points of view that examine cultures that emphasize interdependent living.

Chapter 8 looks at the small group as a system for interaction and growth. It examines various theoretical perspectives on group development and functioning. Concepts related to group dynamics, such as boundaries, leadership, and interactions, are highlighted. In addition, outcomes of group interactions, including social support for members and goal completion for formal groups, are described.

Chapter 9 focuses on the social environment as the context in which individuals and families function. The concept of collective efficacy describes the leadership and engagement of community members in their environment, including leadership positions and effective governance structures. In addition, Bandura's (1977) concept of self-efficacy is applied to larger systems to discuss how aspects of collective efficacy, such as citizen participation and neighborhood identification, can promote competence. Chapter 10 provides tools for evaluating and assessing the competence of individuals, families, groups, neighborhoods, and societies. It also discusses evaluation of effectiveness of social work practice.

Upon completing the text, you should be able to assess client (system) competence (Educational Policy 2.1.10b), use the various theoretical frameworks discussed (2.1.7), describe the issue(s) at hand, infer possible solutions (2.1.10c), and evaluate the effectiveness of a proposed solution (2.1.10d). You should also be able to

> critique theoretical concepts for their congruence with social work values (2.1.2);
>
> use scientific thought related to the concept's empirical effectiveness (2.1.6);
>
> understand adaptive behaviors across the life course (2.1.7);
>
> give attention to differences in clients' sociocultural and historical contexts (2.1.7);
>
> distinguish cultural differences in the expression of competence (2.1.4);
>
> assess individual coping styles (2.1.7);
>
> distinguish people's ability to function competently in a variety of roles and settings (2.1.7);
>
> apply the concept of competence to multi-systemic practice with individuals, families, groups, organizations, and communities (2.1.10); and
>
> arrive at culturally sensitive solutions for client system(s) (2.1.4).

## Social Work Practice: A Working Definition

*Not since more than half a century ago have the political, economic, cultural, and ideological views of the time so dramatically affected how social work practice is defined. While theorists are revisiting debates about how to conceptualize the social work curriculum, social workers are wrestling with how to reformulate theory, practice, and research.*

*—Greene (2005, 38)*

### The Legacy of Freud and Adler

Although there are no specific, precise boundaries to the social work domain, certain landmarks can be identified. Social work practice began at the community level with an interest in both individual enhancement and social reform. Early social work interventions were based on the ideas of pioneer-friendly visitors, such as Mary Richmond and Bertha Reynolds, as well as pragmatic university-based sociologists who dealt with everyday struggles related to adequacy of resources and psychosocial needs.

Starting in the early 1900s social work education had moved to the university, and methods texts placed a heavy emphasis on Freudian theory. Its theoretical assumptions about what helps people function well were translated into practice methods, and many became part of the profession's legacy about how to conduct the helping process (Greene 2008b).

For example, Sigmund Freud, considered by many to be the father of mental health treatment, was the first to suggest in his *The Psychopathology of Everyday Life* that people engage in "faulty acts" and "faulty functions." He argued that some "slips of the tongue" that we now refer to as Freudian slips and symptoms of forgetfulness may be found in healthy people who otherwise have sufficient control of unconscious conflicting emotions. However, those people who cannot control their conflicting emotions and experience neurotic symptoms were seen as benefiting from a therapist's interpretation of their unconscious impulses. Thus, Freud gave birth to the idea that there is an antagonism between civilization (society) and an individual's instinctual forces (Freud 1930). He thought that people who displayed maladaptive behaviors could become better functioning individuals if they received treatment based on *interpretation*, or making explicit what the client is feeling but of which he or she is not yet aware.

Social work practice texts continue to teach that reflecting client feelings is a means of enhancing client self-awareness and thereby leading to better functioning (Compton, Galaway, and Cournoyer 2004; Kadushin and Kadushin 1997). Interpreting feelings that are beyond clients' conscious recognition—a technique used by social workers who adopt ego psychology and cognitive therapies—is often recommended as an intervention so that "people can genuinely learn about themselves" (Boyle et al. 2006, 35; see also Chapter 6). In sum, Freud's ideas about the helping process as a process unique to each individual have shaped the interviewing process.

Freud's contemporary Alfred Adler (1927), considered to be the founder of individual psychology, differed with him about therapeutic principles. In contrast to Freud, he related mental health processes to social transactions. Adler argued that behavior had a conscious purpose as well as a social context that had the potential to be modified through one's experience. He also believed that people strive to achieve significance, to have a unique identity, and to belong. These goals have been called *self-actualization*, *self-expansion*, and *competence* (Lynn and Garske 1985). Thus, theorists such as Adler had an optimistic view of people and about their capacity to change their lives by proactively acting on the environment.

## A Consensus: Person and Environment

Although definitions of competence vary depending on the theoretical orientation of the author, theories adopted for social work practice fall under the rubric of the *ecological perspective* or *person–environment approach* (these terms are used interchangeably here). Although there has been some debate about the efficacy of the ecological perspective as the overarching social work framework (Wakefield 1996), it has nonetheless been a "continuing thread in the historical development of social work" (Gitterman and Germain 2008, 97).

In fact, "interest in the complementarity between person and environment, as embodied in the concepts embraced by the ecological perspective, is, perhaps *the* distinguishing characteristics of contemporary social work practice" (Greene 2008b, 199, emphasis in the original). This perspective has solidified social work's mission, established a conceptual reference point, and delineated the social worker's role in effecting the best adaptation between person and environment (Greene 2008b).

A turning point in the unity of the profession was marked by a CSWE-sponsored curriculum study conducted by Boehm in 1959. This study produced a working definition of social work as a profession concerned with the restoration, maintenance, and enhancement of social functioning (Greene 2005).

About the same time as the Boehm study, the National Association of Social Workers Commission on Practice developed a working definition of *social work* that remains in effect to this day:

> Through the relationship the practitioner facilitates interaction between the individual and his social environment with a continuing awareness of the reciprocal effects of one upon the other. It [the relationship] facilitates change: (1) within the individual in relation to the social environment; (2) of the social environment in its effect upon the individual; (3) of both the individual and the social environment in their interaction. (National Association of Social Workers Commission on Practice, 1958, as cited in Bartlett 1958, 7)

## Person–Environment: Conceptual Point of Reference

*The eco-systems perspective [was] partially in response to ... a half-century long pursuit of a single holistic framework to support social work practice theory. Given the proliferation of disparate treatment models, this unifying idea seems vital for the future coherence of practice in social work.*

—*Meyer (1983, 410)*

The ecological perspective is an approach to examining human behavior that studies the progressive, mutual accommodation between an active growing human being and his or her environment throughout the life course (Bronfenbrenner 1979). It is a multi-theoretical approach without precise boundaries that combines growth-inducing concepts from many different disciplines, including ecology, ethology, stress theory, the Gestalt school of psychology, role theory, anthropology, symbolic interaction theory, general systems theory, and the dynamics of power relationships (see Greene 2008a, for an in-depth discussion).

Moreover, the premises of the ecological perspective serve as a roadmap for organizing the social work knowledge base, describing its philosophical approach, and acting as a "metaphor to guide social work practice" (Gitterman and Germain 2008, 97). Because the profession has such a broad scope of practice, practitioners choose from among the many theories and practice models that fall under the rubric of the person–environment perspective, such as ego psychology, feminist theory, and humanistic psychology (Collins, 1986; Goldstein, 1984; Rogers, 1980).

### Terms and Assumptions

To better understand the theories presented in the text, one needs to consider several terms and assumptions about this person–environment approach. The approach considers the person and environment to be a unitary system in which both are inseparable (Germain 1991). This means that person and situation mutually influence each other; they cannot be dichotomized but must be considered one. "Interest is not in the additive effects of person plus environment, but their interactive, cumulative effects" (Greene 2008a, 207).

The focus of attention is the *transactions* or reciprocal person–environment exchanges (Greene and Watkins 1998). This implies that the social worker can address any difficulties in the client's life space. Thus, the focus is on *process* or what happens across person–environment encounters over time. The practitioner assesses the *goodness of fit* between the person and his or her environment to account for the quality of these encounters, or the match between the person's adaptive needs and the qualities of his or her environment. Do environmental forces support or undermine personal development? Does the individual have a positive or negative effect on the environment? The ultimate goal of intervention is to improve goodness of fit in the person–environment configuration. Consequently, the person–environment focus has allowed social workers to intervene effectively "no matter what their different theoretical orientations and specializations and regardless of where or with what client group they practice" (Meyer 1983, 409).

The person–environment perspective demands that social workers give attention to diversity and context-specific behaviors. Therefore, it is congruent with expectations that social workers be sensitive to

> factors including age, class, color, culture, disability, ethnicity, gender, gender identity and expression, immigration status, political ideology, race, religion, sex, and sexual orientation. Social workers [also] appreciate that, as a consequence of difference, a person's life experiences may include oppression, poverty, marginalization, and alienation as well as privilege, power, and acclaim. (CSWE 2008, 4)

Furthermore, the person–environment perspective is a multilevel model of human development (see Figure 1.1). This multisystemic approach allows practitioners to work with small-scale *microsystems*, such as families and peer groups; the connection between *mesosystems*, such as the family and health care systems; *exosystems*, or systems that do not directly involve the person, such as Social Security and Medicare; and *macrosystems*, or overarching large-scale systems, such as legal, political, and value systems. This suggests the importance of social supports and institutions encompassing friends, family, neighborhoods, communities, networks, workplaces, recreational sites, religious institutions, and political and economic institutions (Greene and Watkins 1998).

Ecological theorists are primarily interested in *competence*, or the ability to be effective in one's environment. From a person–environment perspective, a social work practitioner's major concern

### Figure 1.1 Bronfenbrenner's Model of the Ecology of Human Development

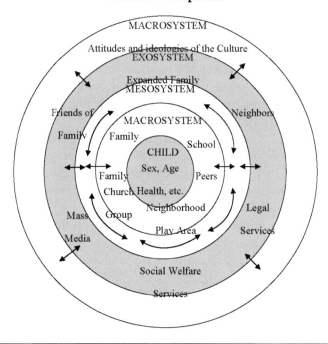

*Source:* Adapted from Bronfenbrenner (1979).

is to ameliorate the negative life experiences that impair social functioning at any time across the life course (Greene 2008a). To achieve this, practitioners need to understand how people develop competence. The most current CSWE educational policy statement underscores that the profession's primary mission, purpose, and focus is to improve societal conditions and to enhance the social functioning of and between individuals, families, groups, communities, and society. This principal purpose of achieving individual and collective well-being is guided by the *person–environment* construct (CSWE 2008).

## The Social Worker's Professional Role

*Social workers strive to enhance person-environment fit by fostering the well-being of individuals, families, groups, organizations, and*

> *communities. They facilitate organizational and societal change in the interest of social and economic justice.*
>
> —*Greene (2005, 54)*

Given the working definition of social work, the practitioner's professional role—improving societal conditions and enhancing the social functioning of individuals, families, and groups—can be more clearly delineated. That is, the profession can rally around the idea that all social work method is grounded in a common paradigm: to intervene effectively in the person–environment configuration (Greene 2005).

## Social Workers and Clients as Agents of Change

A process of social change is set in motion when there is a poor fit between a person and his or her environment. The desired change is agreed upon by the social worker together with the client, and strategies may be directed at personal characteristics of the client, of the environment, or both. The client—whether an individual, family, group, organization, or community—makes the ultimate decision whether a change in behavior or the utilization of resources will help to improve the situation. Practice is then "conducted with an eye to the end result—improved social functioning" (Sheafor, Horejsi, and Horejsi 1997, 97).

This quest focuses the social worker's attention on clients' personal functioning, institutional relationships, and/or economic and social conditions; it requires an approach to practice that concentrates on providing relevant services and advocating for just policies. Thus, the actions social workers take are aimed at helping people, communities, and societies attain a sense of mastery, remain competent, and retain a sense of well-being (Greene 2008a).

## Social Workers as Relationship Facilitators

Providing opportunities for curative and enhancing relationships with others is one method of facilitating change. Interpersonal disruptions are the source of many of the problems in functioning that clients bring to social work practitioners. Difficulties in intimate relationships, such as divorce or widowhood; family problems, such as parenting problems or the stress of caring for older parents; and workplace stressors are examples. The practitioner may work individually with clients who present with relationship issues to achieve change. Group interventions are often encouraged in these situations.

Within groups, clients have the opportunity to learn from the feedback of others as well as to receive supportive help from those who face similar life challenges (Toseland and Rivas 2005). As a result, the group context is a practice ground for learning new competencies that can be introduced in other settings.

Social workers also work as relationship facilitators at the community level. One example is community organizing to promote *collective efficacy* within neighborhoods and community settings. Interventions that promote trusting relationships among neighbors provide a foundation for shared expectations and increased collective efficacy (Ohmer 2007). In this way, social work practitioners use theories of social change at more macro levels to promote more effective functioning within community settings.

### Problems of Living and Help-Seeking Behavior

*At times of distress we may make our experience known to others because we want their advice about what the problem seems to be, what its name is, how they might have experienced it, how they resolved it, and what we might do to find relief as well.*

Green (1999, 51)

Clients' help-seeking may be precipitated by a sudden event or chronic situation that brings about difficulties in everyday life. Problems of living may involve stress or wear and tear that interrupts individual, family, and community functioning during difficult situations (Germain and Gitterman 1996). Help-seeking behaviors and expectations about problem resolution usually begin well before the social worker and client meet. Both the client and practitioner have been socialized into a culture composed of "local knowledge" that includes shared ideas, beliefs, and attempted solutions (Geertz 1983).

Experiencing distress and making the decision to seek care require that clients reflect on what characterizes a capable person and how well they can manage their own affairs (Green 1999). The client will generally have ideas about what works and how things are done in his or her community. Choices about how to cope with a problem are also shaped by the culture in which the client lives. So, too, is what is thought of as undesirable behavior.

James Green (1999) developed a help-seeking model based on the work of Arthur Kleinman (1978). His model provides a preliminary guide for working with clients. It requires that the social worker

(a) recognize that the client defines and understands his or her problem according to local, cultural meanings; (b) listen to and learn from the client narrative that establishes the problem; (c) identify helping community resources and whether they can be utilized; and (d) determine what the client considers a satisfactory resolution of the problem. Thus, Green argued, history, biography, and cultural context are not subordinate to symptom identification, classification, and assessment.

## Theory Selection

*Theories compete to "represent" reality not to "create" reality. Practice realities present themselves to practitioners and theory is deployed to understand those realities.*

*—Floersch (2008, 144)*

The social worker comes to the helping process with knowledge of practice strategies and human behavior theory. A theory addresses attempt to explain why a client behaves as he or she does (see Table 1.1). In fact, CSWE's (2008) *Educational Policy and Accreditation Standards* (EPAS) calls for theories to be critiqued and their usefulness for formulating assessments and planning interventions determined.

### The Target of Change: Social Functioning

The history of social work suggests that there is an ongoing interest in individual and societal well-being, and the knowledge adopted for practice has reflected this interest (Hopps and Lowe 2008). The broad scope of practice requires that the theoretical foundation be anchored in the concept of human competence. How a practitioner defines that concept is central to this. Consequently, the key to the change process is the selection of theoretical assumptions and constructs that delineate what constitutes competent social functioning.

Theory shapes a practitioner's views of human functioning. If a practitioner adopts a particular premise about what constitutes competent behavior, his or her interventions will follow a course of action based on it. Practitioners select certain human behavior constructs because they believe they are the most useful in solving human problems. That is, practitioners initiate a process of change because they hope it will help the client become more effective in his or her environment.

Will such techniques and guidelines help the client achieve the change he or she desires? How human behavior content contributes

13

## Table 1.1 Questions a Theory Should Address

What does the theory offer for understanding development across the life cycle? Life course?

What does the theory suggest about the interactions between biological, psychological, and sociocultural factors of human development and functioning?

What does the theory suggest about healthy/functional and unhealthy/dysfunctional behaviors or wellness?

What does the theory say is adaptive/maladaptive? How does the theory present stress factors and coping potentials?

Is the theory universal in its application? How does the theory lend itself to cross-cultural social work practice or various life contexts? Does the theory address social and economic justice?

What does the theory propose about individuals as members of families, groups, communities, and organizations?

How does the theory serve as a framework for social work practice?

How does the theory lend itself to an understanding of individual, family, group, community, or organizational behavior?

How does the theory suggest the client and social worker go about defining presenting situations, problems, or concerns? Does the theory suggest a strengths perspective?

What are the implications of the theory for social work interventions or practice strategies? Do the principles of the theory emphasize a client's capabilities and resources?

What does the theory suggest the social worker do? What does it suggest the client (system) do?

What role does it propose for the social worker as change agent? What is the aim of treatment/intervention or meaning creation? What does it suggest enhances functioning or promotes change in the client? In society? In societal institutions?

*Source:* From Greene (2008b).

to an understanding of everyday reality is not well understood. What can theory reveal about the social aspects of life and human problems and how any problems may be resolved? Can theory predict what the result of a particular social work intervention is likely to be (Wodarski and Thyer 2004)? This text focuses on how particular theoretical approaches describe human competence and their predicted effects on social functioning. It addresses

> how a theory presents stress factors and coping potentials,
>
> what a theory says are adaptive or maladaptive behaviors,
>
> what a theory suggests social workers do,
>
> what a theory suggests a client (the system) do,
>
> what a theory predicts will be the result of a particular social work intervention, and
>
> what research supports an intervention.

Different theories offer different observations about what is considered competent in a given time and place. A critique of a theory can include whether the theory stems from a positivist school of thought, in which concepts are thought to be universal, or whether the theory emerges from a postmodern tradition, in which meaning is created at the local level. Because what constitutes competent social functioning can differ with evolving historical, political, and sociocultural conditions, case examples are used to illustrate what various theories suggest constitute competent behavior in a given context.

This approach to human behavior examines the mutually beneficial interaction between people and society, and emphasizes the connections between individuals and the various systems that influence their lives (Buckley, 1968; Bronfenbrenner 1979). This viewpoint enables the social worker to conduct multilevel client assessments, gain an understanding of how clients function within their total environment, and plan a range of helpful interventions. The social worker may be interested in how an individual is able to function successfully in the workplace, how a family can be mutually supportive, or how a neighborhood can be made a safe and positive environment.

*Theory Critique*

No theory can explain everything about a given social situation or fit all client contexts (Floersch 2008). In addition, "practice created in one social order is often inappropriate for work in another social order" (McNutt 2008). Compton and Galaway (1999) proposed six criteria for social workers to use in selecting an appropriate theory:

1. Select theories that are supported by empirical testing.
2. Use theories that have been proven effective.

3. Choose theories that are less abstract and delineate interventions.
4. Pick theories congruent with social work values.
5. Choose theories that result in culturally sensitive solutions.
6. Review the theory for its historical context and its person–environment focus (85–90).

As with all aspects of knowledge, theories are dynamic and evolve as information and social conditions change. Practitioners need to assume a critical stance in selecting a theory to help guide practice (Laird 1993). During assessment, practitioners need to evaluate theories to determine how well they apply to a client situation and help make effective decisions about a course of intervention. In addition, theories that have a strong level of empirical support (i.e., a research base) tend to have greater predictive and explanatory power (Gambrill 2003).

## Case Example

Whitney Marks received her social work degree last year and was thrilled when she was hired as a hospice social worker. She could not imagine a more rewarding job than helping people and their families at the final stages of life. In addition, the hospice setting provided her with the opportunity to apply the knowledge and skills that she used in her social work program, as every day brought new situations and challenges!

Within her first few months, Whitney started to work with an eighty-year-old woman, Ms. Pringle, who was diagnosed with terminal cancer. Ms. Pringle had three grown children and seven grandchildren who lived in other states. Although they came to visit her, they were not able to have an ongoing relationship because of distance and expense.

As Whitney learned more about this situation, she started to think about end-of-life developmental tasks. In the Eriksonian theory of life stages (Erikson 1959), the final stage, Integrity versus Despair, includes a sense of integration of one's life. As Whitney learned about Ms. Pringle's relationship with her family, she became aware of the older woman's desire to leave a legacy of family traditions and values for her children and grandchildren. Erikson's theory helped Whitney consider the various ways in which she could work with Ms. Pringle at a time when this woman was expressing a desire to transmit family traditions and culture.

With this in mind, Whitney worked with Ms. Pringle to make a "narrated" photo album. She helped Ms. Pringle look through several photo albums of the family and reviewed special moments and events. Whitney mounted these photographs in a new album and tape-recorded Ms. Pringle telling the story behind the photos. Because of Ms. Pringle's fatigue, this took several days to complete. When each of her sons came to visit during the final months of her life, the photo album and tape recording were available. When she was lucid enough, Ms. Pringle would talk with her family about this history and pass down more information. When she was too incapacitated or sick, her family could still listen and be there with her during her final days. When Ms. Pringle died, she was in the company of all of her sons and daughters-in-law. It was a peaceful time, and the family stated how helpful it had been for them to spend these final weeks of their mother's life in this way.

As part of her work, Whitney used Erikson's theory to help predict and explain the life tasks that Ms. Pringle was facing. She was able to use this information to design a useful intervention and form practice goals to help Ms. Pringle integrate her life experience and transmit family culture and history to future generations. Although the initial work was done by Ms. Pringle, the entire family was helped as they experienced quality final days with their mother and grandmother. In addition, the way in which she died provided a sense of completion for the family. Her oldest son said about his mother, "In these photos I see her as a young woman, a mother, a wife, a friend, and grandmother. I feel that her life was complete."

## References

Adler, A. 1927. *Understanding human nature.* New York: Greenberg.

Bandura, A. 1977. Self-efficacy: Toward a unifying theory of behavioral change. *Psychological Review* 84:191–215.

Bartlett, H. 1958. Working definition of social work practice. *Social Work* 3, no. 2:5–8.

Boehm, W. W. 1959. *Objectives for the social work curriculum of the future: Social work curriculum study.* New York: Council on Social Work Education.

Boyle, S. W., G. H. Hull, J. H. Mather, L. L. Smith, and O. W. Farley. 2006. *Direct practice in social work.* Boston, MA: Pearson Education.

Bronfenbrenner, U. 1979. *The ecology of human development.* Cambridge, MA: Harvard University Press.

Buckley, W. 1968. Society as a complex adaptive system. In *Modern systems research for the behavioral scientist,* ed. W. Buckley, 490–511. Chicago, IL: Aldine.

Collins, B. G. (1986). Defining feminist social work. *Social Work* 31:214–19.

Compton, B., and B. Galaway. 1999. *Social work processes.* 6th ed. Pacific Grove, CA: Brooks/Cole.

Compton, B., B. Galaway, and B. Cournoyer. 2004. *Social work processes.* 7th ed. Monterey, CA: Wadsworth.

Council on Social Work Education. 2008. *Educational policy and accreditation standards.* Alexandria, VA: Council on Social Work Education.

Erikson, E. 1959. *Identity and the life cycle.* New York: Norton.

Floersch, J. 2008. Social work practice: Theoretical base. In *Encyclopedia of social work,* ed. T. Mizrahi and L. E. Davis (Eds.-in-Chief), 20th ed., vol. 2, 141–44. Washington, DC: NASW & Oxford University Press.

Freud, S. 1930. *Civilization and its discontents.* London: Hogarth Press.

Gambrill, E. 2003. A client-focused definition of social work practice. *Research on Social Work Practice* 13, no. 3:310–23.

Geertz, C. 1983. *Local knowledge: Further essays in interpretive anthropology.* New York: Basic Books.

Germain, C. 1991. *Human behavior in the social environment: An ecological view.* New York: Columbia University Press.

Germain, C. B., and A. Gitterman. 1996. *The life model of social work: Advances in theory and practice.* New York: Columbia University Press.

Gitterman, A., and C. B. Germain. 2008. Ecological framework. In *Encyclopedia of social work,* ed. T. Mizrahi and L. E. Davis (Eds.-in-Chief), 20th ed., vol. 2, 97–102. Washington, DC: NASW & Oxford University Press.

Goldstein , E. G. 1984. *Ego psychology and social work practice.* New York: Free Press.

Green, J. W. 1999. *Cultural awareness in the human services: A multi-ethnic approach.* Boston, MA: Allyn & Bacon.

Greene, R. R. 2005. Redefining social work for the new millennium: Setting a context. *Journal of Human Behavior and the Social Environment* 10, no. 4:37–54.

———. 2008a. Ecological perspective. In *Human behavior theory and social work practice,* ed. R. R. Greene, 199–236. New Brunswick, NJ: Aldine Transaction Press.

———. 2008b. *Human behavior theory and social work practice.* New Brunswick, NJ: Aldine Transaction Press.

Greene, R. R., and M. Watkins, eds. 1998. *Serving diverse constituencies: Applying the ecological perspective.* Hawthorne, NY: Aldine de Gruyter.

Hopps, J. G., and T. Lowe. 2008. Social work profession: Overview. In *Encyclopedia of social work,* ed. T. Mizrahi and L. E. Davis (Eds.-in-Chief), 20th ed., vol. 4, 144–56. Washington, DC: NASW & Oxford University Press.

Kadushin, A., and G. Kadushin. 1997. *The social work interview: A guide for human service professionals.* 4th ed. New York: Columbia University Press.

Kleinman, A. 1978. Concepts and a model for the comparison of medical systems as cultural systems. *Social Science & Medicine* 12:85–93.

Laird, J. 1993. *Revisioning social work education: A social constructionist approach.* New York: Haworth Press.

Longres, J. 2000. *Human behavior and the social environment.* Monterey, CA: Brooks/Cole.

Lynn, S. J., and J. Garske. 1985. *Contemporary psychotherapies: Models and methods.* Columbus, OH: Merrill.

McNutt, J. 2008. Social work practice: History and evolution. In *Encyclopedia of social work*, ed. T. Mizrahi and L. E. Davis (Eds.-in-Chief), 20th ed., vol. 2, 138–41. Washington, DC: NASW & Oxford University Press.

Meyer, C. 1983. Selecting appropriate practice models. In *Handbook of clinical social work*, ed. A. Rosenblatt and D. Waldfogel, 731–49. San Francisco, CA: Jossey-Bass.

Ohmer, M. 2007. Citizen participation in neighborhood organizations and its relationship to volunteers' self-and collective efficacy and sense of community. *Social Work Research* 31, no. 2:109–20.

Rogers , C. 1980. *A way of being.* Boston, MA: Houghton Mifflin.

Saleebey, D. 2008. *The strengths perspective in social work practice.* Boston, MA: Allyn & Bacon.

Schriver, J. M. 2003. *Human behavior and the social environment: Shifting paradigms in essential knowledge for social work practice.* Boston, MA: Allyn & Bacon.

Sheafor, B. W., and C. R. Horejsi. 2008. *Techniques and guidelines for social work practice.* 8th ed. Boston, MA: Allyn & Bacon.

Sheafor, B. W., C. R. Horejsi, and G. A. Horejsi. 1997. *Techniques and guidelines for social work practice.* Boston, MA: Allyn & Bacon.

Toseland, R. W., and R. F. Rivas, eds. 2005. *An introduction to group work practice.* 5th ed. Boston, MA: Allyn & Bacon.

Wakefield, J. C. 1996. Does social work need the eco systems perspective? Part 1. Is the perspective clinically useful? *Social Service Review* 70, no. 1:1–32.

Wodarski, J., and B. Thyer. 2004. *Handbook of empirical social work practice: Social problems and practice issues.* New York: Wiley.

# 2

# Infancy and Toddlerhood: The Foundations of Competency

*The ego psychological emphasis on normal coping strategies, adaptation, mastery, competence, cognitive processes, person-environment transactions, biopsychosocial factors in development, and the impact of life stresses and social change holds enormous promise as a unifying theoretical practice.*

*—Goldstein (1996, 194)*

This chapter focuses on how to recognize the behaviors that constitute the competent social functioning of young children. It presents contemporary ideas derived from psychoanalytic theory that can be used to understand the emergence of the building blocks of adaptive human development. Beginning with Freudian psychoanalytic concepts, psychodynamic theories have much to offer about how personality develops during the early years of life. Although some Freudian concepts have been refuted, others are still in use because they support the social work person–environment perspective, which focuses on "the ego—and its relationship to other aspects of the personality and to the external environment" (Goldstein 1996, 191).

Contemporary research on these frameworks expands our knowledge about childhood and parenting practices, providing information about this crucial time in child development and family life (Combs-Orme et al. 2003). Social workers, particularly practitioners in clinical settings such as child welfare agencies, need to be conversant with frameworks that discuss childrearing practices, especially those that might involve inadequate parenting and or maltreatment. Caregiving that does not go well during the first months of life (considered a "sensitive period") may lead to difficulties that will be hard to remedy later in life (Wodarski and Thyer 2004).

Four extensions of Freudian theory about the structure of the personality are presented here. These conceptualizations "do not constitute an integrated and distinct theory, but are bound loosely and are often referred to as psychoanalytic developmental psychology" (Goldstein 1984, 3). They do, however, stem from holistic, humanistic, and growth-oriented premises that can be used by social workers to foster competence in social functioning.

*Ego psychology* (Hartmann 1939/1958) offers an understanding of the role of the ego in developing strong adaptive coping strategies, emphasizing the capacity to deal with anxiety, test reality, and master the environment. *Object relations theory* (Mahler, Pine, and Bergman 1975) describes the gradual emotional separation of mother and child, centering on issues of attachment, individuation, relationship building, and trust. *Attachment theory* (Bowlby 1969) further delineates the process of mother–infant attachment, examining the caregiving relationship. Finally, *psychosocial theory* (Erikson 1959 ) focuses on the attainment of the healthy personality, examining how personality develops in conjunction with significant relationships across the life course.

Most of us are ready to respond to an infant's smile with one of our own. Bronfenbrenner (1989), an ecological theorist, termed such actions *developmentally instigating characteristics*, suggesting that smiles invite parent and child into each other's respective worlds. That is, an infant is both product and producer of his or her development.

"Although infancy is a comparatively brief period, no other stage of life demands more parental time and investment" (Mehall et al. 2009, 17). A child's early developmental trajectory is dramatic, as he or she matures from a seemingly helpless baby to a toddler who can speak, walk, and interact with the environment. In reality, infants are born with the budding capacity to respond to stimuli in their surroundings and develop sensory motor functions as neural connections grow. Being able to recognize and discriminate their parent's face is an indication that infants are biologically equipped to orient "toward social stimuli, which permit infants to participate so readily in the social context upon which their survival depends" (Newman and Newman 2005, 143). By the time children are toddlers, they have begun to control their impulses, interact with others, and explore their individuality.

## The Psychodynamic Approach

*As the originator of psychoanalysis, Freud distinguished himself as an intellectual giant. He pioneered new techniques for understanding human behavior, and his efforts resulted in the most comprehensive theory of personality and psychotherapy ever developed.*

*—Corey (2001, 67)*

Freud was the founder of the psychodynamic approach to personality formation. His influence is so pervasive that it has been contended that "understanding psychodynamic theory is a prerequisite to examining other social work theories" (Payne 1991, 74). It is important to understand the Freudian assumptions and terminology still in use in the literature, especially those that help explain competent social functioning in adults. Because psychodynamic frameworks were originally designed to focus on clients' inner conflicts, they are suitable for use in improving the social functioning of adults who want to work through their conflicting thoughts and feelings (Sheafor and Horejsi 2008).

Freud (1933) considered himself a scientist, and his formulation of the psychosexual stages of development was based on the Darwinian and systems thinking of his era (Erikson 1959). He proposed a controversial deterministic theory in which behavior was based on instinctual sexual and aggressive drives that need to be overcome or repressed if people were to become mature human beings. Freud contended that people do not comply naturally with societal norms. Rather, they must suppress or keep in check their innate motivations. Thus, he saw parental socialization and the force of societal expectations as the major instruments ensuring acceptable social functioning.

*Psychosexual Stages*

Freud used observation methods and self-analysis to develop a psychosexual theory to explain how people achieve mature adult functioning. His model is a *stage theory*, a type of theory that specifies that people must achieve certain behavioral tasks at given times in their lives. Freud outlined psychosexual stages from birth to adulthood during which certain developmental tasks must be successfully completed. The entire model is presented here in brief.

In the *oral stage*, or the first year of life, infants derive pleasure from nursing. As infants emerge from this stage, they must be able to form attachments with others and to *individuate*, or become separate, distinct individuals. This concept, known as *forming object relations*, was adopted by Mahler and Bowlby (see "Object Relations Theory" and "Attachment Theory"). Freud originated the idea that personality features or basic patterns of behavior formed in childhood could be seen in adulthood. As particular feelings and behaviors are formed during a specific stage, they undergird the next stage and finally serve as a prototype for adult behavior. Freud argued that those who are successful during the oral stage will exhibit more trusting behaviors and form more loving relationships as adults. In contrast, those who are not as successful at the task of individuation will exhibit extreme dependency and an inability to form intense relationships in adulthood. In the *anal stage*, between one and three years of age, infants are engaged with parents in bowel control issues. Freud believed that a more successful resolution of this stage results in an adult being able to accept responsibility and negotiate with authority figures.

There are three stages beyond toddlerhood: phallic, latency, and genital. The *phallic stage*, between three and six years of age, is when issues of gender identification and ethical behavior develop. The well-known *Oedipus complex*, according to which a child identifies with the parent of the opposite sex, was said to develop at this time. Although child socialization is still important to developmental theory, more recent research has largely discredited Freud's ideas on the phallic stage of sexual development (cf. Parens 1990). The next or *latency stage* occurs between six and twelve. Freud contended that sexual energy is dormant during this time, but the ego becomes a more active part of the personality. The final or *genital stage* that occurs between the ages of twelve and eighteen is a time of integration of all previous stages, resulting in the emergence of a mature adult.

Freud did not outline the specific outcome of each stage. However, the mental health practitioner can use a process of interpretation and inference of therapeutic content to diagnose aspects of the adult personality interfering with competent social functioning. Freud believed that mature individuals who complete all stages successfully can deal effectively with anxiety, have the ability to love and work, and have the "capacity for enjoyment and of efficiency" (Freud 1916–1917/1963, 457).

## Structural Model of the Personality

Freud proposed that the structure of the personality consists of three discrete components that function as an energy system. The *id*, or the original inherent component, is composed of instinctual aggressive and sexual urges. Thought processes that stem from the id are largely unconscious, are irrational, and remain infantile and pleasure-seeking throughout life. The *superego*, or the moral arm of the personality, mediates the conflicting, selfish thoughts of the id and the more rational, reality-based thoughts of the ego. Finally, the *ego*, or the executive component of the personality, houses goal-directed, organized, reality-oriented thoughts. Freud's compelling ideas about the ego were further developed by ego psychologists.

## Three Levels of Consciousness

Freud proposed that each psychic event is "caused" by or is the result of earlier events. Thoughts about past events may be *conscious*, or known by the individual; *preconscious*, or just beyond the surface and capable of becoming conscious; or *unconscious*, or beyond the awareness of the individual. Psychoanalytic treatment was viewed as an opportunity for patients to become aware of their thoughts and feelings and undergo a corrective experience leading to an understanding and overcoming of negative past events. Freud's idea that some thoughts are hidden from knowledge is still widely accepted in the profession (Payne 1991).

Social work practice often involves the collection of social histories and the use of *interpretation*, or "pointing out, explaining, and even teaching clients the meaning of their behavior" (Corey 2001, 93), to obtain information about problems in social functioning (Greene 2008b). Freud's concept of the hidden purpose of behavior is also widely accepted (Hepworth et al. 2006). Cournoyer (2007), for example, proposed that social workers use active listening, interpretation, and clarification to "go beyond what is said" and help ameliorate the problems at hand (212). In contrast, more recent thinking about individualizing the client suggests a more client-centered practice in which they are viewed as experts on their own life situations (Sheafor and Horejsi 2008).

## The Client–Practitioner Relationship

Freud gave considerable thought to the factors that interfere with healthy, competent behavior (Greene 2008b, 2008c). His psychodynamic framework assumes that less-competent social functioning originates in childhood. When practitioners elect to use interventions derived from these frameworks, their role is to relieve client anxiety and to increase client awareness of underlying and sometimes hidden unconscious purposes of behavior that could lead to nonproductive, sometimes pathological behaviors (Corey 2001).

Freud's ideas about the importance of the early years of development offer practitioners several conceptual tools to use in the helping relationship. Freud, who believed that maladaptive behaviors could be corrected during treatment, introduced two concepts for developing and ensuring a trusting client–practitioner relationship: countertransference and transference. *Countertransference* is defined as the practitioner's reaction to the client based on past events or feelings that can interfere with therapeutic work (Greene 2008b). The idea that the practitioner's unresolved, inappropriate feelings about his or her clients (such as a tendency to personalize client anger) can interfere with clinical work still appears in social work texts today (Sheafor and Horejsi 2008).

*Transference* is the client's special interest in or feelings about the practitioner based on earlier authority relationships that are brought into the clinical experience. When these irrational thoughts about the practitioner (which stem from past events) are revealed in the helping process, they are used to interpret current difficulties in the client's social functioning. Freud's belief that a client is best helped by reexperiencing past feelings within the therapeutic relationship is still emphasized in practice texts (Shulman 2005).

Research supports the view that building a trusting and collaborative client–practitioner relationship is central to *any* form of successful intervention (Hubble, Duncan, and Miller 1999; Lambert 1992). Freud left a legacy that has influenced literature, art, as well as political, social, and economic systems (Greene 2008b). However, Freud's theory was often associated with psychopathology and the medical model—"a perspective with an emphasis on diagnosis, treatment, and cure" (Greene 2008a, 78). By the 1970s, social workers had a growing ambivalence about the use of the medical model and shifted their thinking to a more person-in-environment practice (Meyer 1973; see Chapter 4).

## Ego Psychology

*It is a special instance of social compliance when society, so to speak, corrects an adaptation disturbance: individual propensities which*

> *amount to disturbances of adaptation in one social group or locus*
> *may fulfill a socially essential function in another.*
> —Hartmann (1939/1958, 32)

Heinz Hartmann, a contemporary of Freud and the founder of ego psychology, explored ego autonomy as a scientific approach to understanding the personality. Hartmann described the ego as an autonomous, dynamic force that has the innate ability to cope with internal conflicts and environmental demands. The mediation process of the ego is thought to have originated during the evolution of the species and to be the key to relieving the omnipresent state of tension that motivates people's actions. Hartmann also argued that the social environment shapes the personality and provides the factors that may enhance or impede successful coping.

Focusing on ego growth and mastery, Hartmann contended that even mature individuals experience conflict due to the demands of daily life. Because anxiety was considered a part of the normal human condition, the ego needed to be well defended and to be able to postpone gratification for a person to function well in his or her environment.

### Ego Autonomy

Ego psychologists do not use stage theory to account for problems in social functioning. Rather, they believe that problems in social functioning may occur because of ego deficits, such as an inability to perceive the environment or reality accurately. Ego psychologists believe that there may also be difficulties when there is a poor fit between an individual's needs and capacities and his or her environmental conditions and resources (Goldstein 1995).

Robert White (1959, 1963) proposed that people are born with a drive toward mastery and competence composed of three components: being able to (a) gain and process information, (b) maintain control over their emotions, and (c) interact freely with the environment. White contended that people seek opportunities to master their environment and find pleasure in doing so. This perspective of the innate capacity to strive for competence changed social workers' views of personality development and reinforced the need for interventions that foster self-determination.

By the end of toddlerhood, children who have successfully achieved this ego mastery can take actions to meet goals, delay gratification, explore their surroundings, and recognize when they are in danger. But when difficulties arise in these areas of personality development, social functioning can be less successful and may later become the focal point of therapeutic intervention.

*Ego Defense Structure*

One of the important features of the personality is how the ego manages conflict and deals with anxiety. The need for the ego to exert control over anxiety "in the cause of social responsibility creates further conflict" (Payne 1991, 77). Early in the development of ego psychology, Hartmann described the role of defense mechanisms in adaptation. The more adaptive the *ego defense structure*, or the pattern of use of defense mechanisms, the healthier the individual was said to be (Greene and Ubel 2008). Among the defense mechanisms considered by ego psychologists include *regression* (returning to earlier stages of behavior), *repression* (excluding painful or threatening thoughts and feelings from awareness), *reaction formation* (warding off negative impulses by expressing the opposite impulse), *projection* (attributing to others one's own unacceptable desires), *rationalization* (explaining away failures or losses), *introjection* (taking in the values and standards of others), *identification* (seeing oneself as someone else, usually someone successful), *sublimation* (diverting sexual energies to a higher channel or activity), *undoing* (reconstructing previous actions so that they are less threatening), and *denial* (failing to acknowledge reality). The idea that people may "protect themselves from unbearable emotions" or that "emotionally healthy people experience the full gamut of human emotions within normal limits" can be found in today's social work practice literature (Hepworth et al. 2006, 236)

*Reality Testing*

Ego defenses assist a person coping with anxiety but are only "a way station prior to the individual's engaging in more adaptive, reality-oriented behavior" (Goldstein 1984, 7). Ego defenses can be destructive if they are overused or distort reality. For example, following an adverse event, people may deny how they feel, "putting their heads in the sand" for a time. But if this denial continues, it may cause difficulties dealing with the real world (St. Clair 1999). Thus, Hartmann's theory of ego autonomy helps practitioners understand how people cope with reality under unusual circumstances. Although the emphasis in ego psychology is on freeing and enhancing ego capacity, some practitioners today also incorporate a person-in-situation perspective that examines how clients construct their environment (Saari 2002).

### Adaptation as Conscious Choice

For the most part, ego psychology places a greater emphasis on a person's control over the environment than does orthodox Freudian thought. Ego psychology also gives greater weight to cultural and social influences on the personality (Goldstein 1995). And ego psychologists make another departure from traditional psychoanalytic thought by addressing how people can master impulses and make conscious choices. As early as the 1930s, Hartmann argued that psychoanalysis was concerned with adaptation and how the mental "apparatus" leads to "adapted achievements" (Hartmann 1939/1958, 6). Like Freud, he was concerned with the development of a realistic sense of the world and of oneself: "Ordered thinking is always directly or indirectly reality-oriented" (14).

Furthermore, adaptiveness can only be understood in the context of environmental situations or an organism's "fit" within the environment (Hartmann 1939/1958, 23–24). As Darwin had already expressed it, this fit was a byproduct of the relationship between genotype and environment. In short, "human action adapts the environment to human functions, and then the human being adapts to the environment which he has helped to create" (27; see Chapter 4 on the ecological perspective). In addition, finding new, advantageous environments can lead to better adaptation.

Practice strategies derived from psychodynamic concepts have been infused into social work practice since the 1930s. For example, Perlman (1971) drew heavily on Hartmann to develop a casework model that assumed that all adaptation is about problem solving. Her model proposed that clients can be rational, flexible, and growth oriented, a philosophy still in vogue today. Today, ego psychology concepts have moved away from Freud's interest in patients' pasts, instead emphasizing here-and-now transactions between people and their environments. The practitioner explores a client's ability to cope effectively with life tasks and roles. The extent to which ego anxiety or environmental resources interfere with competent social functioning is examined. The helping process is more client centered or client directed, with the client taking responsibility for his or her choices (Goldstein 1996).

## Object Relations Theory

*The great source of terror in infancy is solitude.*
—James (1890/1950)

Contemporary psychoanalytic theorists suggest that the ego or the self develops through the internalization of psychosocial experiences. This is sometimes called *object relations*. Whereas Freud used the term *object relations* to refer literally to objects that satisfy an infant's needs, such as sucking on a rattle, the term is currently used to describe interpersonal relationships involving a sense of self and attachment to significant others, and the internal representation of these relationships (Corey 2001).

*Phases of the Development of the Self*

Mahler (1968) was key in developing a stage theory about how infants and mothers separate and differentiate themselves. She considered the process of object seeking to be innate and to lead to the development of self as a consequence of experience with others. According to Mahler, four chronologically ordered phases of the development of the self "affect all subsequent interpersonal relations" (Goldstein 1995, 203).

The first phase of the development of the self, *normal infantile autism*, occurs during the first three to four weeks of life. The infant is thought to adapt to physical tensions rather than psychological processes. There is not yet a unified sense of self or whole objects. Rather, ego psychologists believe that the infant's ego is undifferentiated at this time and has not yet been called on to act on the environment. (This is in contrast to the beliefs of ecological theorists such as Bronfenbrenner 1979; see Chapter 4.)

According to Mahler, the second phase, termed *symbiosis*, takes place from the third to eighth months of life. In this phase, the infant has such a strong dependence on the mother figure that he or she might be an "interchangeable part" (Corey 2001, 84). However, toward the end of this phase, the infant recognizes the mother figure as the object that satisfies him or her. This means that the infant is highly in tune with his or her mother.

Mahler's third phase, called *separation/individuation*, overlaps with symbiosis, marking the beginning of the child's development of a sense of independence from the mother. As the infant's attention is directed more to his or her environment, the ego takes on more autonomous functions. This may be likened to Erikson's stage of autonomy versus shame, when toddlers proudly run away from their parents and then return to a parental embrace (see "Psychosocial Stages"). Mahler's fourth and final stage of the development of the self occurs by the third year of life and involves a sense of *constancy of self and object.* This means that a child can relate well to others without fearing the loss of his or her individuality.

Ego psychologists theorize that mature competent adults

> are their healthiest and best when they can feel both independence and attachment, taking joy in themselves and also being able to idealize others. Since mature adults feel a basic security grounded in a sense of freedom, self sufficiency, and self-esteem, they are not compulsively dependent on others but also do not have to fear closeness. (Kohut 1984, as quoted in Corey 2001, 85)

When children do not experience the opportunity to differentiate sufficiently, they may develop a grandiose or exaggerated sense of their importance and become self-absorbed as adults. In addition, poor resolution of the process of individuation is said to result in borderline personality disorder; the characteristics of which include anger, threats of suicide, and suicidal behaviors. According to the American Psychiatric Association (2000), borderline personality disorder is a serious mental health problem, as it involves 2 percent of the general population and 20 percent of psychiatric inpatients.

Traditional outpatient psychotherapy has not proven effective in curing borderline personality disorder, but some trials involving talk and drug therapies have proven effective in reducing or ameliorating the major characteristics of the condition (see Ivanoff, Manuel, and Schmidt 2007). Corey (2001) suggested the use of an integrated object relations theory and cognitive–behavioral treatment that consists of three phases developed by Morgan and MacMillan (1999): (a) The practitioner listens to and assesses a client's stories to learn about his or her feelings of past and present situations that may result in problematic adult relationships. (b) The client is helped to gain insight into the assessment of early relational patterns by engaging in a process to restructure his or her life situations cognitively, taking responsibility for his or her own decisions. (c) Behavioral techniques, such as carrying out homework assignments involving active steps of engaging others, are used in the process of restructuring. This example of combining various treatment philosophies exemplifies an eclectic approach to social work practice.

## Attachment Theory

*Not only must an attachment figure be accessible but he, or she, must be willing to respond in an appropriate way.... Only when an attachment figure is both accessible and potentially responsive, can he, or she, be said to be truly available.*

—Bowlby (1973, 201)

In addition to their Freudian background and observations of children, John Bowlby and his colleague Mary Ainsworth drew on concepts from ethology, cybernetics, information processing, and developmental psychology to develop attachment theory. They postulated that a responsive caregiving dyad and a supportive, economically responsible community are important to positive attachment. Bowlby's major argument was that an infant "should experience a warm intimate, and continuous relationship with his [or her] mother in which both find satisfaction and enjoyment" to be mentally healthy (Bowlby, 1951, as quoted in Bretherton, 1992, 765).

*Attachment* is "the process through which people develop specific, positive emotional bonds with others" (Newman and Newman 2005, 150). Attachment theory examines how a mother's sensitivity to her infant's signals initiates patterns of mother–child attachment (Bretherton 1992). That is, attachment takes place within the caregiving dyad—the infant has an organized pattern of signals to which the caregiver responds. For example, children appear to be "programmed" to recognize their caregiver's face. When an infant turns in the caregiver's direction and smiles, this activity is likely to receive a positive response. In short, the infant's signals are thought to be mirrored in the caregiver's response.

How the caregiver responds to the child's temperament, such as the child's activity level, sociability, and emotionality is another factor that influences the attachment process. A child who is irritable or withdrawn may be less likely to receive positive attention. Sensitivity to touch is another factor that influences positive attachment. Thus, cuddling behaviors are important to a positive bonding experience. In contrast, maternal (caregiver) deprivation may lead to a sense of loss. Thus, the idea that practitioners should pay attention to loss of attachment during the early years of life stems from psychoanalytic theory (Payne 1991).

Mary Ainsworth, Bowlby's research partner, outlined a five-stage theory of attachment. (a) During the first three months of life, an infant sucks, smiles, and gazes to maintain closeness to the caregiver. (b) From three to six months, the baby shows a preference for a particular adult, appearing pleased or upset as that caregiver comes and goes. (c) From six to nine months of age, the infant wants to be close to the caregiver, despite crawling around in his or her familiar environment. (d) From nine to twelve months of age, the child has internalized an "internal working model of an attachment relationship" (Newman and Newman 2005, 151). (e) In toddlerhood and later, children develop a repertoire of behaviors that elicit parental responses. The outcome of this stage process is a prototype of adult-bonding behavior that is necessary for competent social functioning.

Two important concepts that have emerged from attachment theory are stranger anxiety and separation anxiety. *Stranger anxiety* is a baby's discomfort at not being close to the mother figure and at being near unknown adults, whereas *separation anxiety* refers to the extent or degree to which the infant gets upset in the absence of his or her caregiver. Although these reactive patterns are thought to have cultural connotations, Ainsworth conducted a cross-cultural study of mother–child attachment in Uganda. From this she concluded that there is an instinctual bonding of infant and caregiver that is revealed in nursing and clinging child behaviors. Social workers who deliver services in home environments, such as intensive case managers, need to be alert to the cultural nuances and meaning of mother–child bonding, especially in extended family configurations (Combs-Orme et al. 2003; Howes and Guerra 2008).

### Psychosocial Theory

*A healthy personality actively masters his environment, shows a unity of personality, and is able to perceive the world and himself correctly.*

—*Jahoda (1950, 214)*

Erikson's eight-stage psychosocial theory is both similar to and different from traditional Freudian thought. Freud elaborated six psychosexual stages of development, with the process ending at eighteen years of age. His stages are "predetermined periods of time in which there is a shift in the focus of sexual and aggressive energy during the course of maturation." Emotional patterns are formed that determine adult personality as each stage unfolds (Greene 2008a, 79). Development does not continue into adulthood.

In contrast, Erikson's psychosocial theory is "a theoretical approach that explores issues of growth and development across the life cycle as a product of the personality interacting with the social environment" (Greene 2008a, 109). Erikson's optimistic view refocused psychodynamic theory from people's inner psyche to the outer world, contending that more attention needed to be given to "man's ecology" (Erikson 1959, 162; see Table 2.5).

Erikson's *epigenetic principle* proposed that individual growth occurs systematically, with one developmental stage building on another in an orderly pattern over the full life course (Newman and Newman 2005). Each stage is a new plateau for the developing ego as it gains an increased sense of mastery over the environment, resulting in the healthy personality. Unlike in Freud's theory, when a stage is not resolved adequately during its "scheduled" period, support from the environment may result in a further resolution of the developmental crisis at a later period in time.

Erikson (1969) was skeptical about whether the changing ideas of modern psychology were scientific enough or could verify details of the developmental process. Yet he was very interested in how therapeutic observation and his impressions of his applied work could help experts in healthy child development arrive at verifiable knowledge about the healthy personality. He wrote that steps in his clinical thinking began with the general clinical impressions that had led to his development of psychosocial theory. He acknowledged his reliance on clinical insights instead of verifiable knowledge, pointing out that his writings were buttressed by clinical data. Erikson argued that as an expert he could separate fact from theory and knowledge from opinion. He believed that it was his job to know the available techniques to verify statements in the field. He contended, "If ... I were to restrict myself to what is, in this sense, known about the healthy personality, I would lead the reader and myself into a very honorable but very uninspiring austerity" (Erikson 1959/1980, 50).

*Polarities*

Erikson contended that an individual's personality is a function of the outcome of the crisis of each life stage, a state of tension or stress precipitated by societal expectations for an individual's behavior.

The resolution of a psychosocial crisis may be considered less success-ful to very successful, two extremes or poles of the continuum from positive to negative known as *polarities*. That is, the psychological outcome of a crisis is a blend of ego qualities that rests between the two contradictory polarities. For example, although an individual may be perceived as autonomous, the outcome of the second psychosocial crisis is actually a mixture of behaviors that may be characterized as autonomous and shameful.

*Ego qualities* are the positive features that become apparent follow-ing a psychosocial crisis, whereas *core pathologies* are the negative qualities that emerge as a result of severely negative resolutions of a crisis. Ego qualities are the mental states that orient a person to life events. In contrast, core pathologies are negative forces that develop following a crisis and that also guide behavior.

### The Radius of Significant Relationships

Erikson's views greatly expanded the social context in which devel-opment was said to take place. Erikson proposed that the expanding number of significant relationships an individual experiences through-out his or her life is the impetus for development (see Figure 2.1). Significant relationships as a person moves through the life course may include the immediate caregiver, parents, siblings, close relatives, peers, leaders, and coworkers. A person's subculture and mainstream society may also serve as influences, as might the global society.

In addition, Erikson (1959/1980) believed that the society into which one is born strongly influences how that individual resolves the tasks posed by each stage of development. Moreover, he thought that people who share an "ethnic area, a historical era, or an eco-nomic pursuit were guided by a common image of good and evil" (17). This broader developmental context foreshadowed the interest of developmental psychologists in the ecological approach to person in environment.

### Psychosocial Stages

According to Erikson (1950/1963), personality develops through a series of eight psychosocial crises. A psychosocial crisis is not really a crisis but a heightened sense of normal demands that represents "a crucial period or turning point in a person's life when there is increased vulnerability and heightened potential. [That is,] a time when particular efforts must be made to meet a new set of demands

## Figure 2.1 The Radius of Significant Relationships

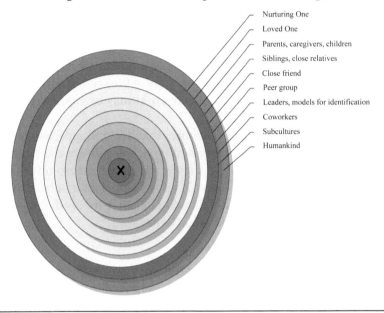

Nurturing One
Loved One
Parents, caregivers, children
Siblings, close relatives
Close friend
Peer group
Leaders, models for identification
Coworkers
Subcultures
Humankind

*Source:* Adapted from Newman and Newman (2005, 48).

presented by society" (Greene 2008c, 231). Erikson's complete model is presented here so the reader can understand it in its totality. Stages 1 and 2 are emphasized here, and the other stages are discussed elsewhere in the text.

*Stage 1: Trust versus mistrust.* Erikson's (1959/1980) first stage, trust versus mistrust, occurs during infancy. Erikson believed that "enduring patterns for the balance of basic trust over basic mistrust" (64–65) were established through positive interaction with a parental caregiving figure. *Trust* is the perception that people are predictable, dependable, and genuine. The capacity for high levels of trust is the "cornerstone of the healthy personality" (56). As stated previously, when a child experiences the warmth and joy of being cuddled or fed, he or she learns trust. In contrast, mistrust may occur as a child senses that he or she is in danger or is not consistently receiving care. In short, Erikson contended that an infant learns trust when he or she learns that care is dependable.

The resolution of this first stage is a blend of trust and mistrust. When the resolution results in a more positive pattern, an adult will exhibit *hopefulness* and a sense of confidence. If the resolution is toward the more negative end of the continuum, the adult may display a tendency to *withdraw* or become socially detached. As Erikson (1959) so aptly stated, the "firm establishment of enduring patterns for the balance of basic trust over basic mistrust is the first task of the budding personality and therefore first of all a task for maternal care" (65).

However, these patterns are not set into adulthood. Rather, he believed that difficulties based on trust could be overcome later in life through positive interaction with a caring adult such as a teacher or a mental health practitioner. This view was underscored by Corey (2001), who suggested that clients often come to counseling with an inability to trust themselves and others.

*Stage 2: Autonomy versus shame.* The crisis of autonomy versus shame occurs in toddlerhood. The development of autonomy rests on a sense of trust. *Autonomy*, or a sense of self-control without a loss of self-esteem, involves the psychosocial issues of "holding on" and "letting go" (Greene 2008c). Autonomy may be displayed when an adult asserts himself or herself during an adverse event (Greene, Graham, and Morano, 2010). In contrast, *shame*, or the feeling of being exposed or estranged from parental figures, involves the feeling of failure. Adults who feel a sense of unresolved shame may be less effective in acting on their environments.

A positive resolution of this crisis allows an adult to experience a sense of *will*, or a better ability to meet his or her goals. In contrast, individuals who have a relatively negative outcome at this stage may develop *compulsions* or repetitive ritualized behaviors. These compulsions may contribute to their feeling that they are less able to be in control of their world (Greene 2008b). According to Erikson (1959/1980), the competent child who emerges from toddlerhood will be more autonomous and "wish to stand on his own feet" (71).

*Stage 3: Initiative versus guilt.* Erikson described six stages of life *after* toddlerhood. The crisis of initiative versus guilt, which occurs at four to six years of age, is the beginning of a child's discovery of what kind of a person he or she is going to be. Erikson (1950/1963) maintained that, during this stage, the family remains the radius of significant relations and children become more concerned with play and with pursuing activities of their own choosing.

As a result of being willing "to go after things" and "to take on roles through play," children develop a sense of *purpose* that continues into adulthood (Erikson 1950/1963). However, children overly thwarted or frustrated in carrying out their plans may develop feelings of *inhibition*, or restraint. When they have matured, they continue to display a "work ethos as well as in recreation and creativity, behaviors relevant to rebalancing of initiative and guilt" (Erikson, Erikson, and Kivnick 1986, 169).

*Stage 4: Industry versus inferiority.* The crisis of industry versus inferiority occurs between ages six and twelve. Erikson (1959/1980) suggested that during this time the central task is to achieve a sense of industry or enthusiasm and self-motivation in relation to work. Developing industry can be recognized in adults who demonstrate "an eagerness for building skills and performing meaningful work" (90). In contrast, inferiority can be seen in adults who do not compare themselves or compete well with others. Friends and peers present social comparisons at this stage.

The crisis of industry versus inferiority can result in the ego quality called *competence.* According to Erikson (1978), competence "is the free exercise of dexterity and intelligence in the completion of tasks, unimpaired by infantile inferiority. It is the basis for cooperative participation in technologies, and it relies, in turn, on the logic of tools and skills" (30). The opposite of competence is *inertia*, or thoughts and actions that prevent productive work.

Erikson (1982) contended that achieving success at "making things together" with one's neighbors and schoolmates is a critical task in a child's expanding physical and social world. Childhood play is a central factor during this phase of development. Erikson, a play therapist himself, argued that modern play therapy follows the pattern of a naturally self-healing process in which the child is allowed to "play it out" (i.e., play out a problem) before a powerful adult (Erikson 1977, 225).

*Stage 5: Identity versus role confusion.* The crisis of identity versus role confusion occurs during adolescence or from ages twelve through twenty-two. Identity is created through a gradual integration of all identifications. During adolescence, an individual struggles with the issues of how "to be oneself" and "to share oneself with another" (Erikson 1959/1980, 179). The peer group becomes the critical focus of interaction. The outcome of these challenges may be fidelity or repudiation. *Fidelity* is an ability to sustain loyalties despite contradictions in value systems, whereas *repudiation* is a rejection of alien roles and values (Greene 2005 it 2008a ).

*Stage 6: Intimacy versus isolation.* The crisis of intimacy versus isolation, or a mature person's ability to form intimate, committed relationships, occurs between the ages of twenty-two and thirty-four. This stage emphasizes one's "being able to lose and find oneself in another" (Greene 2005, 179). The radius of significant relations expands to include partnerships in friendship and love.

*Love*, or a mutual exchange and devotion that can overcome "the antagonisms inherent in a divided function," is the positive ego quality that emerges during this stage (Erikson 1968, 289). *Exclusivity*, or the shutting out others, is a negative sign that an individual has not been as successful in reaching intimacy (see Chapter 4 for a more complete discussion of intimacy).

*Stage 7: Generativity versus stagnation.* The crisis of generativity versus stagnation, which occurs in adulthood between ages thirty-four and sixty, centers on "establishing and guiding the next generation" (Erikson 1968, 290). Generative gifts include acts of altruism and creativity. The radius of significant relations extends to households and the workplace to examine how people share their lives with others.

The ego quality that evolves from the crisis of generativity versus stagnation is the ability to take care of others. *Care* is an ever-widening commitment to take care of all that one has "stored" over a lifetime, passing these strengths to the next generation (67). The inability to care for others sufficiently may result in the negative ego quality *rejectivity*.

*Stage 8: Integrity versus despair.* The crisis of integrity versus despair takes place in old age, from age sixty until death. The issue of this psychosocial crisis is "how to grow old with integrity in the face of death" (1959/1980, 104).

Integrity is realized by individuals who have few regrets, have lived fruitful lives, and cope as well with their failures as with their successes. The person who has achieved a sense of integrity appreciates the continuity of past, present, and future experiences. He or she also comes to have an acceptance of the life cycle, to cooperate with the inevitabilities of life, and to experience a sense of being complete (Greene 2005).

Despair, in contrast, is found in those who fear death and who wish life would give them another chance. Older adults who have a strong feeling of despair believe that life has been too short and find little meaning in human existence, having lost faith in themselves and others. Adults who have successfully resolved the crisis of integrity versus despair exhibit *wisdom*. *Disdain*, in contrast, is an individual's expression of contempt for others and the world around him or her (Newman and Newman 2005).

Although Erikson did not set out to establish treatment protocols or provide guidelines for determining the relative success of the resolution of a psychosocial crisis, his theory has been used to think about a client's relative success in meeting developmental transitions. For example, geriatric social workers may learn that, even during times of great adversity, a client's life course has been positively affected by memories of loving parents during childhood. Understanding the particular life stage of a client provides important considerations about appropriate and effective intervention approaches.

## Critique

This chapter has highlighted the development of competency during the first years of life. Using psychodynamic perspectives, the chapter discussed competence in infants and toddlers in relation to their beginning social attachments and mastery of the environment. It is widely held that "a loving, stimulating environment provides the best foundation to protect against adversity" (Combs-Orme et al. 2003, 438; see also Chapter 7 on risk and resilience theory). From a social work perspective, these theories offer assessment frameworks that help explain where challenges or ruptures to competent social functioning may have occurred.

The focus on the relationship between the infant and his or her physical and social environment varies according to the particular theory base. However, a common element of these theories is that this initial phase of life provides the foundation for subsequent development, growth, and functioning throughout the life course. The theories also assume different styles of *parenting*, or those "behaviors that, given a child's age, developmental needs, and special circumstances, are optimal for promoting the child's healthy growth and development" (Combs-Orme et al. 2003, 440).

However, human behavior theory needs to be understood in the context of the history of scientific thought (Greene 2008b). Developed more than a century ago, psychodynamic theory has been challenged on the following bases:

> Psychodynamic theory, considered scientific in its day, cannot be tested by conventional scientific methods.

> Psychodynamic theory is based on a medical model emphasizing the development of pathological, maladaptive behaviors.

Personality factors were given a greater emphasis than environmental influences on behavior.

Preferring a more here-and-now systemic perspective on client issues, social work theorists turned to systems theory to examine the interacting factors that contribute to human behavior.

Psychodynamic theory is based primarily on a male, white, middle-class model of development, which promotes stereotypes of women.

One of the most important issues that needs to be considered in a critique of human behavior theory is whether the theory's concepts can be considered universal or culture-bound. When practitioners describe illness and mental health, they do not just use the language of empirical reality. Rather, language "reflects ideological beliefs, values, institutional relationships, and cultural mores" (Witkin 1993, 242). Therefore, issues such as caregiving and parenting, child attachment, trust, and competence are related to cultural meanings and family values and beliefs.

*Culture* "refers to societal beliefs, values, and attitudes" (Fitzgerald 2006, 612). Much cultural learning takes place among young children and occurs in the child's culture of origin before age five. As children move outside the home, they are exposed to the dominant culture, which may contrast with familial values (Fitzgerald 2006). For example, attachment theory is said to be universal, but, Pierrehumbert et al. (2009) found that girls expressed more secure attachment representations than did boys; they concluded that further intercultural gender studies were needed.

In a cross-cultural study, Howes and Guerra (2008) explored bonding among low-income children of Mexican heritage and their mothers. Their research revealed that participants constructed secure attachment relationships based on culturally specific meanings and goals for social competence. Their findings were congruent with those of other researchers who argued that it is necessary to examine the intersection of attachment behaviors and culture (Carlson and Harwood 2003; Rogoff 2003). This cautionary statement was underscored by Ogbu (1999), who asked whether it is appropriate for researchers (or practitioners) guided by one set of cultural values to observe and make inferences about people from a different culture or even whether it is possible to adequately sensitize observers to an alternative cultural context.

## Case Example

Parenting programs are often based on a white, middle-class value system, which results in content that is often irrelevant for, insensitive to, and disconnected from other cultural, ethnic, and class values (Estes and Blundo 2007, 140). Estes and Blundo made the following suggestions for developing a culturally sensitive parenting program for African American mothers and grandmothers:

> For parenting classes to reflect the aspirations of the community, a social worker must conduct a cross-cultural assessment.
>
> The development of a culturally sensitive parenting class format begins with a potential member's self-evaluation of her parenting experiences.
>
> During the initial planning for the parenting class, social workers should learn how class members think that racism and poverty have affected them in raising their children.
>
> Information important for the assessment includes learning how a mother who is living in poverty and other harsh circumstances can find the opportunity for self-care to relieve parental stress.
>
> Assessment of family dynamics should occur within a culturally specific context.
>
> Social workers must know the many strengths of the mothers, grandmothers, and community.

In the case example below, parents are involved in classes to help them provide care to underweight infants.

Southern Hospital is a large public hospital in an urban setting. Most of the surrounding neighborhoods have median household incomes below the poverty level, and the area has a higher proportion of teenage parents than the state as a whole. Many of these young mothers receive little or no prenatal care, and a large number of underweight infants are born at this hospital.

Because of the youth and limited resources of many of the mothers, the hospital wanted to know whether the children born there were at increased risk for developmental difficulties. The hospital also wanted to know about the parents' previous parenting experience, the extent of support from family members, and the degree of stress on the family from, for example, inadequate income or housing. In addition, underweight infants could present special medical, dietary, or social needs (Berger and Brooks-Gunn 2005; Wu et al. 2004). Therefore, a needs assessment was conducted to evaluate caregiving challenges and to design the content of the classes.

Southern Hospital has multidisciplinary interventions to help young parents adjust to and manage their caregiving tasks. Part of the program involves in-home support to help configure the home environment to maximize the healthy development of the infant. Developmentally appropriate toys are provided so that infants can begin to engage and advance their skills. Because some young mothers had indicated that they wanted to know more about how to engage positively with their infants, especially those who are premature and underweight, all parents are offered classes about how to interact with their child in terms of feeding, dietary needs, medications, and nurturing.

The goal of the classes is to help young parents learn skills to increase the young child's competence in his or her environment. In addition, the interventions promote a sense of relationship and constancy between the intervention team and parents. A professional team of the pediatric nurse and social worker can provide support for those mothers who have little. This ongoing relationship provides young parents with adult figures that can help them withstand the challenges and frustrations of caring for a medically vulnerable child. Ideally, the same pediatric team would work with the young parents during the first three years of the infant's development. The relationship that develops between the team and the parent helps ensure the ongoing care needed to raise the child and enhance the competence within the family over time. Chapter 3 visits issues of development during adolescence, and Chapter 4 those of family and adulthood.

## References

American Psychiatric Association. 2000. *Diagnostic and statistical manual of mental disorders.* 4th ed., text rev. Washington, DC: American Psychiatric Association.

Berger, L. M., and J. Brooks-Gunn. 2005. Socioeconomic status, parenting knowledge and behaviors, and perceived maltreatment of young low-birth-weight children. *Social Service Review* 79:237–67.

Bowlby, J. 1969. *Attachment and loss: Vol. 1. Attachment.* New York: Basic Books.

_____. 1973. *Attachment and loss: Vol. 2. Separation: Anxiety and anger.* London: Hogarth Press.

Bretherton, I. 1992. The origins of attachment theory: John Bowlby and Mary Ainsworth. *Developmental Psychology* 28:759–75.

Bronfenbrenner, U. 1979. *The ecology of human development.* Cambridge, MA: Harvard University Press.

_____. 1989. Ecological systems theory. *Annals of Child Development* 6: 187–249.

Carlson, V., and R. Harwood. 2003. Attachment, culture, and the caregiving system: The cultural patterning of everyday experiences among Anglos and Puerto Rican mother-infant pairs. *Infant Mental Health Journal* 24: 53–73.

Combs-Orme, T., E. E. Wilson, D. S. Cain, T. Page, and L. Kirby. 2003. Context-based parenting in infancy: Background and conceptual issues. *Child and Adolescent Social Work Journal* 20:437–72.

Corey, G. 2001. *Theory and practice of counseling and psychotherapy.* Belmont, CA: Wadsworth/Thomson Learning.

Cournoyer, B. 2007. *The social work skills workbook.* 5th ed. Belmont, CA: Wadsworth/Thomson Learning.

Erikson, E. H. (1959). Identity and the Life cycle. New York: Norton

Erikson, E. H. 1963. *Childhood and society.* New York: Norton. (Original work published 1950.)

_____. 1968. *Identity, youth, and crisis.* New York: Norton.

_____. 1969. *Gandhi's truth.* New York: Norton.

_____. 1977. *Toys and reason.* New York: Norton.

_____. 1978. *Adulthood.* New York: Norton.

_____. 1980. *Identity and the life cycle.* New York: Norton. (Original work published 1959.)

_____. 1982. *The life cycle completed.* New York: Norton.

Erikson, E. H., J. M. Erikson, and H. Q. Kivnick. 1986. *Vital involvement in old age.* New York: Norton.

Estes, T., and R. Blundo. 2007. Parenting skills among African American mothers and grandmothers. In *Social work practice: A risk and resilience perspective,* ed. R. R. Greene, 138–59. Belmont, CA: Thomson Brooks/Cole.

Fitzgerald, H. 2006. Cross cultural research during infancy: Methodological considerations. *Infant Mental Health Journal* 27:612–17.

Freud, S. 1933. New introductory lectures on psychoanalysis. In *The standard edition of the complete psychological works of Freud,* ed. J. Strachey, vol. 22, 1–267. London: Hogarth Press.

_____. 1963. Introductory lectures on psychoanalysis. In *The standard edition of the complete psychological works of Sigmund Freud,* ed. J. Strachey, vols. 15–16, 9–463. London: Hogarth Press. (Original work published 1916–1917.)

Goldstein, E. G. 1984. *Ego psychology and social work practice.* New York: Free Press.

_____. 1995. *Ego psychology and social work practice.* 2nd ed. New York: Free Press.

_____. 1996. Ego psychology theory. In *Social work treatment interlocking theoretical approaches,* ed. F. Turner, 191–217. New York: Free Press.

Greene, R. R. 2008a. Eriksonian theory. In *Human behavior theory and social work practice,* ed. R. R. Greene, 3rd ed., 85–112. New Brunswick, NJ: Aldine Transaction Press.

_____. 2008b. *Human behavior theory and social work practice.* 3rd ed. New Brunswick, NJ: Aldine Transaction Press.

_____. 2008c. Psychosocial theory. In *Comprehensive handbook of social work and social welfare: Human behavior in the social environment*, ed. B. Thyer, 229–55. Hoboken, NJ: Wiley.

Greene, R. R., S. Graham, and C. Morano. Forthcoming (2010). Erikson's healthy personality, social institutions, and Holocaust survivors. *Journal of Human Behavior and the Social Environment. 20(4), 489–506.*

Greene, R. R., and M. Ubel. 2008. Classic psychoanalytic thought, contemporary developments, and clinical social work. In *Human behavior and social work practice*, ed. R. R. Greene, 57–84. New Brunswick, NJ: Aldine Transaction Press.

Hartmann, H. 1958. *Ego psychology and the problem of adaptation.* New York: International Universities Press. (Original work published 1939.)

Hepworth, D. H., H. Rooney, G. D. Rooney, K. Strom-Gottfried, and J. Larsen. 2006. *Direct social work practice: Theory and skills.* 7th ed. Belmont, CA: Thomson Brooks/Cole.

Howes, C., and A. S. W. Guerra. 2008. Networks of attachment relationships in low-income children of Mexican heritage: Infancy through preschool. *Social Development* 18:896–914.

Hubble, M. A., B. L. Duncan, and S. Miller, eds. 1999. *The heart and soul of change.* Washington, DC: American Psychological Association.

Ivanoff, A., J. Manuel, and H. Schmidt. 2007. Borderline personality disorder. In *Social work in mental health: An evidence-based approach*, ed. B. A. Thyer and J. S. Wodarski, 503–23. Hoboken, NJ: Wiley.

Jahoda, M. 1950, March. Toward a social psychology of mental health. In *Transactions of the fourth conference: Supplement II*, ed. M. J. E. Senn, 211–20. New York: Josiah Macy Jr. Foundation.

James, W. 1950. *The principles of psychology.* Mineola, NY: Dover. (Original work published 1890.)

Lambert, M. J. 1992. Implications of outcome research for psychotherapy integration. In *Handbook of psychotherapy integration*, ed. J. C. Norcross and M. R. Goldstein, 94–129. New York: Basic Books.

Mahler, M. S. 1968. *On human symbiosis and the vicissitudes of individuation.* New York: International Universities Press.

Mahler, M. S., F. Pine, and A. Bergman. 1975. *The psychological birth of the human infant.* New York: Basic Books.

Mehall, K. G., T. Spinrad, N. Eisenberg, and B. Gaertner. 2009. Examining the relations of infant temperament and couples' marital satisfaction to mother and father involvement: A longitudinal study. *Fathering* 7:23–48.

Meyer, C. 1973. Direct services in new and old contexts. In *Shaping the new social work*, ed. A. Kahn, 26–54. New York: Columbia University Press.

Morgan, B., and P. MacMillan. 1999. Helping clients move toward constructive change: A three-phase integrative counseling model. *Journal of Counseling and Development* 77, no. 2:153–59.

Newman, B. M., and P. R. Newman. 2005. *Development through life: A psychosocial approach.* 9th ed. Belmont, CA: Wadsworth/Thomson.

Ogbu, J. U. 1999. Cultural context of children's development. In *Children of color: Research, health, and policy issues*, ed. H. E. Fitzgerald, B. M. Lester, and B. S. Zuckerman, 73–92. New York: Garland.

Parens, H. 1990. On the girl's psychosexual development: Reconsiderations suggested from direct observation. *Journal of the American Psychoanalytic Association* 38:743–72.

Payne, M. 1991. *Modern social work theory.* Chicago, IL: Lyceum.

Perlman, H. H. 1971. *Perspectives on social casework.* Philadelphia, PA: Temple University Press.

Pierrehumbert, B., M. P. Santelices, M. Ibáñez, M. Alberdi, B. Ongari, I. Roskam, Stievenart, M.,Spencer, R., Rodriguez, A. F., and Borghini, A. et al. 2009. Gender and attachment representations in the preschool years: Comparisons between five countries. *Journal of Cross-Cultural Psychology* 40:543–66.

Rogoff, B. 2003. *The cultural nature of human development.* New York: Oxford University Press.

Saari, C. 2002. *The environment: Its role in psychosocial functioning and psychotherapy.* New York: Columbia University Press.

Sheafor, B. W., and C. R. Horejsi. 2008. *Techniques and guidelines for social work practice.* 8th ed. Boston, MA: Allyn & Bacon.

Shulman, L. 2005. *The skills of helping individuals, families, groups, and communities.* 5th ed. New York: Wadsworth.

St. Clair, M. 1999. *Object relations and self-psychology: An introduction.* 3rd ed. Pacific Grove, CA: Brooks/Cole.

White, R. W. 1959. Motivation reconsidered: The concept of competence. *Psychological Review* 66: 297–331.

_____. 1963. Ego and reality in psychoanalytic theory. In *Psychological issues,* ed. R. R. Holt and M. Schur, vol. 2, 38–59. New York: International Universities Press.

Witkin, S. L. 1993. A human rights approach to social work research and evaluation. In *Revisioning social work education: A social constructionist approach,* ed. J. Laird, 239–53. New York: Haworth.

Wodarski, J., and B. Thyer. 2004. *Handbook of empirical social work practice: Vol. 2. Social problems and practice issues.* New York: Wiley.

Wu, S. S., C. X. Ma, R. L. Carter, M. Ariet, E. A. Feaver, M. B. Resnick, et al. 2004. Risk factors for infant maltreatment: A population-based study. *Child Abuse & Neglect* 28:1253–64.

# 3

# Early Life Stages and Identity Formation

*The young individual must learn to be most himself where he means the most to others—those others, to be sure, who have come to mean the most to him. The term identity expresses such a mutual relation in that it connotes both a persistent sameness within oneself (self-sameness) and a persistent sharing of some kind of essential character with others.*

*—Erikson (1959, 102)*

The adolescent years are often portrayed as a time of moratorium, choices, conflict, and turbulence as youth attempt to establish their personal identity. Physical, psychological, social, cognitive, and moral development all come into play. Affiliating with one's peer group, establishing ethnic group identity, feeling that one belongs, and being true to others are the major tasks of this time of life. Many parental and community standards are internalized (Lavoie 1994; Miller 2001; Waterman 1988; Zentner and Renaud 2007). However, there is no single and definable context in which adolescent identity takes place. Rather, several theoretical viewpoints should be considered, as should the historical epoch during which the development takes place (Yoder 2000).

This chapter presents the ideas of major theorists about how these life course challenges are resolved. Erik Erikson (1959), a psychosocial theorist, discussed identity formation as comprising merging one's past identifications, identifying future aspirations, and coming to terms with contemporary cultural issues (Newman and Newman 2005). He believed that identity is historically situated or related to the era in which one lives. In contrast, George Herbert Mead (1934), a social psychologist, formulated a theory of identity that takes into account self-awareness and social acts. He contended that the self emerges as a result of human interaction, the use of language or symbols, and role taking.

Lawrence Kohlberg's theory of moral development, Carol Gilligan's insights about women's development, and Jean Piaget's theory of cognitive development complement these frameworks. Because these various frameworks are limited by their culturally based perspectives, this chapter discusses other diverse perspectives for social work practice (Anderson and Carter 2003; see below). For example, Leon Chestang (1972, 1984) and Dolores Norton (1976, 1978) described the dual perspective, whereas Terry Cross (1998), who suggested a relational worldview based on American indigenous cultures, described identity as "the collective thought processes of a people or a cultural group" (144).

## Psychosocial Identity: Erikson

*A lasting ego identity cannot begin to exist without the trust of the first oral stage; it cannot be completed without a promise of fulfillment which from the dominant image of adulthood reaches down into the baby's beginnings and which creates at every step an accruing sense of ego strength.*

*—Erikson (1959, 96)*

### Erikson's Early Developmental Stages

Erik Erikson, who contended that self-definition is the foundational challenge of adolescence and the transition to adulthood (Schwartz 2005), suggested that three social drives propel personality development: (a) the need for *social attention*, (b) a longing for *competence*, and (c) a desire for *structure and social order*. Erikson's psychosocial theory discusses how the developing self meets the challenges and opportunities of each life stage, merging past identifications into one's present identity.

In addition, Erikson believed that personal development is tied to communal change (Yoder 2000). He contended that people who share ethnic identities, historical eras, or economic pursuits are "guided by common images of good and evil" (Erikson 1959, 17). These socially meaningful models are shaped and limited by the time in which the person lives. For example, as a student of the Sioux Indians, Erikson explored how the ego develops in conjunction with social prototypes. He argued that the growing child must arrive at an identity that incorporates "a successful variant of a group identity and is in accord with its space-time and life plan" (Erikson

1959, 21). Thus, individual identity is ultimately connected to group identity.

The issue of group identity led Erikson to question how the Sioux, a conquered tribe, could reintegrate and restore their marginalized status and personal collective life plan. He pointed out that youth who historically have been discriminated against and marginalized by the broader society may have difficulties integrating their social, historical, and economic pasts into a current positive identity.

In Erikson's first stage of development, the crisis of *trust versus mistrust* is resolved through positive interaction with the maternal figure, establishing an enduring pattern of hopefulness. During this stage, the infant acquires *object permanence*, or the awareness that objects continue to exist even though they cannot be seen. In this stage an infant also develops the underpinnings of goal-oriented actions necessary for competent adult behavior (Vourlekis 2008).

In the second stage, *autonomy versus shame*, parental figures remain paramount and self-control is established. This stage sets the foundation for the child feeling that he or she is ready to meet the world or act on the environment. These behaviors result in an adult's sense of self-efficacy. During the third stage, *initiative versus guilt*, sometimes called the *play stage*, the child develops a sense of purpose. During play, children take on the role of others and develop creative energy. The ability to understand another person's feelings and point of view, known as *empathy*, is increased during this stage. After the person has matured, he or she will use these characteristics to understand the life situations of others and to conduct meaningful work.

The fourth stage, *industry versus inferiority*, occurs between ages six and twelve. Because the strength of a child's need to achieve success is well established by the end of middle childhood, this stage can be precarious or filled with opportunity (Newman and Newman 2005). During this stage, children must master a number of tasks that have a profound influence on their adult functioning. They must create friendships, learn group play, do well scholastically, and, most important, begin to feel that they are a "success." Some children must achieve this while living in an environment in which they experience bullying and or other forms of violence.

In recent years, the problem of violence in families, schools, and neighborhoods has threatened to undermine the quality of psychosocial development and educational attainment for many American children. Children exposed to violence may become more aggressive themselves, and their cognitive and mental health development may be disrupted (Newman and Newman 2005). Youth may also experience barriers to the formation of their *ideal self*—or the representations of the self they would like to achieve (Zentner and Renaud 2007).

Even so, children of this age are intrinsically curious and motivated to achieve, and their natural tendencies to be industrious can also be fostered through school-based programs (Greene 2007). In the words of Erikson (1959, 94), "With the establishment of a good relationship to the world of skills and to those who teach and share the new skills, childhood comes to an end. Youth begins."

### *Adolescent Identity*

*Identity versus identity confusion*, Erikson's fifth stage of psychosocial development, occurs between ages twelve and twenty-two. It requires the youth to "formulate successive and tentative identifications, culminating in an overt identity crisis in adolescence" (Greene 2008, 97). Identity is more than the sum of past identifications. It is based on *ego synthesis*, or the adolescent's perception of his or her sameness and continuity in time. Others also recognize this sameness, hence the saying "She's not like herself." During this stage there is also a growth in self-esteem that reflects the youth's feeling that he or she can master the world.

During this stage of development, adolescents are said to establish *fidelity*, or loyalty to oneself, to other people, and to societal causes. In addition, Erikson (1964) noted that the crisis of identity versus identity confusion takes place during puberty. He argued that youth have a *body self* that encompasses their ideal experience with ideas and images, including of their own body type.

Future aspirations are critical, as youth have to believe that they may be effective as they develop ego identity. For teenagers to experience a sense of competence or successful self-identity, they must overcome a period of role experimentation and alternative choices. They must be committed to their occupational and ideological choices (Marcia 1980; Waterman 1982). Interpersonal relationships become important, and there is some debate about whether interpersonal commitment is more critical to women's development (Gilligan 1982; see below). In addition, youth may wrestle with their political ideology and come to terms with their obligations to society.

## The Cognitive Self: Piaget

*Our views of human potentialities and their unfolding throughout the course of life are profoundly affected by such concepts as mind, reason, and intelligence. These concepts define for us the nature of the mature person.*

*—Labouvie-Vief (1990, 43)*

Cognitive achievements during adolescence "complement" a young person's sense of identity and "add a powerful tool to the tasks of youth" (Erikson 1964, 245). Cognitive theories emphasize "the acquisition and function of human thought and knowledge: how and what one comes to think and know, and the role this plays in what one does and feels" (Vourlekis 2008, 133).

Jean Piaget, a widely known Swiss biological psychologist, developed a stage theory of cognitive development from birth to late adolescence. *Stage theories* describe a psychological reorganization resulting from maturation and the changing demands of the environment (Vourlekis 2008). The child's experiences in the environment are filtered and organized through existing cognitive structures through two complementary mental processes: (a) *assimilation,* which uses cognitive processes to integrate new perceptual information; and (b) *accommodation,* which takes into account new information to create new cognitive schemes. These complementary processes represent the ongoing *adaptation* of the individual to the environment at the cognitive system level or an enhanced person–environment fit (Vourlekis 2008).

### Stages of Cognitive Development

Each of Piaget's cognitive stages involves a new psychological reorganization that stems from the maturation of biological functions and abilities. Piaget outlined how the child emerges from an infant who uses reflexes to act on the environment to an adolescent who is able to use abstract reasoning and formal logic. He contended that children go through four qualitatively distinct universal stages that should culminate in the acquisition and display of true abstract and logical thought:

1. The *sensorimotor stage,* which occurs from birth to two years of age, has similarities with Mahler's normal autism stage. Because infants

must learn to distinguish themselves from their surroundings, this stage is characterized by reflexive motor activity, including sucking and grasping. Infants may repeat certain actions as they become better coordinated and discover ways of obtaining and playing with objects in their environments. By the end of this stage, children have an internal representation or mental image of essential objects around them. For example, they can identify pictures of a cat or dog. However, they have little competence in using language or symbols.

2. During the *preoperational stage*, from two to seven years of age, children begin to master language and the use of symbols. However, they still view the world only from their own perspective, a thought pattern known as *egocentrism.* Egocentric thought is a preoccupation with one's personal worldview rather than an exchange of ideas. Children may engage in vivid fantasies. Practitioners may use these in play therapy to participate with children in the helping process.

3. During the *concrete operational stage*, as children mature, they acquire more logical thought. Through experiments, Piaget demonstrated that children in this stage of development can learn the idea of *reversibility*, or the fact that one can effect change by reversing one's own actions. Children also come to understand the principle of *conservation*, or the fact that the amount of matter remains the same regardless of changes in its shape. Concepts of time and space are also better understood, but there are still limits to abstract thinking.

4. The *formal operational stage*, which begins at about age twelve, is characterized by more logical, abstract thought, and the use of symbols and abstract concepts. "Intellectual excellence has been said to be earmarked by the ability to leave behind the concrete world and to move to the abstract" (Labouvie-Vief 1990, 43). Furthermore, the mature, competent adult is capable of deductive, hypothetical reasoning. By this stage of development, the adolescent has moved from egocentric thought to *socialized thinking*, in which he or she exchanges his or her thoughts with others. Thus, a competent adult "thinks socially, or has his mind's eye on his collaborators or opponents" (Gruber and Voneche 1995, 83).

Although Piaget contended that adolescence marks the end of cognitive development, more recent research suggests that the onset of formal thinking represents only the beginning of cognitive growth (Demetriou 1990). Studies suggest that a formal and post-formal level of cognitive functioning is highly dependent on environmental supports and may not be reached by all individuals (Kuhn et al. 1977). Furthermore, many adults still use egocentric thinking and may be immersed in an imaginary world. According to Piaget, egocentric thought patterns limit a person's ability to effectively deal with reality and to take up adult roles.

The ability to carry out adult roles is in part a cognitive process and a transformation of the adolescent's personality (Gruber and Voneche 1995). This transformation of the self is heightened during adolescence and sets the stage for a sense of self that no longer needs to gauge thought processes on external forces but is able to be self-reflective. That is, the adolescent can struggle with the conflict between society's prescriptive norms and his or her personal sense of integrity and beliefs.

### Cognitive Therapies

Cognitive attributes spurred by brain maturation contribute to the adaptive capacity of the adolescent and his or her development as a competent adult (Gruber and Voneche 1995). Because problem-solving skills and self-awareness are important to behavioral change, a client's cognitive abilities are a critical component of a social work assessment and intervention. The practitioner wants to learn whether an adolescent interprets reality and puts together the abstract reasoning of important life events. What are his or her propositions about the world? That is, how does the adolescent form rules, beliefs, and hypotheses about past and future experiences? Assessing an adolescent's age-appropriate cognitive or intellectual capacity allows the practitioner to adjust interviews so that they can be readily comprehensible and to help clients assess their own strengths, negotiate goals, and plan tasks that are effective (Hepworth, Rooney, and Larsen 2002).

Cognitive therapies focus on a client's self-concept as an important dynamic of social functioning—an area that may be conflicted during adolescence (Vourlekis 2008; see also Chapter 6). The client's personal feelings and perceptions are organized into a belief system about the self, termed *self-efficacy*, or the belief that one is capable of "good" performance (Bandura 1977, 1978). The practitioner capitalizes on the youth's ability to engage in goal-directed behavior, allowing the youth to envision a possible self that he or she would like to become. Self-image, especially body image, is involved. For example, the adolescent is asked whether he or she views himself or herself as likable or too fat. Using these concepts from cognitive theory, Berlin (2002) outlined a problem-solving process for social workers to adopt as a therapeutic model.

# Moral Self-Development: Kohlberg

*On the philosophic side, one is generally offered a culturally universal hierarchical notion with a hard-stage model, which is important for philosophers to take into account [when considering moral development].*

*—Kohlberg (1981, 32)*

Building on Piaget's theory, Kohlberg outlined three developmental stages of moral reasoning, each comprising two sub-stages. He used the hypothetical story of Heinz dilemma to see how individuals would justify the actions of someone faced with a moral dilemma:

### Heinz Steals the Drug in Europe

A woman was near death from a special kind of cancer. There was one drug that the doctor thought might save her. It was a form of radium that a druggist in the same town had recently discovered. The drug was expensive to make, but the druggist was charging ten times what the drug cost him to produce. He paid $200 for the radium and charged $2,000 for a small dose of the drug. The sick woman's husband, Heinz went to everyone he knew to borrow money, but he could only get together about $1,000, which is half of what it cost. He told the druggist that his wife was dying and asks him to sell it cheaper or let him pay later. But the druggist said, "No, I discovered the drug and I am going to make money from it." So Heinz got desperate and broke into the man's store to steal the drug for his wife. Should Heinz have broken into the laboratory to steal the drug for his wife? Why or why not? (Kohlberg 1981)

A core sample of seventy-two boys gave their answers and justifications about what they would do if they were Heinz; from these results, Kohlberg classified each boy into one of the three levels of moral reasoning. Kohlberg's theory suggested that those boys with a higher level of moral development would explain the behavior of stealing the medicine as being based on a higher personal moral code. Heinz went by his own rules that saving a human life supersedes the rules of society. Interpersonal rationales for the theft (e.g., "I would steal the medicine because I love my wife") were scored lower.

1. The person who is at the Level 1 stage of moral reasoning thinks about the direct consequences of his or her actions. This *pre-conventional stage*, common in children, consists of two sub-stages: (a) assuming an obedience and punishment orientation, in which the individual

asks how he or she can avoid punishment (e.g., "It is wrong to steal because you'll be punished"); and (b) taking a self-interest orientation (e.g., "He should not steal because he could get arrested").

2. Level 2, or the *conventional stage* of moral reasoning, involves comparing oneself with societal norms and expectations and takes place during adolescence and adulthood. Two sub-stages are concerned with (a) maintaining interpersonal accord and conformity, in which an individual does not want to incur the disapproval of others; and (b) complying with authority and social order so that law may be upheld. Kohlberg (1973) contended that most people remain at this stage of development, in which moral reasoning is controlled by outside forces.

3. Level 3 of moral reasoning is the *post-conventional stage*. In this stage, people take on their own perspectives about moral reasoning, developing abstract principles about right and wrong. They do not obey the law unquestioningly. Two sub-stages suggest that (a) viewing the world through social contracts in which there are multiple opinions, rights, and values is democratic; and (b) universalizing ethical principles results in a commitment to social justice.

In sum, Kohlberg contended that most adults do not reach the highest level of moral reasoning in which a person puts commitment to social justice above himself or herself.

## The Social Self: Blumer, Mead, and Goffman

*The self .... is essentially a social structure, and it arises in social experience. After a self has arisen, it in a certain sense provides for itself its social experiences ... it is impossible to conceive of a self outside of social experience.*

—Mead (1934, 140)

### Symbolic Interactionism: Blumer

*Symbolic interactionism* is a school of thought that explains how the self emerges through social interaction. Developed in the 1900s at the University of Chicago, its principles had a strong influence on social work pioneer Jane Addams and the settlement house movement as a means of perceiving social activism. The term *symbolic interaction* "refers to the peculiar and distinctive character of interaction as it takes place between human beings.... those human beings interpret or 'define' each other's actions instead of merely reacting to each other's actions" (Blumer 1969, 180). The school's two basic principles are that (a) people develop their personalities through reflection and social engagement, and (b) societal institutions derive their meaning through the social interaction of their members.

The meaning of events and objects cannot be taken for granted, nor does meaning emanate from an event or object itself. Symbolic interactionism emphasizes the aspects of human behavior made possible through language and communication. The theory also focuses on a client's *system of meaning* or internal dictionary that suggests that change in behavior involves developing a new meaning system (Ephross and Greene 1991; see also Chapter 5). For example, Leisenring (2006) conducted a study of forty women who had been abused to understand how they constructed the meaning of the word *victim*. The semistructured interviews revealed that the word was both enabling and constraining: Is a battered woman someone who suffers harm she cannot control? Is she someone who deserves sympathy and/or requires some kind of action? Is she someone culpable for her own experiences? Is she powerless or weak? Many in the study rejected being pigeon-holed and neatly labeled.

A person develops *meaning* through his or her own interpretation of events. For example, there is an interaction between mother and child that designates a stove as "hot." First the child learns to *indicate*, or "to hold it apart"—that is a stove (Blumer 1969, 8). Then he or she communicates to himself or herself the interpretation of danger and the hotness of the stove. In this way, meaning is not superimposed on the child but is created through the interaction of mother and child, and the child gains increased competence in successfully navigating the environment.

Thus, *interaction* involves the reciprocal influence of individuals and the transfer of meaning between people. The interaction in this example involves two kinds of communication: (a) *nonsymbolic interaction*, encompassing gestures, tones of voice, and bodily movements; and (b) *symbolic interaction*, including self-conscious, reflective language. The competent adult must master the symbols of his or her society, thereby developing a definition of self and forging group life and societal institutions (see Chapter 5 for a fuller discussion of meaning making).

*Symbolic Interactionism: Mead*

George Herbert Mead, a social psychologist and one of the founding members of the school of symbolic interactionism, wanted to understand how people understand themselves as well as others. He suggested that once children master the use of symbols, expectations for behavior become crystallized into what he called the *generalized other*—"the internalized organized community or social group which gives to the individual his unity of self" (Mead 1934, 154). Mead proposed that the self consists of two parts: (a) the "I," which refers to the impulsive, spontaneous aspects of the self that are unique to the individual; and (b) the "me," which encompasses the organized expectations of others, social norms, and values. Therefore, the concept of the "me" suggests that the social worker must examine the collective nature of behavior and its social context while also considering how diversity comes into play.

Mead (1934), similar to other theorists, suggested that his approach to the self contributed to an understanding of how people take on adult roles. Here he interjected three stages of role development:

1. The *preparatory stage*, in which children imitate the roles of others meaninglessly;
2. The *play stage*, in which children begin to play the roles of others; and
3. The *game stage*, during which children simultaneously assume a number of different roles.

Mead described the game stage as follows:

> In a game where a number of individuals are involved, then the child taking one role must be ready to take the role of everyone else. If he gets in a [game of baseball] he must have the responses of each position involved in his own position. He must know what everyone else is going to do in order to carry out his own play. He has to take all of these roles. (Mead 1934, 151)

Competent adults also have to understand others' roles to be effective in their family and at work.

### Symbolic Interactionism: Goffman

Erving Goffman, who conceptualized the *dramaturgical approach* to understanding human behavior, suggested that social interaction could be seen as drama. He contended that people learn who they are in a particular situation by their *performance*, or activity in a group. They carry out their role for the *audience*, or team of performers, often to an established *routine*, or preestablished pattern of action. In this case, the peer group of teenager may be thought of as *defining the situation*.

Goffman would say that when teenagers get together, they try to acquire information about one another, "sizing the players up." Are they "nerds" or "geeks"? They may put "others" into categories based on socioeconomic status or intelligence. They are developing a personal self that is "a kind of player in a ritual game who copes honorably or dishonorably, diplomatically or undiplomatically, with the judgmental contingencies of the situation" (Goffman 1967, 31). In this manner, teenagers may eventually learn to deal with the demands of those with power and influence and with their own personal set of meanings.

Because Goffman (1961, 1963) explored the creation of stigmatized roles, such as "mental patient" and "criminal," his works are used by social workers to understand the labeling process. He suggested that once patients receive a label (e.g., "patient"), they start on a *career* (e.g., as a patient) that may be carried throughout the life course. According to this perspective, the psychiatric view of a person becomes significant only insofar as this view itself alters his or her social fate. It is thus a tribute to the power of social forces that the uniform status of mental patient cannot ensure an aggregate of persons a common fate (Goffman 1961).

Identity, however, may change as life situations evolve. For example, researchers and health care practitioners are interested in how illness can influence one's identity. Hinojosa et al. (2008) contended that individuals can construct continuity of the self following illness by using their personal symbolic resources, such as religious beliefs. In contrast, Karner and Bobbitt-Zeher (2006) argued that "caregiving is a process of transformed and reconstructed relations" (550). Because Alzheimer's disease is disruptive to the person with dementia, it also transforms the caregiver. Therefore, the social worker needs to learn what meaning or value each family member puts on the situation and the associated changes in his or her sense of self.

*Stigma* is a social construct or meaning that is developed through perceived negative interactions in a given context and time in history. For example, Marvasti (2006) used Goffman's conceptualization of stigma to examine how Middle Eastern Americans dealt with the suddenness of their "spoiled identity" following the events of September 11, 2001. His autoethnographic study showed that his research group engaged in humor, education, defiance, cowering, and *passing* or concealment to cope with the stereotypes and misrepresentations of their ethnic group, trying to salvage "spoiled identities in disrupted [what prior to September 11 used to be] routine interaction" (544).

Marvasti's study documented that youth who grow up in different sociohistorical times may attribute different meaning to symbols and events. Consequently, practitioners need to learn more about how current events shape the lives of adolescent clients.

## Critique: Alternative Views of the Self

*Vertical models [of stage development] have left no room for the maturing of the mind: for wisdom, emotional depth, for communal responsibility, for moral passions, for mythopoetic awareness, for spiritual concerns*

*—Labouvie-Vief (1990, 52)*

### *The Diverse Self: NASW and CSWE*

The stage theories presented here may provide limited information relative to cross-cultural social work practice, which occurs when a practitioner is helping someone with a different background, values, or lifestyle (Greene 2008; Greene, Watkins, Evans, and David, 2003). The importance of attending to difference is mandated by both of social work's major organizations: the National Association of Social Workers (NASW) and the Council on Social Work Education (CSWE). Diversity, according to NASW standards, requires, among other things, the ability to

assist people of color;

address the interrelationship among class, race, ethnicity, and gender;

assist low-income families;

work with older adults;

address the importance of religion and spirituality in the lives of clients;

explore the development of gender identity and sexual orientation;

understand the dynamics of immigration, acculturation, assimilation stress, and biculturalism; and

help people with disabilities. (NASW 1999, 2001)

Similarly, according to the CSWE (2008), difference is important because

social workers [need] to understand how diversity characterizes and shapes the human experience and is critical to the formation of identity. The dimensions of diversity are understood as the intersectionality of multiple factors including age, class, color, culture, disability, ethnicity, gender, gender identity and expression, immigration status, political ideology, race, religion, sex, and sexual orientation. Social workers appreciate that, as a consequence of difference, a person's life experiences may include oppression, poverty, marginalization, and alienation as well as privilege, power, and acclaim. (4–5)

Social workers, therefore, are asked to critique theories for their suitability before they apply them in their practice (CSWE 2008). For example, Carol Gilligan (1982), a champion of defining psychological theory and women's development, contended that Kohlberg's stages of moral development were gender-biased. She criticized Kohlberg for using an all-male sample. Moreover, she pointed out that Kohlberg's emphasis on abstract principles of formal justice did not take into account the fact that women tend to focus on interpersonal relationships, compassion, and care. Gilligan's critique contrasted the *ethic of justice*, which is based on principled reasoning, with the *ethic of care*, which involves interpersonal contexts. In other words, Kohlberg gave precedence to abstract justice, whereas Gilligan emphasized personal relatedness. It should be understood that there is "some risk of ethnocentrism in projecting the values of one's own culture as a universal standard" (Gump, Baker, and Roll 2000, 79).

Similarly, Akerlund and Cheung (2000) examined identity formation among minority youth, rejecting the literature that tends to focus on deficits. They contended that minority youth, who often face discrimination, move through a nonlinear, dynamic path searching for the meaning of their identity. However, these stages do not necessarily occur in order or sequentially.

Gay and lesbian youth may face the challenges of stigma but generally experience confusing feelings, comparing themselves with others, accepting themselves, understanding that they are different, and associating personal identity with sexual orientation (Akerlund and Cheung 2000). Akerlund and Cheung went on to suggest that if practitioners find stages of development helpful with clients, they adopt models of homosexual identity formation such as that of Cass (1979), who provided a means of understanding six stages gays and lesbians take to positive development: (a) Identity Confusion, (b)

Identity Comparison, (c) Identity Tolerance, (d) Identity Acceptance, (e) Identity Pride, and (f) Identity Synthesis.

*Dual Perspectives: Cooley, Chestang, and Norton*

Recognizing the limitations of theoretical social work practice frameworks to serve oppressed minorities, faculty and staff at the CSWE initiated a project to develop suitable curriculum content (Brown 1978; Francis 1978). Much of the curriculum content developed during the 1970s was based on the earlier works of symbolic interactionists who addressed social aspects of the self. For example, Mead and Goffman used the concept of the generalized other to describe how the self takes on the roles of others; Cooley (1902/1964) coined the term *looking-glass self* to address how the thoughts of others reflect on the self. The looking-glass self-concept, which has been used to understand difference, is composed of three components:

1. How we imagine we must appear to others,
2. What we think about the judgment of that appearance, and
3. How we develop ourselves through the judgment of others. (Yeung and Martin 2003)

From this perspective, the self is seen as an internalization of the perceptions of others. This leads to the question of how competent youths can be raised in oppressive environments. To answer this question, social workers need to learn about "the multiple dimensions of human identity, biculturalism, and culturally defined social behaviors" (Fong and Furuto 2001, 1).

Socialization from the *dual perspective* was first described by DuBois (1903), a freed slave, who said, "One ever feels his twoness—an American; a Negro; two souls, two thoughts, two unreconciled strivings; two warring ideals in one dark body, whose dogged strength alone keeps it from being torn asunder" (17).

Chestang (1972) and Miller (1980) further defined the dual perspective as a process of consciously and systematically understanding the values, attitudes, and behaviors of both the minority and mainstream cultures. These theorists proposed that individuals first learn about their immediate culture in the nurturing family system. People later encounter the majority, sustaining cultural system as they interact with the institutions that control the provision of goods and services, such as schools and health and human services agencies (Norton 1978; see Figure 3.1).

## Figure 3.1 The Dual Perspective

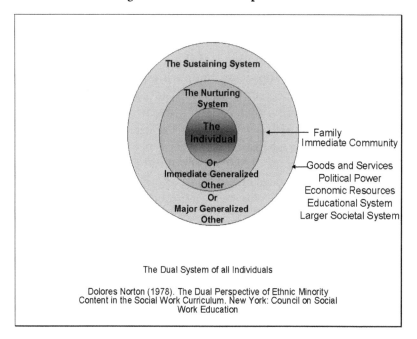

The Dual System of all Individuals

Dolores Norton (1978). The Dual Perspective of Ethnic Minority
Content in the Social Work Curriculum. New York: Council on Social
Work Education

The idea of the dual perspective is, then, that every individual is part of two systems: the smaller system of his or her immediate environment and the larger societal system. For example, Boykin and Toms (1985) found that African American children first develop an understanding of many African cultural forms that are passed on to each generation, and as they go through this development, they also engage with the mainstream ethos.

*Bicultural competence* is a concept related to the dual perspective in which young people take on modes or styles of behavior appropriate for two groups. That is, the ability to be bicultural allows teenagers to learn about and take advantage of mainstream culture without compromising ethnic pride, which enables them to feel effective and well-grounded in both cultures (Greene et al. 2002). As in the case example below, the concept of biculturalism can also be applied to gays and lesbians who live in mainstream and local cultures.

### *The Relational Self: Cross*

Models of human behavior that best address diversity need to be based on the "cultural values and worldviews of marginalized groups"

(Carter 2003, 95). *Worldviews* are the collective thought processes of a people or culture (Gergen and Gergen, 2007). These thoughts and ideas are organized into concepts that are, in turn, organized into constructs and paradigms (Cross 1998; see Chapter 1). The relational worldview has been contrasted with the predominantly linear, mainstream Euro-American philosophy. The *linear worldview* is logical, time oriented, and systematic and is based on a cause-and-effect approach (Schriver 2003). This is reflected in social work assessment protocols that usually involve taking a social history to determine the cause of a problem.

Western theorists have tended to describe the development of the self in deterministic ways, relying on vertical or stage models of development. The aim of such models is to account for universal, consistent, adaptive phenomena. This perspective presumes reason and logical thinking to be superior to wisdom and emotion. Subjectivity is downgraded (Labouvie-Vief 1990). Spirituality and personal and community belief systems that transcend the individual are rarely considered (see Chapter 5).

Furthermore, mainstream Western theorists espouse the idea that the self is housed in the boundaries of the body—or that the body is a "container" for the physiological and psychological factors that compose a person. This perspective is termed the "ideology of the self contained individual" (Gergen 2009, 83). By contrast, the *relational worldview* has its roots in indigenous cultures, is not time oriented, but is intuitive and fluid (see Chapter 5). For example, helping professionals and natural healers may attempt to bring people into balance or harmony among four major forces as represented in the medicine wheel (see Figure 3.2). The four quadrants are the following:

1. *Context:* A history of oppression is a major context for American indigenous cultures. Children are socialized to pick up subtle clues about danger and develop sharpened survival skills. History and heritage are central to communal life.
2. *Mind:* Youth may adopt ego defenses such as denial as mechanisms for surviving oppression. Storytelling is the major vehicle for learning strategies to interact with the world.
3. *Body:* The physical aspect of the self refers to the individual's body but also to family and kinship.
4. *Spirit:* Spirituality practices may include faith, prayer, meditation, healing ceremonies, and positive thinking.

The relational worldview can only be understood by considering all

## Figure 3.2 A Relational Worldview Model

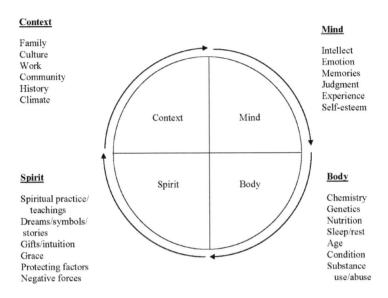

**Context**

Family
Culture
Work
Community
History
Climate

**Mind**

Intellect
Emotion
Memories
Judgment
Experience
Self-esteem

**Spirit**

Spiritual practice/
    teachings
Dreams/symbols/
    stories
Gifts/intuition
Grace
Protecting factors
Negative forces

**Body**

Chemistry
Genetics
Nutrition
Sleep/rest
Age
Condition
Substance
    use/abuse

*Source:* Adapted from Newman and Newman (2005, 48).

*Note:* The items listed are examples only. All of life and existence is included in the circle. Balance of all four parts brings harmony, and harmony equals health. Nothing in the circle can change without every other thing in the circle changing as well. The circle is constantly changing because of the cycles of the days, weeks, and seasons and because of different developmental experiences. Individuals are considered ill if the circle becomes out of balance. Lack of balance causes "dis-ease." In this view of health and mental health, healing may come from any or all of the four parts of the circle as indicated by the arrows surrounding the circle.

four properties together and the interdependence among them that maintains individual, family, and community balance.

## Case Example

Tony Rodriguez, a fourteen-year-old Latino boy, was referred to the school social worker for fighting on the school campus. Tony was significantly overweight and the target of teasing by other children, especially the boys. At the freshman dance, Tony had been on the dance floor when boys had started mocking him and making degrading noises. In addition, they shouted racial and homophobic slurs. This was particularly troublesome to Tony, as it was done in front of a girl he admired. Finally, at the breaking point, Tony had punched one of the tormentors. As a result, Tony and another boy were suspended from school and were required to meet with the school social worker upon return.

In his meeting with the social worker, Tony started to discuss the experience that had gotten him suspended. As a Latino boy and an overweight adolescent, he felt different from the more "popular" boys in his school. To cope, he tried to keep a low profile; however, this did not seem to work, as he continued to be targeted by a group of older boys. Teachers had spoken with the tormenting students, but this also did not seem to alleviate the problem. Because his parents were undocumented aliens, they did not want to call attention to their family and wanted little contact with the school. As a result, Tony felt unprotected and unable to function at school. The dance was the first time that he had really tried to do something social at school, and the end result had been devastating to him.

The social worker started a plan with Tony that involved several levels of intervention. One was to have him get involved with the local Boys and Girls Club to allow him to form a new identity with peers away from his school. The Boys and Girls Club offered recreational and educational programs and pulled students from across multiple schools, which provided an opportunity for them to form a new peer group. In addition, the social worker contacted the Boys and Girls Club staff to help provide Tony with a positive entree into the club. Tony had a strong interest in music, and the staff asked him to participate in a program that featured local musicians. This gave him an opportunity to showcase some of his knowledge of the local music scene and to assume a valued role among his peers.

Tony was also referred to a Spanish-speaking pediatrician who could speak with his family about his weight and body image. The physician spoke with Tony's parents about the health risks that Tony was facing at such a young age, including diabetes, high blood pressure, and cardiac risks. For Tony, however, the importance of being more physically fit had more to do with fitting in with the other boys.

The hardest part was managing the issue at school. The social worker worked with teachers to implement a sensitivity program within the curriculum. This content involved the students reviewing various scenarios and looking at "right and wrong" behavior and at different ways to deal with others, especially those who were different in some way. As a final component of the intervention, a student panel was established for cases like Tony's. Students who violated the conduct code (e.g., by swearing or fighting) had to go before a student-run panel that was elected from the student body as a whole. Although the administration had the ultimate decision about sanctions, this student group had the opportunity to provide input about ways in which social infractions should be handled at the school. Such transformational dialogues can be a powerful intervention for bringing people in conflict together (see Chapter 5).

## References

Akerlund, M., and M. Cheung. 2000. Teaching beyond the deficit model: Gay and lesbian issues among African Americans, Latinos, and Asian Americans. *Journal of Social Work Education* 36:279–92.

Anderson, J., and R. W. Carter. 2003. *Diversity perspectives for social work practice.* Boston, MA: Allyn & Bacon.

Bandura, A. 1977. Self-efficacy: Toward a unifying theory of behavior change. *Psychological Review* 84:191–215.

_____. 1978. The self system in reciprocal determinism. *American Psychologist* 33:344–58.

Berlin, S. 2002. *Clinical social work practice: A cognitive-integrative perspective.* New York, NY: Oxford University Press.

Blumer, H. 1969. *Symbolic interactionism.* Englewood Cliffs, NJ: Prentice Hall.

Boykin, A. W., and F. D. Toms. 1985. Black child socialization: A conceptual framework. In *Black children*, ed. H. P. McAdoo and J. L. McAdoo, 33–52. Beverly Hills, CA: Sage.

Brown, E. G. 1978. Minority content in the first-year practice course. In *The dual perspective*, ed. D. Norton. New York: Council on Social Work Education. Pp. 23–30

Carter, R. 2003. Ethnic-centered: Afrocentric framework. In *Diversity perspectives for social work practice*, ed. J. Anderson and R. Carter, 95–112. Boston, MA: Pearson.

Cass, V. 1979. Homosexual identity formation: A theoretical model. *Journal of Homosexuality* 4, no. 3:219–35.

Chestang, L. W. 1972. *Character development in a hostile society* (Occasional Paper No. 3). Chicago, IL: School of Social Service Administration.

_____. 1984. Racial and personal identity in the black experience. In *Color in a white society*, ed. B. W. White, 83–94. Silver Spring, MD: NASW Press.

Cooley, C. H. 1964. *Human nature and the social order.* New York, NY: Scriber's. (Original work published 1902.)

Council on Social Work Education. 2008. *Educational policy and accreditation standards.* Alexandria, VA: Council on Social Work Education. http ://www.cswe.org/NR/rdonlyres/2A81732E-1776-4175-AC42-retrieved July 28, 2008

Cross, T. 1998. Understanding family resiliency from a relational world view. In *Resiliency in Native American and immigrant families*, ed. H. I. McCubbin,

E. A. Thompson, A. I. Thompson, and J. E. Fromer, 143–58. Thousand Oaks, CA: Sage.

Demetriou, A. 1990. Structural and developmental relations between formal and postformal capacities: Towards a comprehensive theory of adolescent and adult cognitive development. In *Adult development: Vol. 2. Models and methods in the study of adolescent and adult thought*, ed. M. L. Commons, C. Armon, L. Kohlberg, F. A. Richards, T. A. Grotzer, and J. D. Sinnott, 147–73. New York, NY: Praeger.

DuBois, W. E. B. 1903. *Souls of black folk.* Chicago, IL: McClurg.

Ephross, P., and R. R. Greene. 1991. Symbolic interactionism. In *Human behavior theory and social work practice*, ed. R. R. Greene and P. Ephross, 203–26. Haworth, NY: Aldine de Gruyter.

Erikson, E. H. 1959. *Identity and the life cycle.* New York: Norton.

———. 1964. *Insight and responsibility.* New York: Norton.

Fong, R., and S. Furuto. 2001. *Culturally competent practice: Skills, interventions, and evaluations.* Boston, MA: Allyn & Bacon.

Francis, E. A. 1978. Integrating Black minority content into social welfare policy and services. In *The dual perspective*, ed. D. Norton. New York: Council on Social Work Education . Pp. 48–57.

Gergen, K. 2009. *Relational being: Beyond self and community.* New York: Oxford University Press.

Gergen , K., and M. Gergen. 2007. *Social construction: A reader.* Los Angeles, CA: Sage. (Original work published 2003.)

Gilligan, C. 1982. *In a different voice.* Cambridge, MA: Harvard University Press.

Goffman, E. 1961. *Asylums.* New York, NY: Anchor Books.

———. 1963. *Stigma: Notes on the management of spoiled identity.* Englewood Cliffs, NJ: Prentice Hall.

———. 1967. *Interaction rituals.* New York, NY: Anchor Books.

Greene, R. R. 2007. *Social work practice: A risk and resilience perspective.* Monterey, CA: Brooks/Cole.

———. 2008. *Human behavior theory and social work practice.* New Brunswick, NJ: Aldine Transaction Press.

Greene, R. R., N. Taylor, M. Evans, and L. A. Smith. 2002. Raising children in an oppressive environment. In *Resiliency: An integrated approach to practice, policy, and research*, ed. R. R. Greene, 241–75). Washington, DC: NASW Press.

Greene , R. R., M. Watkins, M. Evans, V. David, and E. J. Clark. 2003. Defining diversity: A practitioner survey. *Arête* 27, no. 1:51–71.

Gruber, H. E., and J. J. Voneche. 1995. *The essential Piaget.* Northdale, NJ: Jason Aronson.

Gump, L. S., R. C. Baker, and S. Roll. 2000. Cultural and gender differences in moral judgment: A study of Mexican Americans and Anglo-Americans. *Hispanic Journal of Behavioral Sciences* 22, no. 1:78–93.

Hepworth, D., R. Rooney, and J. Larsen. 2002. *Direct social work practice.* Pacific Grove, CA: Brooks/Cole.

Hinojosa, R., C. Boylstein, M. Rittman, M. S. Hinojosa, and C. Faircloth.

2008. Constructions of continuity after stroke. *Symbolic Interaction* 31: 205–24.

Karner, T., and D. Bobbitt-Zeher. 2006. Losing selves: Dementia care as disruption and transformation. *Symbolic Interaction* 28:549–70.

Kohlberg, L. 1973. The claim to moral adequacy of a highest stage of moral judgment. *Journal of Philosophy* 70:630–46.

———. 1981. *Essays on moral development: Vol. I. The philosophy of moral development.* San Francisco, CA: Harper & Row.

Kuhn, D., J. Langer, G. Kohlberg, and N. S. Haan. 1977. The development of formal operations in logical and moral judgment. *Genetic Psychology Monographs* 95:97–188.

Labouvie-Vief, G. 1990. Modes of knowledge and the organization of development. In *Adult development: Vol. 2. Models and methods in the study of adolescent and adult thought,* ed. M. L. Commons, C. Armon, L. Kohlberg, F. A. Richards, T. A. Grotzer, and J. D. Sinnott, 43–62. New York, NY: Praeger.

Lavoie, J. C. 1994. Identity in adolescence: Issues of theory, structure and transition. *Journal of Adolescence* 17:17–28.

Leisenring, A. 2006. Confronting "victim" discourses: The identity work of battered women. *Symbolic Interaction* 29:307–30.

Marcia, J. E. 1980. Identity in adolescence. In *Handbook of adolescent psychology,* ed. J. Adelson, 159–87. New York: Wiley.

Marvasti, A. 2006. Being Middle Eastern American: Identity negotiation in the context of the war on terror. *Social Interaction* 28:525–47.

Mead, G. H. 1934. *Mind, self, and society.* Chicago, IL: University of Chicago Press.

Miller, J. 2001. Family and community integrity. *Journal of Sociology and Social Welfare* 28, no. 4:23–44.

Miller, S. 1980. Reflections on the dual perspective. In *Training for service delivery for minority clients,* ed. E. Mizio and J. Delany, 53–61. New York, NY: Family Service of America.

National Association of Social Workers. 1999. *Code of ethics of the National Association of Social Workers.* http://www.naswdc.org/pubs/code/code.asp (accessed September 11, 2007).

———. 2001. *NASW standards for cultural competence in social work practice.* http://www.socialworkers.org/practice/standards/NASWCulturalStandards.pdf (accessed August 1, 2007).

Newman, B. M., and P. R. Newman. 2005. *Development through life: A psychosocial approach.* 9th ed. Belmont, CA: Wadsworth/Thomson.

Norton, D. G. 1976. Working with minority populations: The dual perspective. In *Social work in practice,* ed. B. Ross and S. K. Khinduka, 134–41. New York: National Association of Social Workers.

———. 1978. *The dual perspective: Inclusion of ethnic minority content in social work curriculum.* New York, NY: Council on Social Work Education.

Schriver, J. M. 2003. *Human behavior and the social environment: Shifting paradigms in essential knowledge for social work practice.* Boston, MA: Allyn &

Bacon.

Schwartz, S. 2005. Predicting identity consolidation from self-construction, eudaimonistic self-discovery, and agentic personality. *Journal of Adolescence* 29:777–93.

Vourlekis, B. S. 2008. Cognitive theory for social work practice. In *Human behavior theory and social work practice*, ed. R. R. Greene, 133–63. New Brunswick, NJ: Aldine Transaction Press.

Waterman, A. S. 1982. Identity development from adolescence to adulthood: An extension of theory and a review of research. *Developmental Psychology* 18:341–58.

_____. 1988. Identity status theory and Erikson's theory: Communalities and differences. *Developmental Review* 8:185–208.

Yeung, K., and J. L. Martin. 2003. The looking glass self: An empirical test and elaboration. *Social Forces* 81:843–79.

Yoder, A. E. 2000. Barriers to ego identity status formation: A contextual qualification of Marcia's identity status paradigm. *Journal of Adolescence* 23:95–106.

Zentner, M., and O. Renaud. 2007. Origins of adolescents' ideal self: An intergenerational perspective. *Journal of Personality and Social Psychology* 92:557–74.

# 4

# Living in Systems: Work and Love

*Humans are never just individuals trying to meet their own needs. They are social in nature and live out their lives in the context of social systems and their constituent roles. The meeting of individual needs is intimately caught up in the dynamics of the system as a whole.*
*—Longres (2000, 45)*

A primary function of human behavior theory is to offer explanations of how people make transitions across the life course by carrying out their roles in various social systems. Whereas youngsters must learn how to behave within their families, adults must deal effectively with family and workplace issues. In this chapter we discuss how to recognize behaviors that constitute competent social functioning in family systems and in the workplace. General systems and role theories complement one another to explain the interactions within these systems, including patterns of organization and communication. Both theories are part of the *structural functionalist school* of sociology that examines the properties of social systems. Theories in this category address how a system reaches its goals, maintains itself, and adapts to new conditions. Furthermore, they are a means of understanding how families nurture and conduct their economic functions or roles (Parsons 1961).

During the 1970s, as practitioners sought better articulated person–environment theoretical approaches, the popularity of the psychodynamic approach to social work practice began to wane (Meyer 1973; Strean 1971). Social workers focused their attention from studying cause-and-effect relationships, in which A causes B (a linear view), to identifying patterns of family and group interaction (a reciprocal, circular perspective). This person-in-environment perspective also explored the complex interactions between clients at all levels of social systems (Andreae 1996).

By the 1990s, practitioners had a choice of modalities to effect change and promote optimum functioning. They sought a view of human behavior that explained peoples' interrelationships and interdependence, taking into account the influence of various systems and subsystems on client functioning. "Of all the theoretical paradigms utilized by social workers, general systems theory perhaps most clearly articulates this reality," especially interactions in families (Andreae 1996, 610). As practitioners began to give more attention to family dynamics, they found that role theory was an important complement for understanding the rights and obligations of family members (Greene 2008a, 2008b; Perlman, 1962). In addition, "role theory carries a considerable freightage of meaning in social work because it implies a means of individual expression as well as dimensions of social behavior" (Strean 1979, 318).

## General Systems Theory

The purpose of general systems theory is "to assist social workers in maintaining a focus on the dynamic interplay of the many biological and social systems that affect client behavior" (Sheafor and Horejsi 2008, 87). General systems theory is not in itself a body of knowledge; rather, it is a content-free *model*—a set of highly abstract assumptions or rules that can be applied to understand systemic change (Buckley 1967, 1968). Models, which provide a means of examining selected aspects of reality, are at a higher level of abstraction than a theory; they simplify this reality while retaining its essential features (Chin 1961). Therefore, models do not describe the real world. Rather, they are a map or transparency that can be superimposed on social groupings to show their relatedness (Greene 2008a).

*Terms*

As they go about the helping process, social workers come into contact with an array of social systems. Before one can understand the basic assumptions of how systems function effectively, it is necessary to define the major terms of general systems and how they are used in assessment. A *social system* is "an aggregation of interrelated and interconnected people who form an identifiable, organized, and functioning whole" (Sheafor and Horejsi 2008, 87).

One of practitioners' first tasks in assessment is to identify a focal system that will receive primary attention, which includes ascertaining the difficulties and resources that may be addressed (Longres

2000). The family is the focal system that is examined in this chapter. A *family* is a social system consisting of individuals who are related to one another by reason of strong reciprocal affection and loyalties and who comprise a permanent household or cluster of households that persist over time (Fields and Casper 2000).

Some theorists use the terms *functional* and *dysfunctional* to describe family functioning (Corey 2001). *Functional systems* are said to be more open to outside influences and more flexible, adaptable, and goal achieving; in contrast, *dysfunctional systems* are considered to be relatively closed and are apt to be inflexible and less effective. However, some practitioners have found these problem-like descriptions unacceptable and have shifted the focus to family adaptability and task performance. For example, according to Goldenberg and Goldenberg (2003),

> A family is a natural social system with properties all its own, one that has evolved a set of rules, is replete with assigned and ascribed roles for its members, has an organized power structure, has developed intricate overt and covert forms of communication, and has elaborated ways of negotiating and problem solving that permit tasks to be performed effectively. (3)

Thus, family competence is likened here to the ability to perform tasks, adapt to new circumstances, and ensure reciprocal emotional attachments.

Competence also depends on a shared sense of history, purpose, and meaning. Bronfenbrenner (1990) outlined five propositions that describe the processes that foster the development of human competence and character. At the core of these principles is a child's emotional, physical, intellectual, and social need for ongoing, mutual interaction with a caring adult—and preferably with many adults. Although their functions continue to evolve, families often provide for the rearing and socializing of children, offer intimacy and a sense of belonging, assist family members who are vulnerable, act as an economic unit, and provide legal and social identity.

As adaptation and competence may vary by family form, social workers need to learn from their client families how they organize themselves. Family forms include *reconstituted or blended families* composed of a husband and wife who bring children from previous unions; *extended families*, which include parents, unmarried children, grandparents, married children, and aunts and uncles; *consanguine families*, which consist of people who place an emphasis on blood relationships; and *same-sex couples or partnerships* composed of two people of the same sex with or without children.

A family's form determines its boundaries. The *boundaries* of a family system give the practitioner an indication of who is "in" and who is "out," or who is a member of the family. Because systems are organizations of individuals united in some form of regular interaction or interdependence (Walsh 2006), each system takes on a unique character or a defined structure based on the identified membership. For example, a competent family may be composed of two fathers and a child or many "aunties." Therefore, the practitioner may ask who the members might include in their family system.

*Structure* refers to the pattern of stable relationships of family system members and is usually based on the functions and roles that each person carries out. Family interactions contribute to a recognizable, discernible pattern of organization that comes about through repeated interaction between family members. *Organization* refers to the grouping(s) or arrangement(s) of the system members. A competent structure is one that is capable of carrying out family tasks. Consequently, the social worker observes and confirms with the family members the nature of their organizing principles.

One structural family feature that the practitioner learns about is *hierarchy*, or the "division of labor" and "pecking order" associated with family membership. Understanding family hierarchy involves discovering who is in charge of particular aspects of family functioning. In some cultures it is expected that the father will have parental control; however, no one structure is considered more adaptive. For example, Russians have a saying about parent roles: "Although the father is the head of the family, the mother is the neck. And the head must move in the direction of the neck!" This demonstrates the pivotal role that women hold within the Russian family system (Kropf, Nackerud, and Gorokhovsky 1999). Regardless of the cultural background of the family, the structure must work to keep the family stable and to provide positive nurturing. Therefore, practitioners assess whether the family's hierarchical structure interferes with or promotes positive family life.

Another feature of a family's structure is its *subsystems*, or the components of a system that have a system of their own, such as systems based on generation, gender, interest, or function. The nature of subsystem formation is often fluid, depending on family interaction and the task at hand. How a family organizes and reorganizes its subsystems over time is an important aspect of its adaptiveness. The practitioner observes and listens for information about how well each family member fits in the family system (Sheafor and Horejsi 2008, 20). For example, family therapists believe that a family is more adaptive if the parent subsystem is in charge of the child subsystem.

Another important property of family systems is communication. *Communication*, or the flow of information within and from outside the system, represents an exchange of energy. Practitioners need to assess the family system's means of transmitting information between two or more individuals, as this serves as the basis for the evolving relationships between its members (Walsh 2006). It is through communication that family members express their needs and expectations. When a family has a relatively freer flow of communication or energy within and from outside the system, it is considered to be relatively *open*. That is, members are willing to discuss how their family "gets its job done" and are comfortable reaching out to other systems for assistance and recreation. When there is little exchange with the environment, the family is considered *closed*. The closed system has unclear communication among members and is less likely to be involved with other systems. Some families may feel more vulnerable or less supported by the community. Practitioners will find that systems exist along a continuum from relatively open to closed (Goldenberg and Goldenberg 2003).

Communication or *energy* permits the family to perform its functions and is critical to the family's adaptiveness (Greene 2008a). For example, energy may take the form of, for example, a paycheck. Systems take in energy (*input*) and use a *feedback mechanism* to process the information and maintain a *steady state*, or equilibrium. If a family loses a job (a paycheck) during a recession, it must use the information to restructure its economic activities. *Output*, or interactions with other social systems, such as taking a job training course, may also contribute to the stability of the system. Cybernetic principles also play out in the transactions that occur among members of the system. Understanding this process of *circular change*—in which one member influences another in a ripple effect—is a major contribution of general systems theory.

The social worker's examination of *family development* provides an understanding of the family life cycle. Although there is no single developmental pattern, normative or expected rhythms are sometimes referenced (Carter and McGoldrick 2005). Family changes across the life cycle result in relationships shifting and altering to meet member needs over time. In addition, internal and external demands can bring about new circumstances, sometimes stressing the family system (see Figure 4.1). Carter and McGoldrick (1999) developed a schema to depict the stress of everyday life. It consists of a horizontal axis representing time (family development) and a vertical axis illustrating variously sized social systems.

Horizontal stressors depicted on the schema include:

> developmental events, such as life cycle transitions and migration;
>
> unpredictable events, such as the untimely death of a friend or family member, chronic illness, accident, and unemployment; and
>
> historical events, such as war, economic depression, the political climate, and natural disasters.

Vertical stressors include:

> racism, sexism, classism, ageism, consumerism, and poverty;
>
> the disappearance of community, more work, less leisure, the inflexibility of the workplace, and no time for friends;

### Figure 4.1 The Context for Assessing Stress in Families

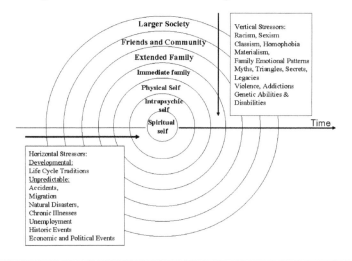

*Source:* Adapted from Carter and McGoldrick (1999, 6).

family emotional patterns, myths, triangles, secrets, legacies, and losses;

violence, addictions, ignorance, depression, and lack of spiritual expression or dreams; and

genetic makeup, abilities, and disabilities. (Carter and McGoldrick 1999, 6)

Families that are more *closed* may experience increased *stress* or *tension*, whereas family systems that are relatively *open* have a freer flow of energy and are thought to be more adaptable. Family systems that are less able to maintain stability become disorganized, a process known as *entropy*. Responding successfully to stress requires that family behaviors change, bringing about a time of transition. At times, stress may bring about disorganization, at which time families may seek help from social service agencies (Compton & Galaway, 1989; Hepworth et al. 2006).

*Basic Assumptions*

Ludwig von Bertalanffy (1962), a leading systems theorist, argued that to understand a system, the social worker cannot view any one part in isolation. He pointed out that a system has a Gestalt pattern or a holistic property that cannot be observed separately from its parts. Therefore, it is necessary for the social worker to assess the relationships among family members, considering any one individual's behavior to be a consequence of the total social situation (Walsh 2006).

The idea that every family member's behavior affects everyone else is known as *circular causality* (Andreae 1996). The communication system of the family regulates and controls its ability to function, and principles for how these controls function are borrowed from the field of cybernetics. Goldenberg and Goldenberg (2003) pointed out that the term *cybernetics* comes from the Greek for *steersman*, suggesting the piloting of a ship through rough waters by means of a feedback mechanism. Because a change in one member affects all, change creates a ripple effect and brings about a different family configuration. Family therapists keep this principle in mind as they help a family adapt by reconfiguring its structure and/or communication patterns.

"Perhaps the major contribution that systems theory makes to an understanding of human behavior in the social environment is an explanation of how systems maintain stability as they grow and change" (Greene 2008a, 181). Social systems tend to be adaptable, but they are in constant interaction with environmental demands, which often creates tension that may upset their balance. Family members' interactions with the environment influence the internal workings of the family system. (These systems' levels include the micro, meso, and macro and are discussed in Chapter 1.) When imbalances occur, the system attempts to right itself by discriminating, mapping, and responding to the environment. This process of "structuring, deconstructing, and reconstructing" the family system may come about naturally or as a result of practitioner intervention (Buckley 1968, 494). Sometimes a family may even reach a higher level of organization by reconstructing itself.

Thus, the competent family may first resist change or be thrown off balance by change produced by stress, but at the same time it may be attempting to right itself. Family members may try to restore family balance by obtaining new resources, using new problem-solving strategies, reducing demands, or changing their perception of their situation (Kropf and Greene 2002). The *belief system*, or the perception of events, affects a family's ability to change, especially when undergoing a crisis. What is the family members' shared purpose? Can they frame their situation more optimistically? Belief systems may foster family change through expectations for the future, confidence in overcoming odds, spirituality, and/or creativity (Walsh 2006).

*Family-Focused Treatment*

General systems theory has given birth to many schools of family therapy, all of which assume that "change in one part of the unit reverberates throughout other parts" (Corey 2001, 387). Consequently, the goal of family-focused social work practice is to change, alter, or improve family relationship patterns. This form of intervention can be viewed according to a continuum from A to Z. The practitioner who represents the idealized Type A polarity of intervention views the family as a circular interchange of emotion (Ackerman 1972). This practitioner's methods are psychodynamically oriented, and the goal is to develop insight into negative aspects of family functioning. Therapists who adopt the Type Z form of intervention may see themselves as family coaches who help families meet the goal of restructuring (Bowen 1971; Minuchin 1974). These social workers assist families in achieving their goals by pointing out what might be problematic behaviors as observed in the here and now.

Depending on the school of thought adopted by the practitioner, the goal of treatment may be

> repairing the family's self-defeating interactive patterns,
>
> opening up the style and manner of communication,
>
> strengthening the structure of the family unit, or
>
> relieving a family member of symptoms. (Goldenberg and Goldenberg 2003, 7)

Social workers may use a *genogram* to depict the inner workings of the family constellation. In this process, the family that has asked for help is asked to outline three generations of family relationships. The practitioner uses the genealogical tree to obtain information on "ethnic and religious background, major family events, occupations, losses, family migrations and dispersal, identifications, role assignments...communication patterns" (Hartman and Laird 1987, 215; see also Hartman 1978).

The ability of families to change their unit is called *plasticity*. Plasticity enables the system to maintain a system–environment fit that is necessary for effective family functioning. The family may reach the same endpoint through different routes. This concept, which is known as *equifinality*, accounts for differences in families at different points in time. As social systems evolve or develop over time, each member takes on differentiated roles. *Differentiation*, or a change in behavior, occurs when new expectations are placed on members and on the system, such as providing care for an older relative. To enable family members to accomplish such tasks, a differentiation of roles within the family occurs (Greene 2008b).

For example, *kin keeping* or *kinship care*, which refer to arrangements in which relatives step into the parenting role, have always been latent family resources (Chan and Elder 2000; Hirshorn, 1998; Kolomer 2000). However, census data suggest that the number of grandparent-headed families is increasing dramatically. In addition, the number of children in what is called a *skipped generation household*, or a household that is headed by neither biological parent, is also on the rise. As already stated, changes in any one family member have a ripple effect throughout the system, stretching, reorganizing, and redefining the relationship between family members. The case below shows that these life course role transitions do not occur according to "usual" expectations but rather seem to violate the expected timetable and thus are termed *off time* (Greene 2008b).

*Case Example*

Ms. Anderson is a sixty-two-year-old grandmother who is raising her two grandchildren. She has been doing this for about three years, because her daughter became a drug addict and was less able to raise her young sons. Instead of finding foster care, Ms. Anderson brought them into her home and has been their primary caregiver.

Making this decision at age sixty-two has had various consequences. One is that as a result of taking in her two grandsons, Ms. Anderson has had less time to spend as a grandmother to her other grandchildren.

In addition, her daughter periodically sobers up and returns to see her two sons. When she does returns, there is a great deal of disruption within the family, as the boys are confused about their allegiances. Their mother is indulgent, letting them stay up late and miss school. Ms. Anderson, who tries to maintain stability, insists that they stay on their schedule. This creates confusion and divided loyalties. When their mother leaves again, the boys are despondent. They are unable to deal with the re-abandonment they feel when their mother leaves them.

In addition, Ms. Anderson has been widowed for five years, so she is raising these two children as a single parent for the first time in her life. As an off-time caregiver, she feels that her friends and peers do not understand what she is experiencing, as they are not in the same situation with their own grandchildren.

## Role Theory

*The discharge of tensions in the "doing" of a role, the feedback from other persons or from circumstances that give evidence of competence and "payoff"—all these moving forces are involved in active performance of vital roles.*

*—Perlman (1968, 3)*

During the 1960s and early 1970s, a renewed focus on the environmental factors that influence personality prompted social workers' interest in role theory (Strean 1979). Role theory was originated by social scientists who wanted to explain the relationship between a social structure and the way individuals enact their socially designated or normative behaviors.

Earlier, human behavior theorists and practitioners had empha-sized intrapsychic processes, moving away from social activism (see Chapter 2). According to Hamilton (1958), social workers' increased attention to the concept of social role represented a "revolution" in the social sciences, offering social and cultural insights that would provide an understanding of a client's "ethnic, class, and other sig-nificant group determinants of behavior" (xi).

The construct of role was introduced into social work practice as a way of "studying and describing the interaction of members of a social group as they adjust to each other within a social system" (Turner 1996, 319). The assumptions of role theory are often used in conjunction with systems theory to bring about more culturally sensitive interventions. The construct of role theory allows for an exploration of interpersonal systems and the underlying assumptions about family definitions, gender roles, and hierarchical structures that are based on role relationships (Carter, McGoldrick, and Bloch 2004). Role theory is also used "to clarify and describe the nature of a client's difficulty in performing role-related behaviors," such as difficulty in the workplace (Sheafor and Horejsi 2008, 264).

As role theory evolved, it focused on a number of issues of inter-est to social work, including how an individual is socialized into role behavior, the stresses that may emerge as an individual performs multiple roles, and the impact on an individual when he or she does not live up to normative or prescribed behaviors. In addition, role theory helps the practitioner examine the relationship between client status, power, and access to resources (Davis 1996).

## Terms

Talcott Parsons (1961), a sociologist interested in the "plurality of individual actors" (5) in the family and other systems, examined system communication, culture, and shared symbols. He contended that each social action is actually a "process in the actor-situation system" (4). For example, parents are expected to provide children with food, protection, shelter, and guidance, and children have the right to be cared for. Therefore, one role must be viewed in reference to other roles, such as parent–child or client–social worker. Because roles are interrelated, what constitutes a claim for one party is an obligation for another. *Role expectations*, or what is deemed appro-priate by a reference group or by a given society, are also anticipated in school settings (e.g., a teacher is expected to teach and motivate a student, who in turn is expected to learn what the teacher selects as important; Sheafor and Horejsi 2008). Consequently, each action has a collective meaning.

A role may also be thought of as a *social position* or a social category, such as employer and employee. Although an individual carries out a role related to a certain social position, he or she must carry out behaviors with another person in particular situations. Positions may be *ascribed* (dependent on the accident of birth) or *achieved* (earned through a person's efforts). A person's *status* refers to the value placed on his or her role—prestige, power, or authority. When social workers work with clients who have lower status in their community, empowering them is part of the helping process.

Role theory examines the attitudes and behaviors expected of people in particular positions and suggests that others' expectations always influence the expectations of the self. Because roles are simultaneously "an element of the individual and an element of a social system," the concept of role exemplifies the person-in-environment paradigm (Longres 2000, 41; see Figure 4.2). Figure 4.2 shows that some roles are specific to (a) the microlevel of family and friends, (b) the mesolevel of community and other nonfamily small groups or organizations, and (c) the macrolevel of national (or global) organizations. Still other roles may be thought of as cutting across the micro-, meso-, and macrolevels. This suggests that roles are influenced by and must be assessed at multiple cultural levels.

*Types of Roles*

Role theory is a means of operationalizing the person–environment perspective by addressing issues in social functioning. In 1981, the National Association of Social Workers began a project to classify problems in social functioning called the *Person-in-Environment System*. The organizing taskforce believed that most social work clients seek help because they are having difficulties performing social roles. The taskforce identified environmental problems, mental health problems, physical health problems, and four major role categories:

1. *Family roles* play out in a family context and consist of the subcategories of parent, spouse, child, sibling, other family role, and significant other.
2. *Other interpersonal roles* are enacted in interpersonal relationships between individuals but not between members of the same family.

## Figure 4.2 Types of Roles: Levels and Categories

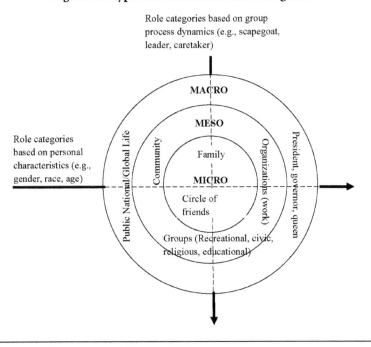

Role categories based on group process dynamics (e.g., scapegoat, leader, caretaker)

Role categories based on personal characteristics (e.g., gender, race, age)

MACRO

MESO

Family

MICRO

Circle of friends

Groups (Recreational, civic, religious, educational)

Public National/Global Life

Community

Organizations (work)

President, governor, queen

*Source:* From Thompson and Greene (2008).

These may consist of lover, friend, neighbor, member, and other interpersonal roles.

3. *Occupational roles* are performed in the paid or unpaid economy and consist of worker, home worker, volunteer, student, and other occupational roles.

4. *Special life situation roles* include consumer, inpatient, outpatient, probationer, prisoner, legal immigrant, undocumented immigrant, refugee, and other special life situation roles (Karls and Wandrei 1994, 25–26).

Also developed during the Person-in-Environment System project was a means of assessing problems in role functioning by severity and duration, as well as a means of assessing the coping skills of the client. Assessment eventuates a mutual understanding of how a client is experiencing challenges in role performance. These challenges stem from the fact that people occupy multiple roles, such as parent, child, social worker, and/or clergy.

According to Thompson and Greene (2008), conducting a role analysis includes determining all of the demands that contribute to a client's social functioning. For example, a woman may be a wife, a mother, a daughter, and a worker. She is expected to fulfill these roles in highly particular ways shaped by past as well as current contexts and the woman's reference groups. A comprehensive role assessment must also include knowledge of the normative role expectations specific to the client's geographic locale, which in turn gives further context to each role performance. Hence, role analyses require the inclusion of socioeconomic, cultural, and biopsychological data.

Negative outcomes in role performance may include the following:

> *role ambiguity*, which may arise when a person is uncertain about the behaviors associated with a particular role;
>
> *role conflict*, which may arise when a person has contrary or incompatible demands in several roles, such as going to university classes and getting to work on time;
>
> *role incapacity*, which may exist when an individual cannot perform a role, such as with an injured soldier;
>
> *role incongruity*, which may occur when two or more people disagree about the expectations for a specific role, such as what makes a "good" professor;
>
> *role overload*, which may occur when a person occupies more roles than he or she can perform adequately, such as when a woman must work, be a parent, and be a caregiver when her husband becomes sick; and
>
> *role strain*, which can arise when an individual experiences too many demands in one role, such as when a student has multiple assignments due on one day. (Compton, Galaway, and Cournoyer 2005; Sheafor and Horejsi 2008)

### *The Work Role: Assessment*

Because individuals perform many roles in a given day, role theory is particularly helpful during assessment. Practitioners learn what difficulties a client has in fulfilling the various roles expected of him or her and what role changes are causing distress. In today's world, stress related to the workplace is on the rise, and many workers report role overload accompanied by feelings of being overwhelmed and overtired (Schwartz 2004). Galambos, Livingston, and Greene (2007) reminded practitioners that "work commands the majority of waking hours for millions of Americans" (201).

Mager and Pipe (1997) proposed four questions for analyzing job-related performance stressors:

1. What is the nature and degree of discrepancy between actual performance and role expectations?
2. Is the discrepancy caused by a lack of knowledge or skill?
3. If the discrepancy is caused by a lack of knowledge or skill, how best can the problem be addressed?
4. If the discrepancy is caused by a rejection or a lack of interest in the role, how can the problem be addressed? (as summarized from Sheafor and Horejsi 2008, 265)

To reduce workplace stressors and be more competent in the workplace, workers cannot overlook signs of stress and need to take actions to relieve it. However, employee assistance workers deal with more than role strain or the competing nature of multiple demands. They must also address workplace organization, management styles, and communication. The following case illustrates the need for better supervisor training to create a more supportive workplace environment.

### Case Example

When Brenda Matthis majored in computer science at her university, she was one of only a handful of African American women in the department. As she watched others in the program, mostly young white men, receive opportunities to participate in research projects with the professors, she became more aware of how more mentoring could have helped her. The lack of guidance and close relationships with faculty members left Brenda feeling like an outsider in her own major.

Upon graduating, Brenda received a good job in her field. However, she felt a nagging sense that she should be doing more to help attract and mentor young women into the field of computer science. As part of a National Science Foundation grant, a local university received funding to help attract young women of color into the science and math fields, in which they had historically been underrepresented. Although one other African American worked at the firm, Brenda was selected to serve as the internship coordinator. Brenda was initially thrilled, as she could see the importance of this program in the lives of young women.

However, the responsibilities of leading the internship were greater than she had imagined. The interns were expected to complete several required experiences, and these were not part of the work that the company typically performed. Because she was a relatively new hire, Brenda did not have the authority to institute new computing procedures, so the interns could meet the requirements of the grant. In addition, there was no one in the organization to serve as a source of information and support, so Brenda received limited guidance on how best to handle these issues.

Over time, Brenda's excitement started to turn to feelings of stress and being overwhelmed. The responsibilities of coordinating the internship and working with the young interns started compromising the other work to which Brenda was assigned. As a result, she started losing sleep and feeling fatigued and irritable.

## Critique

The general systems and role theories were developed during a period of family and societal stability when the dominating paradigm was functionalist. This paradigm placed an emphasis on the nuclear family of two adults living together with their children. Roles were socially determined, with the male roles associated with public and political activities and female roles, expressive and caring activities. Although it was accepted that patterns would vary from family to family as well as within each family over time, this process of understanding systems was generally accepted as an innovative means of working with families (Herr and Weakland 1979).

However, as families evolve and diverse family forms became more recognized, the idea that families have fixed roles and life cycles came under question (Laird 1996). For example, same-sex partners do not have the legal rights of traditional couples. In addition, feminists such as Betty Friedan joined theory with political action and took exception to the place of prescribed gender roles. It is here that socialization comes into play, as children are taught rules for gender identification or how to treat people who are "different" (Van Voorhis 2008; see Chapter 2). Ironically, Parsons (1964) believed that as society evolved there would be a more complex division of labor and differentiation of roles. In fact, Parsons thought of himself as a cultural determinist, believing that family members were socialized to the particular mores and emotional tone operating within a family system at a particular time and place.

Linton (1936/1976), another founder of role theory, described a *role* as "the sum total of the cultural patterns associated with a particular status" (76). Because a given society defines the norms for how behaviors are to be performed, the behaviors that result are considered to be normative. *Normative behaviors* are those valued in a particular community or culture and consist of behaviors that "ought to be." However, one's personal beliefs and assumptions about a particular role may not conform to those defined by others or the society in general (*role conception*).

Because roles are often viewed through a cultural lens, it may be difficult for the practitioner to help a client sort out what constitutes appropriate or effective role performance. This fine-tuning of role performance gives it particular meaning in a specific cultural system. Several areas of research have analyzed various cultural-, gender-, and age-related patterns of social roles. Because social workers need to take a learning stance and become familiar with the *mores* of particular families—the cultural expectations, customs, and norms by which the families live—more attention is needed to how theories fit with various family forms (Laird 1993).

Because roles are socially constructed perceptions of behaviors, there are different expectations for role functioning across different subpopulations. For example, research on gender roles among African American adolescents provides evidence that attributes of feminine and masculine roles are created based upon historical trends within the family (Palapattu, Kingery, and Ginsburg 2006). Researchers measured both the gender role orientations of adolescents and adolescents' level of adherence to "traditional" female and male role behaviors. The results showed that the adolescents had a high level of role fluidity in the form of women expressing more traditional male behaviors. The researchers suggested that these patterns evolved from the era of slavery, when women assumed male traits of assertiveness, confidence, and leadership.

Research on African American nonresidential fathers has also indicated that flexibility in role expectations can enhance competency and adjustment within the family. In a study of separated and divorced fathers, lower levels of involvement with their children were partially explained by retaining a definition of the fatherhood role based upon a model of residing within the same household (Leite and McKenry 2006). Those fathers who were more involved with their children were able to adapt their role expectations and create ways to maintain connection and involvement even when they were no longer within the same household.

Other research has looked at gender role relationships within families with various racial/ethnic identities. These studies suggest that family competence is enhanced when parents are not restricted to gender-based role functions. In immigrant families, for example, the process of acculturation with the concomitant process of adjusting to new norms, social relationships, and expectations requires individuals to be more flexible in their role expectations (Pinto and Coltrane 2009; Qin 2009). These families often face numerous challenges that affect role functioning. For example, men and women may struggle to find work in their new country that has comparable intrinsic meaning and extrinsic rewards. A teacher or engineer may become a laborer or small business owner because comparable jobs are unavailable. In addition, the relationships between parents and children, and the subsequent family dynamics, can lead to intergenerational conflicts (Lee et al. 2009; Updegraff, Delgado, and Wheeler 2009). The ability of the family to function harmoniously may be challenged as generations adapt in different ways to new communities and social roles.

Families also have to negotiate and balance demands of multiple systems when caring for older family members. As systems theory indicates, exchanges take place between a family system and the larger environment. The workplace is one such system. It creates a sense of purpose within the adult role and provides financial benefits that promote family functioning. When families are caring for older family members, however, the balance of work and family life can create challenges and stresses within personal and work-related roles.

Although much of the caregiving literature has focused on women's experiences, there is evidence that men and women both struggle with eldercare responsibilities. Findings from a study on men's and women's work–family conflicts in caregiving indicated that women and men have different experiences in enacting their roles (Barrah et al. 2004). Married men with greater eldercare responsibilities reported the greatest amount of family-related interference in their work roles. Married women associated higher levels of stress with being a woman, working more hours, lacking the support of a supervisor, and lacking a flexible work schedule. Although this research suggests that both genders experience caregiving stress that compromises their sense of role competence, men and women do not have the same set of challenges.

When individuals in social roles do not fulfill the expected associated behaviors, they may receive messages of deviance or experience stress. Two different areas of research indicate that behaving differently than expected can create challenges for both the individual and the surrounding social systems. One area of research that supports this premise is in sex role stereotyping and sexual orientation. Various studies have indicated that stereotypes of people who are gay and lesbian abound (England 1992; Madon 1997). In a study of various social roles and gay men, researchers reported that "nonstereotypical" gay men were the most perplexing for respondents to understand (Fingerhut and Peplau 2006). When shown a picture of a gay male truck driver, for example, respondents had a more difficult time assessing his level of masculinity than when shown pictures of more stereotypical gay men (e.g., a hairdresser).

The other area of research has indicated difficulties associated with individuals demonstrating unexpected role behaviors. In a study of nursing home care, residents who had declining levels of health were classified into categories corresponding to possible end-of-life situations (Bern-Klug 2009). Findings indicated that end-of-life care was facilitated when the residents' behaviors and prognoses were congruent. That is, social interactions between staff, the family, and the patient were optimized for end-of-life care when the resident who was dying evidenced those behaviors and experiences that are typically associated with the dying role (Fandetti & Goldmeir, 1988). A lack of congruence (i.e., when people acted as if they were dying but really were not) created more stress within care plans and expectations.

The following case example integrates system and role theories to examine the experience of gay fathers. In general, childrearing continues to be a role that is associated more with women and feminine gender role characteristics. As a result, gay fathers can benefit from the support of others in similar family types as well as from support in redefining the role of parent to be more expansive and less gender bound. Social workers can provide assistance in helping gay fathers with these tasks.

## Case Example

Jerry Atkins is a social worker at an elementary school in a large metropolitan environment. The school represents a very diverse population of students by race/ethnicity, religion, and family structure.

Jerry has been instrumental in developing and offering several programs at the school to both honor the differences the students' families represent as well as bring together families with similar backgrounds to meet and create support networks as part of the school community.

One of these groups is of children in same-sex families. Jerry has reached out to gay fathers in particular to provide a forum for these men to meet. Several of the men share custody of their children with their ex-wives, whereas others have adopted children into their families. The program provides social times (e.g., a picnic and some play dates at the school) as well as a connection between these families to support the men in this role.

As a unique group of parents, the fathers have expressed that certain aspects of fatherhood are challenging for them. One of these is the message they receive that they do not have the same ability to parent children as women in terms of being nurturing or empathetic. In addition, fathers of boys seem to be questioned about their "maleness" and about whether they are appropriate role models for their sons.

As a result of the school program, several of the fathers have formed friendships and a support group outside of the more formal structure. They meet for coffee on a regular basis and often discuss issues of raising children in an environment that continues to privilege the woman as the model parent. As a result of Jerry's efforts, these men have been able to forge bonds and create a social structure that promotes a sense of efficacy in their parenting role.

## References

Ackerman, N. 1972. Family psychotherapy-theory and practice. In *Family therapy: An introduction to theory and technique*, ed. G. D. Erikson and T. P. Hogan. Monterey, CA: Brooks/Cole .

Andreae, D. 1996. Systems theory and social work treatment. In *Social work treatment*, ed. F. Turner, 610–16. New York: Free Press.

Barrah, J. L., K. S. Shultz, B. Baltes, and H. E. Stolz. 2004. Men's and women's eldercare-based work-family conflict: Antecedents and work-related outcomes. *Fathering* 2:305–30.

Bern-Klug, M. 2009. A framework for categorizing social interactions related to end-of-life care in nursing homes. *The Gerontologist* 49:495–507.

Bowen, M. 1971. Aging: A symposium. *Georgetown Medical Bulletin* 30, no. 3:4–27.

Bronfenbrenner, U. 1990. Discovering what families do. In *Rebuilding the nest: A new commitment to the American family*, ed. D. Blankenhorn, S. Bayme, and J. B. Elshtain. New York: Family Service America . Pp. 27-38

Buckley, W. 1967. Systems and entities. In *Sociology and modern systems theory*, ed. W. Buckley, 42–66. Englewood Cliffs, NJ: Prentice Hall.

_____.1968. Society as a complex adaptive system. In *Modern systems research for the behavioral scientist*, ed. W. Buckley, 490–511. Chicago, IL: Aldine.

Carter, B., and M. McGoldrick. 1999. *The expanded family life cycle: Individual, family, and social perspectives.* 3rd ed. Boston, MA: Allyn & Bacon.

_____ 2005. *The expanded family life cycle: Individual, family, and societal perspectives.* Boston, MA: Allyn & Bacon.

Carter, E. A., M. McGoldrick, and D. A. Bloch. 2004. *The expanded family life cycle: Individual, family, and social perspectives.* Boston, MA: Allyn & Bacon.

Chan, C. G., and G. H. Elder. 2000. Matrilineal advantage in grandchild-grandparent relations. *The Gerontologist* 40:179–90.

Chin, R. 1961. The utility of systems models for practitioners. In *The planning of change: Readings in the applied behavioral science*s, ed. W. G. Bennes, K. D. Berne, and R. Chin, 90–113. New York: Holt, Rinehart & Winston.

Compton , B., and B. Galaway. 1989. *Social work processes.* 4th ed., 131–32. Chicago, IL: Dorsey.

Compton, B., B. Galaway, and B. Cournoyer. 2005. *Social work processes.* 7th ed. Monterey, CA: Wadsworth.

Corey, G. 2001. *Theory and practice of counseling and psychotherapy.* Belmont, CA: Wadsworth/Thomson Learning.

Davis, L. V. 1996. Role theory. In *Social work treatment*, ed. F. J. Turner, 581–600. New York: Free Press.

England, E. M. 1992. College student gender stereotypes: Expectations about the behavior of male subcategory members. *Sex Roles* 27:699–716.

Fandetti , D. V., and J. Goldmeier. 1988. Social workers as culture mediators in health care settings. *Health and Social Work* 13, no. 3:171–79.

Fields, J., and L. M. Casper. 2000. *American families and living arrangements* (Current Population Report No. P20-537). Washington, DC: U.S. Government Printing Office.

Fingerhut, A. W., and L. A. Peplau. 2006. The impact of social roles on stereotypes of gay men. *Sex Roles* 55:273–78.

Galambos, C., N. Livingston, and R. R. Greene. 2007. Workplace stressors: A preventive resilience approach. In *Social work practice: A risk and resilience perspective*, ed. R. R. Greene, 196–214. Belmont, CA: Thomson Brooks/Cole.

Goldenberg, I., and H. Goldenberg. 2003. *Family therapy: An overview.* Monterey, CA: Brooks/Cole.

Greene, R. R. 2008a. *Human behavior theory and social work practice.* New Brunswick, NJ: Aldine Transaction.

_____. 2008b. *Social work with the aged and their families.* New Brunswick, NJ: Aldine Transaction.

_____. Forthcoming (2010). A Holocaust survivorship model: Survivors' reflections. *Journal of Human Behavior and the Social Environment . 20(4), 569-579*

Hamilton, G. 1958. Foreword. In *Social perspectives on behavior*, ed. H. D. Stein and R. A. Cloward, xi–xiv. New York: Free Press.

Hartman, A. 1978. Diagrammatic assessment of family relationships. *Social Casework* 59:465–76.

Hartman, A., and J. Laird. 1987. Family practice. In *Encyclopedia of social work*, ed. A. Minahan (Ed.-in-Chief), vol. 1, 18th ed., 575–89. Silver Spring, MD: National Association of Social Workers.

Hepworth, D. H., H. Rooney, G. D. Rooney, K. Strom-Gottfried, and J. Larsen. 2006. *Direct social work practice: Theory and skills.* 7th ed. Belmont, CA: Thomson Brooks/Cole.

Herr, J. J., and J. H. Weakland. 1979. *Counseling elders and their families.* New York: Springer.

Hirshorn, B. A. 1998. Grandparents as caregivers. In *Handbook on grandparenthood*, ed. M. E. Szinovacz, 200–14. Westport, CT: Greenwood Press.

Karls, J. M., and K. E. Wandrei. 1994. *Person-in-environment system.* Washington, DC: NASW Press.

Kolomer, S. R. 2000. Kinship foster care and its impact on grandmother caregivers. *Journal of Gerontological Social Work* 33, no. 3:85–102.

Kropf, N., and R. R. Greene. 2002. People with developmental disabilities. In *Resiliency: An integrated approach to practice, policy, and research*, ed. R. R. Greene, 293–320. Washington, DC: NASW Press.

Kropf, N. P., L. Nackerud, and I. Gorokhovsky. 1999. Social work practice with older Soviet immigrants. *Journal of Multicultural Social Work* 7, no. 1/2:111–26.

Laird, J., ed. 1993. *Revisioning social work practice.* New York: Haworth Press.

———. 1996. Family-centered practice with lesbian and gay families. *Families in Society* 77:559–72.

Lee, R. M., K. R. Jung, J. C. Su, A. G. T. T. Tran, and N. Bahrassa. 2009. The family life and adjustment of Hmong American sons and daughters. *Sex Roles* 60:549–58.

Leite, R., and P. McKenry. 2006. A role theory perspective on patterns of separated and divorced African-American nonresidential father involvement with children. *Fathering* 4:1–21.

Linton, R. 1976. *The study of man.* New York: Appleton-Century-Croft. (Original work published 1936.)

Longres, J. 2000. *Human behavior in the social environment.* 3rd ed. Monterey, CA: Wadsworth.

Madon, S. 1997. What do people believe about gay males? A study of stereotype content and strength. *Sex Roles* 37:663–85.

Mager, R. F., and P. Pipe. 1997. *Analyzing performance problems, or, you really oughta wanna: How to figure out why people aren't doing what they should be, and what to do about it.* 3rd ed. Atlanta, GA: Center for Effective Performance.

Meyer, C. H. 1973. Direct services in new and old contexts. In *Shaping the new social work*, ed. A. J. Kahn, 26–54. New York: Columbia University Press.

Minuchin, S. 1974. *Families and family therapy.* Cambridge, MA: Harvard University Press.

Palapattu, A. G., J. N. Kingery, and G. S. Ginsburg. 2006. Gender role orientation and anxiety symptoms among African American adolescents. *Journal of Abnormal Child Psychology* 34:441–49.

Parsons, T. 1961. *Theories of society: Foundations of modern sociological theory.* New York: Free Press.

———. 1964. Age and sex in the social structure. In *The family: Its structure and functions,* ed. R. L. Coser, 251–66. New York: St. Martin's Press.

Perlman , H. H. 1962. The role concept and social casework: Some explanations. *Social Service Review* 36:17–31.

———. 1968. *Persona: Social role and responsibility.* Chicago, IL: University of Chicago Press.

Pinto, K. M., and S. Coltrane. 2009. Divisions of labor in Mexican origin and Anglo families: Structure and culture. *Sex Roles* 60:482–95.

Qin, D. B. 2009. Gendered processes of adaptation: Understanding parent-child relations in Chinese immigrant families. *Sex Roles* 60:467–81.

Schwartz, J. 2004. Always at work and anxious: Employees' health suffering. *New York Times,* September 5, 1.

Sheafor, B. W., and C. R. Horejsi. 2008. *Techniques and guidelines for social work practice.* 8th ed. Boston, MA: Allyn & Bacon.

Strean, H. S. 1971. *Social casework theories in action.* Metuchen, NJ: Scarecrow.

———. 1979. Role theory. In *Social work treatment,* ed. F. J. Turner, 314–42. New York: Free Press.

Thompson, K., and R. R. Greene. 2008. Role theory. In *Human behavior: A diversity framework,* ed. R. R. Greene and N. Kropf, 2nd ed., 101–22. New Brunswick, NJ: Aldine Transaction.

Turner, F. J. 1996. *Social work treatment.* New York: Free Press.

Updegraff, K. A., M. Y. Delgado, and L. A. Wheeler. 2009. Exploring mothers' and fathers' relationships with sons versus daughters: Links to adolescent adjustment in Mexican immigrant families. *Sex Roles* 60:559–74.

Van Voorhis, R. 2008. Feminism. In *Human behavior theory and social work practice,* ed. R. R. Greene, 265–90. New Brunswick, NJ: Aldine Transaction.

von Bertalanffy, L. 1962. General systems theory: A critical review. *General Systems Yearbook* 7:1–20.

Walsh, F. 2006. *Strengthening family resilience.* New York: Guilford Press.

# 5

# Meaning-Making:
# Self-Affirmation and
# Transcendence

*This sense of profound cultural change, accumulated technologies of
the twentieth century ... were radically altering the character of my life
and those around me. The effects seemed both promising and perilous.
The firm sense of self, close relationships, and community were being
replaced by the multiplicitous, the contingent, and the partial.*

*Gergen (2000, xiv)*

Previous chapters in this text have described stage theories, such
as those originated by Freud, Kolberg, and Piaget, to explain the
development of the self in relation to *individuation*, or separation
and independence from others. Object relations theory, for example,
emphasizes how infants split from a symbiotic, or conjoined, relationship with their parent caregiver, developing a unique, distinct
personality.

In this chapter we discuss existential, humanistic, and social
constructionist theories and build on the symbolic interactional
perspective of the self—one that arises from interaction with others.
*Self-transcendence* expands the assumptions of the social basis of
the self, discussing theories that provide an understanding of how
people gain a higher sense of consciousness about their inner selves.
From this perspective, people not only form their personalities in
unity with others, but also they connect with meaning beyond their
own immediate personal concerns. *Transpersonal theories* are used
to reconnect clients with their significant others and to foster their
sense of community and spirituality.

Transpersonal theories focus on people's highest aspirations and
potential, emphasizing "love, meaning, creativity, and communion
with others and the universe" (Robbins, Chatterjee, and Canda 2006,
386). Theorists focus on these aspects of human development are

interested in the development of the whole person—body, mind, and spirit—offering a nonsectarian framework for dealing with spirituality.

Human behavior theories reflect the sociohistorical times in which the theorist explains human functioning. Since the end of War World II, these theories have expressed increasing concern with the "erosion of the centered self" (Gergen 2000, xiv). Major threats to psychological stability such as domestic and foreign terrorism have prompted a demand for theories that address dealing with life's daily uncertainties and overcoming a sense of amorphous anxiety (Lifton 1999).

Social work practice models also reflect "the needs of the times, the problems they present, the fears they generate, the solutions that appeal, and the knowledge and skills available" (Reynolds 1969/1985, 55). In the twentieth century, models of psychoanalytic theory that emphasized intrapsychic phenomena expanded into a psychosocial approach to the study of human functioning. By the 1980s, systems theory and the ecological perspective were widely adopted, culminating in the pluralistic multi-systemic practice of the 1990s (Cowley 1996; Greene 2008).

This approach involved a change in *paradigm*, or how people perceive reality. *Modernists* or *positivists* focus on using the scientific method to develop normative stage theories, whereas *postmodernists* give less credence to scientists' ability to discover the ultimate truth, instead emphasizing art, intuition, spirituality, and the creation of meaning within a cultural, historical, and sociopolitical context (Weick 1993).

Each successive theory increased the understanding of human growth and development. This process has been described by Cowley (1996) as the *Four Forces of Psychology* (London 1974, 1986). The *First Force*, dominated by Freudian thought, was based on deterministic views of psychological development and provided an explanation of psychopathology or mental distress. Practitioners helped to uncover and ameliorate unconscious motivations for negative, socially unacceptable behaviors, and people were portrayed as guilt ridden and repressed.

The *Second Force* stressed giving relief to symptomatic, observable behavior. Evidence to document the effects of interventions was sought. Structural and cognitive therapies were said to provide for practitioner accountability. The *Third Force* focused on the search for self-fulfillment and self-actualization. It encompassed *humanistic theory*, involving people's innate potential for love, creativity, and spirituality; *experiential/client-centered theory*, addressing how people can fully experience repressed emotion; and *existential theory*, including the need to clarify values and find meaning in a seemingly meaningless world. The Third Force expanded psychological thought to less observable and measurable subjects, searching for the "farther reaches of human nature" (Maslow 1971).

Theorists and clinicians of the *Fourth Force* are more immersed in models that incorporate spiritual concerns. Technology is said to have produced global connections and introduced people to multiple perspectives, but with a negative impact on the human process of relating well to others. The aim of treatment frameworks that stem from the Fourth Force is to reconnect the seemingly autonomous self with a "completion or fulfillment of self in communion with others" (Robbins, Chatterjee, and Canda 2006, 389).

### Existential Theory: Frankl, Rollo May, and Yalom

*One of the few blessings of living in an age of anxiety is that we are forced to become aware of ourselves. When our society, in its time of upheaval in standards and values, can give us no clear picture of "what we are and what we ought to be," ... we are thrown back on the search for ourselves.*

—Rollo May (1953, 7)

The existential philosophical movement arose in Europe during the 1940s and 1950s as a way of reflecting on dilemmas of an everyday life involving anxiety, alienation, and meaninglessness. Existential theorists suggested that people develop the capacity for self-awareness, experience freedom of action, take responsibility for themselves, construct their personal identities, establish intimate relationships, clarify their values, and search for meaning in life in response to feelings of anxiety and despair. However, existentialists contend that people must accept certain *givens*, such as their gender or the inevitability of anxiety, stress, and death (Corey 2001; Yalom 1980).

Rollo May (1953), who introduced existential philosophy to the United States, stated that "anxiety strikes us at the very 'core' of ourselves: it is what we feel when our existence as selves is threatened" (40). Although many therapies are designed to relieve anxiety, existential therapists believe that it is necessary for people to live with ambiguity and use the debilitating effects of anxiety "constructively" (43).

This means that in order for people to become competent they need to address the conflict within themselves, to mobilize their creative selves, and to discover life's purpose and meaning.

Creating new meaning, even in cases of severe stress or adversity, is at the heart of existential philosophy (Frankl 1959/2006; Yalom 1980). Victor Frankl, a psychiatrist who had been a slave laborer in a Nazi concentration camp during World War II, was a key figure in the development of existential thought and therapy. He believed that inner life becomes more intense when people facing adversity appreciate the beauty of nature and human love. He recorded his impression about the remarkable process of finding meaning even while in captivity:

> In spite of all the enforced physical and mental primitiveness of the life in a concentration camp, it was possible for spiritual life to deepen. Sensitive people who were used to a rich intellectual life may have suffered much pain.... but the damage to their inner selves was less. They were able to retreat from their surroundings to a life of inner riches and spiritual freedom. (36)

Frankl was a student of Freud, but he took a different view of human nature. He believed that a person's capacity to *create meaning* is central to his or her well-being or competence. Frankl contended that a person's true sense of meaning is created through the decisions he or she makes. These decisions may be made by looking at the past or by considering the future. *Regressive* decisions made by reviewing the past may lead to unproductive conformity. Decisions made with future possibilities in mind may provoke a certain amount of anxiety but can ultimately facilitate growth. By emphasizing the future, a person is more likely to achieve intimacy and depth in relationships, characteristics of competent individuals.

This ongoing process of *freedom of choice* and taking *responsibility* for one's own actions, which can be fostered by therapy, is critical to the development of authenticity and maturity. Although anxiety may accompany new ideas, it is essential to experience discomfort, to take responsibility, and to move ahead with decisions (Corey 2001).

*Transformational coping*, the process of taking responsibility and clarifying values, is developmental. Children can be taught to approximate success as they learn to face daily challenges, "stretching to accomplish something and succeeding" (Lynn and Garske 1985, 199). Children who receive encouragement to construct their own meaning of events use their own imagination and judgment. "At the heart of *transformational learning* is meaning-making—the act of 'making sense' of an experience" (Courtenay, Merriam, and Reeves 1998, 65). The mechanism of transformational learning involves interpreting an event from a new set of expectations. In adolescence, youths adapt to their failures and accept more responsibility, particularly if they have positive role models. As a result, they become competent adults who "are highly differentiated, being able to recognize the many nuances of events and processing many values" (Lynn and Garske 1985, 198). From this perspective, values are the outcome of deciding what way of living is consistent with one's sense of being.

*Self-awareness* is at the root of a developmental process in which adults learn that they do not have to look to others for approval, but can feel a sense of self-affirmation. Once self-acceptance is achieved, an individual is ready to commit to others and to his or her society. Tillich (1952) called this aspect of the self *the courage to be.*

Surviving crises throughout the life course is an important aspect of courage. Consider, for example, being diagnosed with cancer. From Frankl's (1959/2006) perspective, such a diagnosis, while emotionally stressing, can be a "catalyst for meaning" (49). Indeed, Laubmeier, Zakowski, and Bair (2004) analyzed various ways that cancer patients coped with their diagnosis and treatment. They suggested that finding meaning through spirituality, even with the perceived life threat, is associated with better quality of life. They found that patients with higher levels of existential well-being (i.e., a greater sense of purpose and meaning in life) had lower levels of stress and a better quality of life than those with lower levels of existential well-being.

### Existential Therapy

From the existential perspective, "striving to find meaning in one's life is the primary motivational force" (Frankl 1959/2006, 99). Frankl developed *logotherapy*, or therapy through meaning, to help clients take responsibility, find answers to their problems, and fulfill the tasks that life inevitably sets for them. The aim of active, directive social work interventions is to help clients deal with a crisis of meaning. Thus, the practitioner helps clients trust their capacity to uncover new values congruent with their way of being (Corey 2001). Clients also learn that they are not victims of the past unless they choose to be.

Logotherapy is less retrospective about past events (than, say, psychodynamic theory) and more introspective about future aspirations.

The practitioner might use *paradoxical intent* to confront the client to wish for what he or she fears most. *Dereflection* is another technique in which the client is diverted from his or her problems to something else meaningful in life. The primary role of the practitioner is to help the client sort out the meanings and values that are most important to him or her.

Feelings of dissatisfaction with a career are precipitating reasons for seeking therapy for a significant number of adults. Pines (2000) applied an existential perspective to career burnout and the resulting lack of involvement and investment. She believed that the cause of burnout was that "people's need to believe that their life is meaningful, and that the things that they do—and consequently they themselves—are important and significant" (633). When people choose a career for a particular reason, for example, to help others or to be successful, failure to achieve this may result in repeated negative feelings (e.g., "I'm not good enough" or "I'll never amount to anything"), producing feelings of career burnout.

According to Pines (2000), treatment of career burnout using logotherapy involves three steps: First, identifying conscious and unconscious reasons for an individual's career choice and the intended meaning of the career; second, identifying reasons why the individual has failed to derive a sense of significance in his or her work; and third, identifying changes that enable the individual to derive significance from work.

As individuals move through the therapeutic process, they can focus on outcomes, enabling them to create a greater sense of meaning in their careers.

## Humanism: Rogers and Maslow

*In a wide variety of professional work involving relationships with people—whether as a psychotherapist, teacher, religious worker, guidance counselor, social worker, clinical psychologist—it is the quality of the interpersonal encounter with the client which is the most significant element in determining effectiveness.*

—*Rogers (1957, 103)*

Existentialists and humanists both believe in the worth of the individual, the right to self-determination, and the human capacity to self-actualize. Therefore, social work practice models often apply the principles of Carl Rogers (1959) and Abraham Maslow, and many social work practice texts call for client–practitioner relationships that support growth and client autonomy (Hepworth et al. 2006).

*Rogers' Facilitative Conditions*

Carl Rogers is best known for his client-centered therapeutic relationship. He proposed that the quality of the client–social worker relationship matters more than the social worker's training or clinical orientation. He argued that *client-centered* practitioners can build relationships and contribute to a client's constructive personal growth by imparting his or her *genuineness*, which is related to congruence or authenticity; *empathy*, or the ability to deal sensitively and accurately with client feelings; and *nonpossessive warmth*, or unconditional acceptance of the client as an individual (Fischer 1978; Rogers and Dymond 1957).

The practitioner who is genuine engages the client without a façade or front. Thus, the social worker "*is* what he *is*" (Rogers and Stevens 1967, 86, emphasis in the original). The social worker who is empathetic experiences an accurate understanding of the client's private world, and the social worker who has unconditional positive regard for the client has positive feelings without reservation and evaluation.

These characteristics of effective helping professionals are at the heart of Rogerian theory and are known as the *core conditions* or *essential facilitating conditions* of the helping relationship (Cournoyer 2007). Forty years of outcome research, including Rogers' own, have proven that the core ingredients are necessary to *any* successful intervention (Asay and Lambert 1999; Frank and Frank 1991; Hubble, Duncan, and Miller 1999; Norcross and Newman 1992). Moreover, research suggests that these principal elements of therapy accounting for client improvement may be a form of healing.

*Self-Awareness, the Valuing Process, and Self-Actualization: Rogerian Therapy*

The key to a person-centered approach, and central to much of social work practice, is an optimistic perspective and the belief in the client's ability to achieve self-awareness and growth. Rogers (1980) suggested that each client brings the need to achieve self-awareness to the therapeutic relationship: "It seems to me that at bottom each person is asking: Who am I really? How can I get in touch with this real self, underlying all my surface behavior? How can I become myself?" (357). Therefore, according to Rogers, the goal of the helping

101

process is raising the level of client self-awareness so that he or she can have new, constructive responses to events in the everyday world (Greene 2008). As an outcome of the therapeutic process, the client will become a more autonomous, spontaneous, and confident person who can enjoy life.

Rogers believed that the helping process enables clients to move away from living with values "introjected from others to values which are experienced in themselves in the present" (Rogers and Stevens 1967, 41), trusting their experiences and feeling joy in their uniqueness. Thus, the competent adult believes that he or she can say, "I can live myself, here and now, by my own choice" (46). By valuing one's self and one's life experiences, a competent self is transformed from a child, to an adult, to an older person. Self-regard is a central self-concept, and "the basic goal of client-centered therapy is to release an already existing capacity for self-actualization in a potentially competent individual" (Rowe 1996, 78).

Person-centered therapy has been integrated into various forms of practice and various client situations (e.g., see Chapter 8 for a Rogerian approach to groupwork). Rogers' nondirective approach, with its emphasis on the client's personal growth and development, affords the client the opportunity to focus on most salient issues without a practitioner controlling the direction of therapy or the topic. Person-centered approaches are well-suited to addressing a variety of client issues, including those that might involve a degree of shame or stigma. As Kirshenbaum (2004) stated, "[Rogers's approach] relied exclusively on the client for who he or she is—no matter how confused or anti-social that might be at the moment—and skillfully reflected back the client's feelings" (118).

Working with men who are violent toward women is an example of a difficult client situation. Weaver (2008) argued that using a person-centered approach allows perpetrators to explore the complexity of their feelings and beliefs and that "cruelty against one's partner may [also] be bound up with denying one's sense of inadequacy to face or fulfill the demands and responsibilities of being an intimate partner, husband or father" (178). Practitioners espousing a Rogerian perspective would allow men to uncover and explore the sense of who they are instead of taking a confrontational or challenging perspective. This therapeutic method would involve valuing the whole person beyond the sum of his or her current behaviors, feelings, and attitudes. As Barrett-Lennard (2007) stated, it would involve "being deeply receptive to the other's felt experience without evaluating that person for *having these feelings*" (129, emphasis in the original). The outcome would be acceptance of one's self in the entirety, including its imperfections and flaws. Such awareness exposes "the gap between the real and ideal self and serves to motivate the individual toward narrowing the gap" (Cepeda and Davenport 2006, 2).

### Maslow's A Pyramid of Needs

Maslow (1959) is best known for the conception of a pyramidal hierarchy of needs: *physiological needs*, including breathing, food, and homeostasis (an optimal level of tension); *safety needs*, encompassing personal and financial safety, security, health and personal well-being, and protection from accidents and illness; needs for *belonging and love needs and esteem needs*, involving friendship, intimacy, and family as well as self-respect; and *self-actualization*, referring to living up to one's own potential (see Figure 5.1). The bottom, or largest, level of the pyramid contains *deficiency needs*, or those that are required for human survival and that if not met make a person anxious and tense. The motivation to achieve higher level needs brings a person closer

**Figure 5.1 Maslow's Hierarchy of Needs**

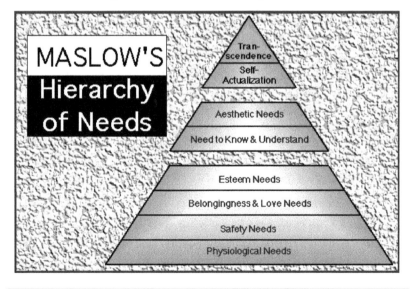

*Source:* From Huitt (2007).

to self-actualization and a higher degree of human consciousness, or *peak experiences.*

### Self-Actualization

Maslow (1968) used data from twelve years of his clinical practice to support the view that people have a natural, innate propensity for self-understanding, personal change, and growth. He suggested that if people lived in environments that met their basic needs, they could move from a deficit situation to one that is more and more satisfying.

The process of self-actualization begins in childhood, when the infant spontaneously explores, manipulates, and experiences his or her environment. That is, the child naturally strives for pleasurable experiences. When he or she feels safe, there can be positive growth. The conflict between fearing that one is not safe and being a whole person continues to some degree throughout life, but is most striking during childhood.

Maslow (1968) constructed a profile of healthy people who have sufficiently met their basic needs for safety, belongingness, love, respect, and self-esteem. He found that once these basic needs are met, individuals are able to self-actualize, reach their potential, and engage their full capacity and talents. In other words, subsistence needs must be met before people are able to attend to creative and spiritual needs. Maslow also believed that the tendency to attain a unique sense of self was more profound among individuals who have accepted themselves and others, are spontaneous, possess strong problem-solving abilities, can function autonomously and appreciate their environment.

Self-actualization involves growth or moving toward attainable goals. In this process, the person transcends his or her ego, engages in spontaneous activities, and enjoys creative pleasures. He or she is also self-searching, contemplative, and striving for self-improvement. The self-actualized person achieves a higher level of maturity. In sum, he or she becomes more competent.

### Peak Experiences

Maslow's (1968) description of *peak experiences* can be likened to the subjective experience of delight beyond one's ego boundaries. This developmental process begins spontaneously in children who are not overly fearful, are self-accepting, and seek to experience delight. "The peak experience is felt as a self-validating, self-justifying moment," carrying its own intrinsic value (90). Creative energy may be released and a disorientation in time and space experienced, but peak experiences are by their very nature "good and desirable" (92).

According to Maslow (1971), peak experiences are characterized by

| | |
|---|---|
| Wholeness | unity, integration |
| Perfection | inevitability, completeness |
| Completion | ending, fulfillment |
| Justice | fairness, orderliness |
| Aliveness | self-regulation, full-functioning |
| Richness | complexity, intricacy |
| Simplicity | honesty, abstractness |
| Beauty | aliveness, rightness |
| Goodness | benevolence, desirability |
| Uniqueness | individuality, novelty |
| Effortlessness | ease, grace |
| Playfulness | fun, joy |
| Truth | beauty, purity |
| Self-sufficiency | environment transcendence, autonomy |

Because Maslow understood peak experiences to be connected to the "whole of being," he thought they are similar to spiritual and or religious experiences.

### The Implications of Maslow's Work for Social Work Practice

Maslow provided few explicit guidelines for practice, but his hierarchy of needs is still referred to by authors examining oppression-related issues (Greene 2002). Implications for practice also include the idea that basic needs must be met for people to live in resilient communities. As did Rogers, Maslow believed that clients should be approached as unique individuals and should not be labeled or seen simply as members of certain homogenous groups.

An interesting application of Maslow's theory was carried out in The Netherlands involving a group of adults with intellectual disabilities (Kreuger, van Exel, and Nieboer 2008). Residents of a residential facility were surveyed to determine the importance of physical, social, and structural factors to their quality of life. Safety needs were rated highest, followed by preferences for a consistent structure of their day. Social priorities were further down the list, but researchers found that residents wanted to form closer relationships with other residents and get to know staff better. The residents' strongest preferences, that is, the factors that most influenced their quality of life, were related to safety, part of the initial stage of Maslow's hierarchy. From a practice perspective, this indicates that the safety concerns of people living in long-term care or congregate group settings need to be a primary consideration in facility management.

## Social Construction: Gergen

*Many are drawn to constructionist ideas because they offer a bold invitation to build new futures. Transforming ourselves, our relationships, or our culture need not await the intervention of some expert, set of laws, force of arms, bold leaders, public policies, or the like. As we speak together right now, we participate in creating the future—for good or ill.*

*—Gergen (2009b, 12)*

### Relational Selves

The relational self was first introduced in Chapter 2, which focused on identity formation. It is reviewed here to clarify how personal and community-based meaning-making emerges through human interaction. Gergen (2009b) credited the symbolic interactionists with being among the first to introduce theories that addressed a "socially embedded view of the self" (9), pioneering a transpersonal social constructionist view of human development.

This emphasis on relationships is important, as it holds that in order for people to be well-grounded, competent adults, and build viable community institutions, they must live out their lives in authentic relationships. Social constructionists such as Kenneth Gergen (2009a, 2009b) believe that relationships are a necessary aspect of meaning-making. They contend that "nothing exists for us as an intelligible world of objects and persons until there are relationships" (Gergen 2009a, 6).

The relational worldview contrasts with the predominantly linear, mainstream Euro-American philosophy. The linear worldview is logical, time oriented, and systematic, based on cause-and-effect

(Schriver 2003). This is reflected in social work assessment protocols that often involve taking a social history to determine the cause of a problem. In contrast, the relational worldview has its roots in indigenous cultures; it is not time oriented but intuitive and fluid. Its aim is for helping professionals and natural healers to have clients reach a state of balance and harmony.

For example, consistent with aboriginal beliefs, social workers in northern Ontario, Canada, use a practice framework as a means of connecting all of creation. Indigenous people generally believe that nature is not apart from us; rather, it is an extension of our being and is part of creation and that makes life itself sacred (Nabigon and Mawhiney 1996). Existence and healing is thus an important aspect of individual balance and community meaning-making at the local level.

*Epistemology and Basic Assumptions*

There is no single theory of social construction, and only recently has it begun to coalesce into patterns of ideas. Terms for the theory and descriptions of how it is used include:

1. *Constructivism*, a philosophy of learning, which is based on the assumption that people construct their understanding of the world based on interpretations of their own experience;
2. *Social constructivism*, which focuses on the collaborative nature of learning; and
3. *Social constructionism*, which is concerned with how people and groups perceive reality (see Blundo and Greene 2008).

Social construction theory began as a "new thought system" for examining social work practice (Turner 1986). Its philosophy tends to be concerned with the nature of knowledge and how people understand reality. That is, the social constructionist movement is an alternative *epistemology*—the study of how people know things—to the positivist, scientific approach that attempts to reveal and prove universal laws and theories.

The challenge posed by the social constructionist perspective is to undo a mechanistic sense of reality and explore peoples' day-to-day realities. This involves taking a radical step away from "the taken-for-granted conventions of understanding, and simultaneously [inviting ourselves] into new worlds of meaning and action" (Gergen 1993, 116).

There are four assumptions underlying this meaning-making stance:

1. How people study the world is based on available concepts, categories, and scientific or research methods, and these are a product of language.
2. The various concepts and categories people use vary considerably in their meanings and vary from culture to culture, as well as over time.
3. The popularity or persistence of certain concepts and categories depends on their usefulness rather than on their validity; ideas tend to persist if they are congruent with cultural values.
4. The way people describe or explain the world is a form of social action that has consequences; for example, theories built on male experiences may deny women's values and processes (Gergen 1985).

*Defining Meaning–Making*

Social construction theory views the person–environment as the creation and re-creation of meaning through discourse in a specific cultural tradition (Blundo and Greene 2008). *Meaning-making*, therefore, is then a communal process that depends on people's understanding of self and interaction with others. Language is the vehicle for this natural or innate process. It is used to give significance to objects and ideas in the world around us. A familiar example is the use of eighteen different words for snow by the Inuits. From this perspective, meanings are ideas constructed by humans. In the process of meaning-making, people draw meaning from their experiences and give meaning to events and experiences.

Studies of the Holocaust suggest that meaning-making played a central role in how survivors recreated their daily lives. Those who attributed importance to reestablishing families, obtaining education, and contributing to the community gave new meaning to their lives (Greene 2009). Armour (2009) hypothesized that this occurs "when survivors act in ways that are congruent with their inner convictions, [and] their acts of inferred meaning produce an internal resonance and personal coherence that is self-affirming. The internal experience of the individual is that 'I make sense'" (457).

"Meaning [then] is the underlying motivation behind thoughts, actions and even the interpretation and application of knowledge" (Krauss 2005, 763). Human behavior theory and patterns of the life course can be thought of in this same vein. For example, "developmental concepts such as 'child,' 'adolescent,' or the 'elderly' are social constructs, always in transition within differential contexts" (Blundo and Greene 2008, 248). During the Middle Ages, people did not identify teenagers as adolescents, and people were considered old at fifty. Furthermore, what constitutes our real self and whether we view ourselves as competent may be understood in the same way (see Chapter 4).

Moreover, *culture*, which emerges in the context of human interaction, can be explored as the "expression of historically shared meanings of a community of people" (Blundo and Greene 2008, 251). Culture and the collective meaning-making in a given time and place results in a sense of community, the creation of societal institutions, and the belief system and traditions of the society. Thus, attributing meaning to the world is a means of organizing experience into a coherent, shared experience, sometimes known as a *story* or *stories*. As Randall (1995) states,

> Not only might we be *a* story.... But we might be *many* stories as well—of many kinds on many levels, with many subplots and versions. Also, given [an] emphasis on the stories that *we* are, it points beyond the individual dimension of our existence to the communal one. It reminds us that, in the end, none of us is an island whose saga can be separated from the story of a particular family, from the stories of colleagues and friends, from the countless larger stores of which our world is constructed or individual from history as a whole. (10, emphasis added)

The story or narrative, then, can become the vehicle of social work intervention.

*Examining Diversity*

Just as social construction theory can be used to understand culture, it can also be used to better understand diversity or differences among people. Social constructionists contend that a strong individualistic tradition can create a world in which some people are perceived as less desirable or worthy. Social constructionists also reject the idea that human behavior can be studied objectively apart from gender, race/ethnicity, religion, age, sexual orientation, and so forth. They argue that the self-contained individual, a singular self, must be replaced by the *relational* being, or a person who relates to others and sometimes to the cosmos. From this perspective, the self is ever evolving in relation to diverse others. That is, the human being is never completely developed; rather, he or she grows throughout the life course through human discourse and in connection with his or her community of meaning or culture (Blundo and Greene 2008).

*Social Construction Interventions*

Although the theoretical position of social construction that there is no objective world goes back to the ancient Greek philosopher Protagoras, practice perspectives and treatment approaches are more recent developments. Social workers are asked to take a learning stance and listen to the client's subjective account of life events. This may help the client deal with stress and alleviate trauma and the impact of grief and loss (Greene 2007). Treatment methods, including narrative therapy and solution-focused treatment, are often used following highly stressful or adverse events disrupt meaning (Janoff-Bulman and Berger 2000).

*Narrative therapy* is based on the idea that people construct meaning in life through stories that embody their personal life and family, community, and cultural environmental views. When problems arise, clients create a negative narrative. Social constructionists contend that a "problem" is often an internalized oppressive view of self that a client has adopted. In addition, a person may hold competing possibilities within a story. This means that a dysfunctional narrative may be displaced by a more functional narrative that is also true. Therefore, the practitioner helps the client *re-story* his or her narrative by *externalizing the problem*, or separating it from the client. This may take the form of asking the client for evidence that he or she is competent enough to stand up, defeat, or escape an oppressive experience (O'Hanlon 1994, as summarized by Corey 2001). The practitioner then asks a series of questions that help the client search for *outcomes unique* to his or her situation. This approach is then a form of meaning-making (White and Epston 1990). In addition, the narrative is used to facilitate a therapeutic conversation promoting spiritual integration and healing (Greene 2009).

As an example, an older woman was depressed as a result of her decreasing levels of independence (Kropf and Tandy 1998). Her initial narrative was one of dependence and frailty. Through work in narrative theory, however, her narrative changed from one of dependence to one of survivorship. This more functional narrative promoted a sense of competence and resilience in moving forward, in spite of some health challenges.

*Solution-focused therapy* also aims to create new meaning in collaboration with the client. It can help the client examine his or her goals for the future. The method is known for the therapist's use of the miracle question: "If you could solve the problem overnight, what would be different?" (de Shazer 1985, 1988). The solution-focused method is also associated with the scaling question, which asks clients to assess how close they are on a scale of 1 to 10 to solving their problem. Again, these techniques may be characterized as ways of helping the client achieve a new sense of meaning and gradually determining alternative ways to achieve success and competence.

Finally, social constructionists seek to bring about community change. Their ideas focus on helping individuals not to compete with one another but to create a dialogue in which meaning is co-created (Gergen 2009a, 2009b). Leaders of these seemingly opposing traditions are brought together to construct new, harmonious policies. This process is intended to resolve community or intergroup conflict and is known as *transformational dialogue*. Transformational dialogue, which is congruent with social work values and activism, aims to arrive at new and promising relationships.

### Critique: Theories of Spiritual and Faith Development

Although social work theorists have only recently returned to the spiritual aspects of human functioning, transpersonal theories tend to encompass a spiritual or religious dimension. *Faith* has been defined as an individual's inner system of beliefs about the meaning of life. It often includes a relationship with the transcendent or God. *Religion* is an outward expression of belief in a faith community, including ethical codes and forms of worship (Conrad 1999).

Most stage theories did not encompass spiritual content into the life span (Robbins, Chatterjee, and Canda 2006). Recognizing this void, practitioners turned to other frameworks that took spiritual dimensions into consideration. This was typified by Fowler's (1981) faith development model (Cowley 1996) and Hodge's (2001) spiritual assessment instrument (Greene 2008). Fowler's model consists of six stages during which the child moves from obedience to parental authority to a worldview of faith beyond that of the family. During adolescence, the youth becomes aware of his or her own belief system. In the fifth stage, adulthood, is when some individuals realize that they may hold prejudices about other faiths and beliefs. Fowler believed that the sixth and final stage, in which people believe that they are the spirit of an inclusive and fulfilled human community, is reached by few adults.

A spiritual self-assessment instrument developed by Hodge uses a narrative/anthropological approach. It raises questions about a family's belief system and the individual's feelings of communion with a higher power. Research suggests that a person's faith or belief system depends greatly on his or her social support network (Farris 2006).

## Case Example

Arthur and Kendra Moore are couple in their mid-forties who sought therapy about eight months after the death of their middle child, Keith, age sixteen, in a car accident. Arthur is an elementary school principal and Kendra is a registered nurse in an oncology clinic. Both have returned to work, but their grief process is affecting their marriage and their relationship with their other two children.

The social worker, Anna Hastings, started the initial session by having each of them discuss their motivation for seeking treatment. Arthur spoke about his need to hold on to Keith's memory while simultaneously moving forward with his own life and family. Kendra talked about her desire to "hold time still" to preserve their life as it had been while Keith was alive. The precipitating factor for entering therapy was a disagreement that involved cleaning Keith's room. Arthur felt the need to clean out Keith's closet and some of his belongings. Kendra, however, wanted Keith's bedroom to stay just as it had been prior to his death. She stated, "I'm not ready to let Keith go."

In the therapy sessions, Anna used a client-centered perspective to determine how each of the parents was experiencing the grief process. Anna listened and reflected with each parent, enabling both Arthur and Kendra to explore and share their own grief without needing to take on the other's experience. Arthur talked about making a place in the family for Keith to remain their son as they moved on with their family life. With Kendra, Anna explored the meaning of "letting Keith go" and Kendra's guilt about moving forward with her own life and her relationships with Arthur and her other two children.

As part of the therapy, Anna explored the stories the parents told about Keith and the meaning of his being a part of their family. Both Kendra and Arthur spoke about Keith's kindness and his passion for helping others and his career goal to become a teacher like his father, as he enjoyed being with younger kids and helping them learn. For example, Keith had volunteered as a tutor at the local Boys and Girls Club.

As the parents talked more about Keith, they both started to speak more fluently about the past and the future. Arthur was able to reminisce about Keith's life and his mark on the family and community; Kendra was able to discuss how Keith's legacy would continue even though his life had ended so soon. As part of their therapy, Kendra and Arthur came to a decision that they would approach the Boys and Girls Club about setting up a scholarship in Keith's name for someone to tutor at-risk children so that the community could also participate in maintaining and honoring Keith's legacy.

## References

Armour, M. 2009. Meaning making in survivorship: Application to Holocaust survivors. *Journal of Human Behavior in the Social Environment* 20: 440–68.

Asay, T. P., and M. J. Lambert. 1999. The empirical case for the common factors in therapy: Quantitative findings. In *The heart and soul of change*, ed. M. A. Hubble, B. L. Duncan, and D. Miller, 23–55. Washington, DC: American Psychological Association.

Barrett-Lennard, G. T. 2007. The relational foundations of person-centered practice. In *The handbook of person-centered psychotherapy and counseling*, ed. M. Cooper, P. F. Schmid, M. O'Hara, and G. Wyatt, 127–39. Houndsmills: Palgrave Macmillan.

Blundo, R., and R. R. Greene. 2008. Social construction. In *Human behavior theory and social work practice*, ed. R. R. Greene, 237–64. New Brunswick, NJ: Aldine Transaction Press.

Cepeda, L. M., and D. S. Davenport. 2006. Person-centered therapy and solution-focused brief therapy: An integration of present and future awareness. *Psychotherapy: Theory, Research, Practice, Training* 43, no. 1:1–12.

Conrad, A. P. 1999. Professional tools for religiously and spiritually sensitive social work practice. In *Human behavior theory and social work practice*, ed. R. R. Greene, 2nd ed., 63–72. New York: Aldine de Gruyter.

Corey, G. 2001. *Theory and practice of counseling and psychotherapy*. Belmont, CA: Wadsworth/Thomson Learning.

Cournoyer, B. 2007. *The social work skills workbook*. 5th ed. Monterey, CA: Brooks/Cole.

Courtenay, B., S. Merriam, and P. Reeves. 1998. The centrality of meaning-making in transformational learning: How HIV positive adults make sense of their lives. *Adult Education Quarterly* 48, no. 2:65–84.

Cowley, A. 1996. Transpersonal social work. In *Social work treatment*, ed. F. Turner, 663–98. New York: Free Press.

de Shazer, S. 1985. *Keys to solutions in brief therapy*. New York: Norton.

____. 1988. *Clues: Investigating solutions in brief therapy*. New York: Norton.

Farris, K. 2006. The role of African-American pastors in mental health care. In *Contemporary issues of care*, ed. R. R. Greene, 159–82. New York: Haworth Press.

Fischer, J. 1978. *Effective casework practice: An eclectic approach.* New York: McGraw-Hill.

Fowler, J. W. 1981. *Stages of faith.* New York: Harper & Row.

Frank, J. D., and J. B. Frank. 1991. *Persuasion and healing: A comparative study of psychotherapy.* 3rd ed. Baltimore, MD: Johns Hopkins University Press.

Frankl, V. 2006. *Man's search for meaning.* Boston, MA: Beacon Press. (Original work published 1959.)

Gergen, K. J. 1985. The social constructionist movement in modern psychology. *American Psychologist* 40:266–75.

____. 1993. *Refiguring self and psychology.* Lebanon, NH: Dartmouth Press.

____. 2000. *The saturated self.* New York: Basic Books.

____. 2009a. *An invitation to social construction.* Los Angeles, CA: Sage.

____. 2009b. *Relational being: Beyond self and community.* New York: Oxford University Press.

Greene, R. R. 2002. Holocaust survivors: A study in resilience. *Journal of Gerontological Social Work* 37, no. 1:3–18.

____. ed. 2007. *Social work practice: A risk and resilience perspective.* Belmont, CA: Thompson Brooks/Cole.

____. 2008. Carl Rogers and the person-centered approach. In *Human behavior theory and social work practice*, ed. R. R. Greene, 113–31. New Brunswick, NJ: Aldine Transaction Press.

____. 2009. A Holocaust survivorship model: Survivors' reflections. *Journal of Human Behavior in the Social Environment* 20:569–81.

Hepworth, D. H., H. Rooney, G. D. Rooney, K. Strom-Gottfried, and J. Larsen. 2006. *Direct social work practice: Theory and skills.* 7th ed. Belmont, CA: Thomson Brooks/Cole.

Hodge, D. R. 2001. Spirituality assessment: A review of major qualitative methods and a new framework for assessing spirituality. *Social Work* 46:203–14.

Hubble, M. A., B. L. Duncan, and S. Miller. 1999. *The heart and soul of change.* Washington, DC: APA Press.

Huitt, W. 2007. *Maslow's hierarchy of needs.* Retrieved from the Educational Psychology Interactive website: http://www.edpsycinteractive.org/topics/regsys/maslow.html www.abraham-Maslow.com/m

Janoff-Bulman, R., and A. R. Berger. 2000. The other side of trauma: Towards a psychology of appreciation. In *Loss and trauma: General and close relationship perspectives*, ed. J. H. Harvey and E. D. Miller, 29–44. Philadelphia, PA: Brunner-Routledge.

Kirshenbaum, H. 2004. Carl Rogers's life and work: An assessment on the 100th anniversary of his birth. *Journal of Counseling & Development* 82:116–24.

Krauss, S. E. 2005. Research paradigms and meaning making: A primer. *The Qualitative Report* 10:758–70.

Kreuger, L., J. van Exel, and A. Nieboer. 2008. Needs of persons with severe intellectual disabilities: A Q methodological study of clients with severe behavioral disorders and severe intellectual disabilities. *Journal of Applied Research in*

*Intellectual Disabilities* 21:466–76.

Kropf, N. P., and C. Tandy. 1998. Narrative therapy with older clients: The use of a "meaning-making" approach. *Clinical Gerontologist* 18, no. 4:3–16.

Laubmeier, K. K., S. G. Zakowski, and J. P. Bair. 2004. A role of spirituality in the psychological adjustment to cancer: A test of the transactional model of stress and coping. *International Journal of Behavioral Medicine* 11, no. 1:48–55.

Lifton, R. J. 1999. *The protean self: Human resilience in an age of fragmentation.* Chicago, IL: University of Chicago Press.

London, P. 1974. From the long couch for the sick to the push button for the bored. *Psychology Today* 8, no. 1:63–68.

———. 1986. *The modes and morals of psychotherapy.* New York: Hemisphere.

Lynn, S. J., and J. P. Garske. 1985. *Contemporary psychotherapies: Models and methods.* Columbus, OH: Merrill.

Maslow, A. H. 1959. Creativity in self-actualized people. *General Semantics Bulletin* 24–25:45–50.

———. 1968. *Toward a psychology of being.* 3rd ed. New York: Van Nostrand.

———. 1971. The farther reaches of human nature. *Journal of Transpersonal Psychology* 1, no. 1:1–19.

May, R. 1953. *Man's search for himself.* New York: Delta Book by Norton.

Nabigon, H., and A. Mawhiney. 1996. Aboriginal theory: A Cree medicine wheel guide for healing first nations. In *Social work treatment*, ed. F. Turner, 18–38. New York: Free Press.

Norcross, J. C., and C. F. Newman. 1992. Psychotherapy integration: Setting the context. In *Handbook of psychotherapy integration*, ed. J. C. Norcross and M. R. Goldfried, 3–45. New York: Basic Books.

Pines, A. M. 2000. Treating career burnout: A psychodynamic existential perspective. *Journal of Clinical Psychology* 56:633–42.

Randall, W. L. 1995. *The stories that we are: An essay on self creation.* Toronto, ON: University of Toronto Press.

Reynolds, B. C. 1985. *Learning and teaching in the practice of social work.* Silver Spring, MD: National Association of Social Workers. (Original work published 1969.)

Robbins, S., P. Chatterjee, and E. R. Canda. 2006. *Contemporary human behavior theory: A critical perspective for social work.* Boston, MA: Pearson.

Rogers, C. 1957. The necessary and sufficient conditions of therapeutic personality change. *Journal of Consulting Psychology* 21:95–103.

———. 1959. A theory of personality and interpersonal relationships as developed in the client-centered framework. In *Psychology: A study of science formulations of the person and social context*, ed. S. Koch, vol. 3, 184–256. New York: McGraw-Hill.

———. 1980. *A way of being.* Boston, MA: Houghton Mifflin.

Rogers, C. R., and R. F. Dymond. 1957. *Psychotherapy and personality change.* Chicago, IL: University of Chicago Press.

Rogers, C. R., B. Stevens. 1967. *Person to person: The problem of being human.* Walnut Creek, CA: Real People Press.

Rowe, W. 1996. Client-centered theory: A person-centered approach. In *Social work treatment*, ed. F. Turner, 69–93. New York: Free Press.

Schriver, J. M. 2003. *Human behavior and the social environment: Shifting paradigms in essential knowledge for social work practice.* 4th ed. Boston, MA: Allyn & Bacon.

Tillich, P. 1952. *The courage to be.* New Haven, CT: Yale University Press.

Turner, F. 1986. *Social work treatment: Interlocking theoretical approaches.* New York: Free Press.

Weaver, L. 2008. Facilitating change in men who are violent towards women: Considering the ethics and efficacy of a person-centered approach. *Person-Centered and Experiential Psychotherapies* 7, no. 3:143–84.

Weick, A. 1993. Reconstructing social work education. In *Revisioning social work education: A social constructionist approach,* ed. J. Laird, 11–30. New York: Haworth.

White, M., and D. Epston. 1990. *Narrative means to therapeutic ends.* New York: Norton.

Yalom, I. D. 1980. *The theory and practice of psychotherapy.* New York: Basic Books.

# 6

# Cognitive and Behavioral Approaches

*If we are to use the methods of science in the field of human affairs, we must assume that behavior is lawful and determined. We must expect to discover that what a man does is the result of specifiable conditions and that once these conditions have been discovered, we can anticipate and to some extent determine his actions.*
*—Skinner (1953, 6)*

Cognitive and behavioral theories stem from several streams of thought and are integrated into an approach to social work practice that focuses on how behavioral change is related to change in cognitive functions. In this chapter, we explore the major premises of human behavior cognitive function as initially developed by Alfred Adler (1959), sometimes called the father of the cognitive approach; Albert Ellis (1977, 1994), known for rational emotive behavior therapy; Aaron Beck (1976, 1995), who described cognitive events, processes, and structure; and Albert Bandura and B. F. Skinner, most associated with social learning theory or behaviorism. In addition, many social workers who use a cognitive–behavioral (CB) orientation have been influenced by the work of theorists such as Berlin (1980) and Meichenbaum (1985).

Unlike the more psychodynamically oriented theorists, cognitive and behavioral theorists pay only limited attention to the intrapsychic complexities that are fundamental components of the work of Freud and those who followed his lead. Cognitive theorists emphasize the role that cognitive factors play in maladaptive behavior, whereas behavioral theorists are empirical in their approach and focus their attention on observable outcomes such as how people behave in multiple contexts and situations (Thyer 1994; Thyer and Myers 1997). These theorists are particularly concerned about how people learn dysfunctional behaviors, including phobias, violent acting out, and depression. The central questions that arise from CB approaches to understanding human functioning include the following: What

117

conditions create problematic behaviors for clients? What situations and circumstances decrease the competence of individuals? And, how can these situations be eradicated so that individuals can function more competently?

The conceptualization of time is another major difference between CB approaches and more psychodynamically oriented approaches. As discussed in Chapters 2 and 3, Freud and Erikson viewed current functioning as being rooted in earlier life experiences. Behavioral and cognitive theorists consider past experiences important only as they affect current situations and functioning. From a therapeutic perspective, little emphasis is placed upon past conditions. Cognitive and behavioral therapists are more likely to focus on clients' current thoughts or the conditions that shaped behavior in the present. Past experiences are only considered relevant to the extent that they impact functioning today.

From the cognitive and behavioral perspectives, *competence* is viewed as functioning without interference from faulty and irrational thoughts, associations, or maladaptive behaviors. Practitioners using cognitive and/or behavioral approaches strive to understand behaviors from the client's viewpoint. There might be situations in which a client appears to be functioning competently yet may actually be behaving in a way that involves escaping a problematic situation. For example, the current emphasis on exercising has prompted some people to choose to walk up stairs instead of taking the elevator. On one hand, walking up the stairs appears to be a sound decision and can be evidence of someone's good judgment involving improving his or her health. Yet the same decision (i.e., avoiding the elevator) may also be the result of a fear of being in a confined space, which creates a sense of panic. A person may avoid his or her claustrophobia by taking the stairs. Although the stair-climbing behavior looks healthy from an external perspective, the person's functioning is limited because a sense of fear, panic, or anxiety limits how he or she can navigate the world.

In this chapter, various theoretical orientations that are part of the cognitive and behavioral orientation to understanding human functioning are summarized and discussed.

### Behavioral Approaches: Adler, Skinner, and Bandura

*Give me a dozen healthy infants, well-formed, and my own speci-*
*fied world to bring them up in and I'll guarantee to take any one*
*at random and train him to become any type of specialist I might*

> *select—doctor, lawyer, artist, merchant-chief and, yes, even beg-*
> *gar-man and thief, regardless of his talents, penchants, tendencies,*
> *abilities, vocations, and race of his ancestors.*
> —*Watson (1930, 82)*

Behavioral theory, which is closely associated with social learning theory, focuses on an "analysis of the contingencies that affect behavior, particularly the individual and the environmental events that occur before and after behavior itself" (Garvin 1991, 151). This involves finding out why certain behaviors occur and what can be done to change behaviors by changing *contingencies* or possible events.

### Alfred Adler

In the early years of his career, Adler collaborated with Freud in developing the psychodynamic approach, but he later broke away from Freudian concepts. Adler espoused an approach that suggested that people view the world and behave according to their values, beliefs, goals, and interests. Not only was Adler at the forefront of the subjective approach to psychology, known as *phenomenology*, but he argued that all behavior is purposeful and goal oriented. Furthermore, he contended that people "have the capacity to interpret, influence, and create events" (Corey 2001, 109). This viewpoint suggests that clients are not "sick" and in need of "cure"; rather, they can be helped by therapy, which is a form of education. The goal is to learn new ways of thinking about themselves, others, and the world. Adler believed that people who are able to clarify their goals and interests and address incorrect thoughts and belief patterns are better able to cease feeling inferior and to contribute to society, a mark of good mental health.

Adler asked clients to express their immediate thoughts and concerns. He gave encouragement by building rapport with clients and prompting them to try solutions to problems they had not tried. To make his assessment, Adler explored clients' subjective experiences of reality, referring to thoughts, convictions, and conclusions; lifestyle, including the themes that characterized one's daily life; social interests, encompassing a person's attitudes toward the social world; and birth order or sibling relationships. He contended that birth order affects family dynamics and the competence of the individual as an adult:

> Because the oldest child receives much attention, he or she may be
> spoiled, but he or she is expected to be a high achiever.

The second child receives less attention and must strive for recognition.

The middle child is squeezed and as a result acts more sociably.

Because the youngest child is the "baby," he or she is pampered and tends to go his or her own way.

The only child may be pampered, may be expected to be a high achiever, and may want center stage.

### Ivan Pavlov

One of the origins of behavioral approaches is in the work of Ivan Pavlov. A physiologist by training, Pavlov was interested in the stimuli that caused certain behaviors. His work was based on biological principles beyond the scope of this chapter. However, in his most famous experiments with animals (i.e., Pavlov's dogs), he turned to measurable behaviors such as the amount of saliva secreted in response to various stimuli. His work on conditioning formed the foundation for several other branches of behavioral theory and analysis.

In his experiments, Pavlov paired various stimuli to condition the dog to salivate in circumstances that typically do not produce saliva. To do this, he paired a neutral stimulus (i.e., ringing a bell) with a saliva-producing stimulus (i.e., food). After repeated paired presentations of the bell and food, the dog began to salivate when the bell rang—whether or not food was present. At that point, the bell had become an antecedent to atypical behavior. This type of experiment has been called *paired association.*

Based on these experiments, Pavlov developed a theory of conditioning. In the example of the dog, the food, and the bell, the food is the *unconditioned stimulus.* The unconditioned stimulus typically creates an *unconditioned response,* such as a baby smiling when his or her mother's face appears. The *conditioned stimulus* is a condition that typically does not create the response. When the unconditioned stimulus and the conditioned stimulus are paired so that they occur simultaneously, the *conditioned response* occurs when the unconditioned stimulus is presented alone. When the unconditioned stimulus and the conditioned stimulus are paired so that they occur simultaneously, after a time the *conditioned response* will occur when the unconditioned stimulus is presented alone. For example, if a particular song is paired with the appearance of the mother, the expected outcome is that the baby will smile when the song is played even though the mother does not appear.

## John B. Watson

John B. Watson is often considered to be the father of behaviorism, as he furthered research and theory on classical conditioning in the United States. He emphasized the importance of the environment on how people act and behave and, like Pavlov, he made little reference to the emotional life of the individual. In the nature versus nurture debate about human development, Watson strongly emphasized nurture.

In one of his best known experiments, Watson furthered understanding of *stimulus generalization* (Watson and Rayner 1920). He set out to answer three questions:

> Can an infant be conditioned to fear an animal that appears simultaneously with a loud fear-arousing sound?
>
> Would such fear transfer to other animals or to inanimate objects?
>
> How long would such fear persist?

To answer these answers, he selected an infant who showed no fear of any particular animal. The child, Little Albert, was exposed to a white rat and showed no adverse reaction to the rodent. As the experiment continued, a loud noise was paired with the appearance of the rat. This made Little Albert cry. The boy became afraid of the rat, as predicted by classical conditioning theory. However, his generalized distress went beyond the original stimulus to include other fuzzy objects. He demonstrated fear when exposed to a rabbit, a dog, and even a bearded Santa Claus. The Little Albert experiment demonstrated how response to one stimulus can broaden to a variety of similar objects, resulting in panic or anxiety.

Classical conditioning has been used to explain some individuals' responses to trauma such as violence or maltreatment. For example, posttraumatic stress responses involve the association of a neutral stimulus to a traumatic event, such as experiencing or witnessing an act of brutality or violence. A soldier who witnessed a horrific act that killed colleagues or that compromised his or her own safety may associate feelings of fear, helplessness, and aggression with a neutral stimulus that was present during the event (Litz et al. 2000). For example, certain smells or sounds that are present at the time of a tragedy may become paired with the horror of the trauma. The conditions are unconnected to the traumatic event but may become paired in a person's mental schema. As a result, the smell or sound can trigger a charged emotional response even in the absence of any overt danger. Recently, there has been more neurobiological research on the impact of traumatic events on brain chemistry and functioning (Garakani, Mathew, and Charney 2006).

### B. F. Skinner

B. F. Skinner (1985) contended that culture "consists of descriptions of contingencies of reinforcement in the form of advice, maxims, instructions, rules of conduct, the laws of governments and religion, and the laws of science" (294). He argued that people can be taught to be more competent in their environments by bringing about behavioral change (Thyer 1994). Skinner (1966, 1974, 1988) developed operant conditioning, another form of behaviorism. Differing from classical conditioning, Skinner's form of radical behavioral analysis focused on understanding behavior as a consequence of the environmental factors that reinforce it. His interest was in the reinforcers and punishments that either promoted or extinguished behaviors. According to this perspective, individuals (or animals, as many of Skinner's experiments were conducted with birds or animals) seek to increase positive outcomes and decrease negative outcomes by acting on the environment. Some of his most famous experiments involved teaching pigeons to obtain food pellets by pecking at a lever. If pecking behavior results in food, a pigeon's pecking behavior will increase. If the pigeon pecks at the lever and no reward is forthcoming, the behavior will cease. This stimulus–response paradigm is the basis for operant conditioning.

There are several behavioral contexts in operant conditioning (see Table 6.1). *Reinforcers* can be either positive or negative, but both types can increase the occurrence of a certain behavior. Positive reinforcement involves receiving a reward or pleasurable outcome as a result of the behavior, whereas negative reinforcement involves the removal of an unpleasant or unrewarding experience. Praising a child or giving him or her a treat for behaving well in the classroom is an example of positive reinforcement. The goal is to increase the amount of time a child is behaving positively in school. Individuals may also engage in some behaviors as a way to avoid certain experiences. A study on gender and motivation for smoking found differences in tobacco use by college-age men and women (Morrell, Cohen, and McChargue 2010).

**Table 6.1 Reinforcement and Punishment in Operant Conditioning**

|  | Definition | Outcome |
|---|---|---|
| Positive reinforcement | An outcome that is positive or rewarding | Increase in behavior |
| Negative reinforcement | The removal of a negative or unrewarding behavior | Increase in behavior |
| Positive punishment | The occurrence of some negative or undesired outcome | Decrease in behavior |
| Negative punishment | The withdrawing of a pleasurable or desired outcome | Decrease in behavior |

Women were found to be more likely than men to use cigarettes to alter negative mood states, such as depression. From a behavioral perspective, cigarettes served as negative reinforcers for the women, as they expected to feel better (i.e., avoid feeling depressed) by smoking.

In addition to reinforcers, certain behaviors can be followed by *punishments*. These have the overall outcome of decreasing the occurrence of a behavior and can also be either positive or negative. Positive punishment involves following a behavior with an unpleasant or unrewarding stimulus. It has been used in the treatment of addiction by using certain prescription drugs to create feelings of nausea when taken with alcohol. If drinking alcohol decreases as a result, the drug has worked as a positive punisher. Negative punishment involves a pleasurable or rewarding stimulus being withdrawn following a behavior. A common example of this is when a child has a tantrum and, as a result, the parent takes away a favored toy. The removal of the toy, a negative punishment, is expected to decrease the child's troublesome behavior so that he or she does not have to forfeit the desired object again. With both forms of punishment, the desired outcome is to decrease problematic or undesirable behavior.

The four major consequences that follow behavior were summarized by Thyer (1994) as follows: "Something good is presented (positive reinforcement), something bad is taken away (negative reinforcement), something bad is presented (positive punishment), or something good is taken away (negative punishment)" (138).

From this perspective, individuals' sense of competence erodes when their behaviors create barriers to their ability to function.

A woman who has a fear of flying, for example, begins to limit her traveling. In a most extreme form, she might make life decisions to keep from experiencing forms of distress such as panic attacks, which include hyperventilation, feelings of disconnection of mind and body, sweating, and rapid heartbeats. However, avoiding panic attacks by not traveling by plane could limit the woman's job advancement if this includes air travel.

### Albert Bandura

Social learning theorists such as Bandura (1977) contend that behavior can be influenced by both the environment and the person. This view is known as *reciprocal causation*. Social learning theory extends behavioral theory by hypothesizing that learning takes place through individuals' perceptions of events and the behaviors of others. Although social learning theory concerns how individuals *behave*, Sheldon (1995) stressed that this process is primarily a cognitive one (i.e., one that involves how we view ourselves in a given situation and how repeating these actions will lead to a satisfying outcome).

Bandura (1977) is well known for his research on social modeling, which showed that behaviors can be taught or strengthened by showing the learner a certain skill. People are more likely to model behaviors they value. He also stressed that behaviors such as those seen on television shows and commercials may be imitated. In a classic experiment, children were exposed to the aggressive acts of adults. After watching an adult punch or kick a Bobo doll, children copied this behavior, acting similarly toward the doll (Bandura, Ross, and Ross 1961). Bandura's research suggests that these children evaluated the behavior of the adult in a way that had a significant impact on how they themselves later behaved. This is called *vicarious learning*, and it involves individuals learning from social situations in which they have evaluated how others have acted. When their appraisal is positive, others will adopt these behaviors and act in a similar fashion.

The concept of modeling is primary in social learning theory. The modeling of behavior can lead to different outcomes for different people, depending on the people themselves and how they appraise the situation. Hudson and Macdonald (1986) described modeling as follows:

> A person sees someone performing an action and pays attention to it.

The person who is observing codes how the action is carried out and what outcome is achieved.

The observer identifies those circumstances in which the behavior has occurred and what the outcomes have been; that is, the observer contextualizes the behavior.

When similar situations arise, the observer enacts or repeats the behavior with the belief that he or she will evoke a similar response.

Although modeling happens across the life course, there are certain times or situations when it can be used to help individuals function competently, or less competently. One time is during adolescence, when childhood norms and behaviors are disappearing but adult forms have not yet been fully developed. Teens adopt the behaviors of others as a way to begin to separate from family and parents and to begin the process of forming their own identity (see Chapter 3). A national study of the use of nonprescription drugs found that adolescents who abused these drugs had a greater number of peers who were also abusing such medications (Ford 2008). This suggests that exposure to others who are abusing nonprescription drugs may influence teens to adopt these behaviors.

Modeling is also particularly useful during major life transitions. When individuals have limited understanding of how to function competently, they observe those who are acting effectively and adopt similar behaviors. The outcomes can be either positive (enhancing the competence of the individual in the new situation) or negative (promoting problematic and challenging conditions). When students enter college, for example, they encounter a number of new circumstances. With increased freedom and the decreased structure of high school and home life, they may adopt the new behaviors of those around them, possibly including alcohol use. In one study on drinking behavior on college campuses, researchers reported that especially for men, the quality and stability of peer relationships was prominent in decisions about whether to drink (Borsari and Carey 2006). Young men who had social networks populated by other young men who drank alcohol were themselves more likely to drink.

Another aspect of the appraisal process is how people evaluate observed actions in the contexts of their lives. Bandura (1977) described this process as *perceived self-efficacy*, or the self-appraisal of one's ability to perform particular tasks or actions. This concept is directly related to competence, as an individual is more likely to carry out a behavior he or she feels capable of executing it successfully. Cross-national research on children supports the premise that there are differences in perceived self-efficacy based upon both gender and culture (Pastorelli et al. 2001). That is, what constitutes efficacious and appropriate behavior is defined by both cultural and gender role norms and values.

## Cognitive Approaches

*Cognitive theory argues that behavior is affected by perception or interpretation of the environment during the process of learning. Apparently, inappropriate behavior must therefore arise from misperception and misinterpretation.*

*—Payne (1997, 115)*

Whereas behavioral approaches focus on the environmental conditions and influences that shape behavior, cognitive and CB approaches focus on the internal experiences of the individual. According to these theoretical approaches, competence is inhibited by faulty thinking processes that decrease a person's ability to functioning effectively. In order to increase competence, the therapist challenges distorted thinking to help the client discard it and replace it with thinking that is more productive.

The Swiss psychologist and philosopher Jean Piaget was a major influence in developing cognitive theory for practice and intervention. Piaget's (1948) work on the moral reasoning of children provided a foundation for understanding the development of cognition processes. As described in Chapter 3, Piaget conceptualized four developmental stages: *sensorimotor* (birth to two years), *preoperational* (ages two to seven), *concrete operational* (ages seven to eleven), and *formal operational* (ages eleven through adulthood). As children progress through these stages, they exhibit a greater ability to process more complex conditions and understand their environment.

### Cognitive Therapy (CT): Beck

In the decade following the work of Piaget, other theorists incorporated cognitive understanding of the ways in which an individual's functioning becomes challenged or he or she develops problems interacting with others and/or the environment. Aaron Beck used three basic concepts to delineate cognitive function: (a) *cognitive events*, or the stream of thoughts and images that are somewhat automatic and not frequently attended; (b) *cognitive processes*, or the processes by which people process, search for, and store information; and (c) *cognitive structures*, or the underlying mechanisms that allow people to attend to events. The interdependence of these three concepts must be addressed in treatment in order for clients to become more competent in understanding and influencing their own cognitive processes and self-regulatory activity.

Cognitive theorists and practitioners integrate concepts about cognition into various methods of intervention. In particular, CT approaches have a strong evidence base of being successfully used to treat depression and anxiety across the life course (Dobson and Dobson 2009; see Chapter 10). For example, Aaron Beck, who was both a psychiatrist and a researcher, applied cognitive principles to the remediation of depression. He is noted for developing the Beck Depression Inventory (BDI; Beck et al. 1961), which is one of the most commonly used instruments for measuring depression. The BDI has several forms and has been translated into a number of languages. Behavioral symptoms represented in the BDI include feelings of sadness, loss of sexual drive, and changes in appetite and sleep patterns. Respondents rate the magnitude of these experiences on a scale from 0 to 3. Higher scores on the BDI represent greater depressive symptomatology.

Cognitive theory and therapy originally stemmed from a shift away from behaviorism. However, therapists had an appreciation that both approaches to psychotherapeutic treatment focused on a "here-and-now" approach to client problems. As a result, cognitive therapy (CT) has become effective for alleviating numerous mood and anxiety disorders as well as compromised social functioning. A review of various meta-analyses of studies that have used CT found strong evidence for its effectiveness across a variety of conditions (Butler et al. 2005). In particular, adult depression, anxiety, social phobia, post-traumatic stress, and childhood depression and anxiety have been treated effectively using CT. Moderate success was also found in the treatment of several other conditions, including anger management, marital distress, chronic pain, and childhood somatic symptoms.

The premise of cognitive theory and practice is that faulty thinking leads to distortions that create problems in functioning and hinder competence. For example, an introverted and shy man may have a self-perception that no women would be interested in dating him. If he got up enough nerve to ask someone out and was turned down, his faulty thinking would lead him to believe that he will never have a relationship. In this cognitive paradigm, there is no alternative possibility about this experience, such as "She wasn't right for me" or "Even though this date didn't work out, I will eventually find someone." Instead, the explanation about the rejection becomes a dominant theme in the man's perspective of himself as a desirable partner.

Cognitive techniques have been combined with behavioral methods (CBT) and can be applied across a variety of different client systems. In individual settings, the therapist uses techniques to help the client identify and challenge his or her faulty thinking processes. CBT is also used in group work (see Chapter 8), in which members work collectively to identify distorted thinking and challenge one another when such thinking is presented and shared within the group. As a result, the group members can attain a degree of competence as they become more aware of their own and others' problematic thinking.

CBT is also used with couples and families. In a study on child maltreatment, fifty-five families were reviewed to determine the impact of various types of treatment on reducing violent behavior (Kolko 1996). Sessions with the parents included interventions to help them be more competent in their caregiving role, learn alternative methods of dealing with the challenging behaviors of their child, and restructure their thought process about their parenting role. Parents who completed the CBT intervention had lower rates of violence and risk of harm to their children and lower levels of parental distress compared to those parents receiving routine service plans.

CBT interventions have also been used to assist families with medical conditions and diagnoses. CBT methods can be provided to caregivers, including spouses and other family members. For example, one long-term follow-up study involved eighty-eight patients with osteoarthritis. The patients were randomly assigned to one of three treatment conditions: (a) spouse-assisted treatment, (b) intervention with no spousal involvement, and (c) arthritis education with spouse support (Keefe et al. 1999). After twelve months, the patients in the spouse-assisted CBT condition (Group 3) had significantly higher overall self-efficacy and showed greater improvement than those in the other groups. Patients who reported improved marital relationships as a result of the training had lower levels of psychological and physical disability and reduced pain levels at a twelve-month follow-up.

*Rational Emotive Behavioral Therapy (REBT): Ellis*

Albert Ellis is the founder of rational emotive behavioral therapy (REBT), previously called *rational emotive therapy*. Like many other prominent clinicians of his time, Ellis was a student of Freudian psychoanalysis during the early stages of his career. His disillusionment with psychoanalytic theory was based upon his growing awareness of the clinical importance of assisting the client in identifying the various aspects of irrational thinking that create problems in competent functioning. Ellis believed that irrational beliefs could be self-defeating and thus overcome. Like CBT, REBT is an approach that can be used with individuals, couples and families, and groups.

REBT is founded on a theoretical A-B-C paradigm. The *A*dverse condition (also called the *A*ctivating event) leads to particular *Con*sequences for an individual. The person's *B*elief about the event or situation "intervenes" in the outcome. Therefore, two individuals may experience the same adverse condition, yet their particular beliefs about the occurrence can lead to dissimilar outcomes or consequences.

Within REBT, cognition and emotion are viewed as interrelated processes. Ellis (1994) stated that "the theoretical foundations of [REBT] are based on the assumption that human thinking and emotion are *not* two disparate or different processes, but that they significantly overlap and are in some respects, for all practical purposes, essentially the same thing" (55, italics in the original). That is, problems in human functioning or barriers to competence are a result of faulty belief systems that arise from a person's understandings and feelings about an event or situation.

REBT has been used to help clients cope with and gain competence in a range of challenges and situations. This approach is particularly useful with clients who are dealing with health and functional limitations. For example, REBT has been successfully used to assist clients with the challenges of deafness and hearing impairment (Gough 1990) and during the transition from a serious health problem to rehabilitation (Gandy 1999). In these and related circumstances, clients are challenged to confront their irrational thoughts about the situation they are facing (e.g., "Because I have X condition, my life is over"). By disputing these negative thinking processes, clients can become more open to viewing functional ways in which to enhance their sense of mastery and competence despite some of their challenges.

REBT has also been used with clients with maladaptive behaviors. For example, this approach has been used to challenge incarcerated populations in terms of thinking about their present situation within prison as well as to improve their ability to function competently after their release (Kopec 1995). Another situation in which this approach has been implemented is with regard to pathological gambling (Angelillo 2001). Examples of distorted thinking, such as continuing to believe that "a big win" is right around the corner or that they are "owed" something, are challenged. REBT approaches help clients who are struggling with problematic behaviors determine alternative and more competent ways of thinking and behaving.

### Cognitive Social Work: Berlin

Cognitive social work is based on empirically derived learning theories. It can incorporate techniques such as operant conditioning and modeling. As with all social work practice, cognitive interventions stem from a person–environment perspective and include social work values (Thyer 1994). Rimm and Cunningham (1985) made the following contrast between cognitive social work and other forms of intervention:

1. As compared to psychotherapy, behavioral interventions focus on behavioral processes or overt behavior.
2. Behavioral interventions emphasize the here and now.
3. Behavior theory assumes that maladaptive behaviors are learned.
4. Behaviorists believe that learning can be an effective means of changing maladaptive behavior.
5. Behavioral interventions involve setting well-defined goals.
6. Behavioral interventions stress empirically supported techniques.

Social work practitioners may combine several techniques in treatment, such as *extinction* (or not rewarding a client's negative behavior) and *desensitization* (or gradually teaching a client to overcome fear by learning to relax in the presence of noxious stimuli). Clients may also receive *assertiveness training*, which involves giving themselves permission to stand up for themselves in a socially appropriate manner. In addition, *positive reinforcement*, or a process of rewarding a response, may be used.

A basic principle of CB practice is that learning can change a client's negative behavior. The client and practitioner set goals intended to target and change or modify negative behavior and achieve more competent functioning. Integrating concepts from cognitive theory, Berlin (2001) outlined a problem-solving process for social workers to adopt as a therapeutic model, and contended that clients have "real-life reasons for feeling down and out" (2). She wanted to develop a clinical social work approach that provided an in-depth assessment of a client's cognitive–emotional patterns. She argued that people are natural meaning-makers and can be helped to translate new information they gain in therapy into new meanings:

> All the important meaning in our lives—who we are, how we stand in relation to others, what kind of prospects and options we have—are a function of the nature of the information we encounter and our patterns or systems of organizing these informational cues—in other words our schema (Berlin 2001, 9).

The therapeutic encounter is a proactive time when client and social worker jointly create plans, acquire skills, and think about positive possibility. It is a safe time to explore old negative thought patterns and behaviors as new ones are learned.

## Critique

Because of the more rote-like nature of Pavlovian experiments, erroneous conclusions can be drawn about behavioral therapies. This view of the deterministic nature of behavioral therapy was fueled by the more controversial aspects of social learning theory espoused by B. F. Skinner. In his political novel *Walden Two* (1948), Skinner envisioned a decentralized society in which a utopia is created through his theory of reinforcement.

Walden Two is an experimental rural community of 1,000 members in which people subscribe to a code of conduct based on behaviorism. Members are ruled by an elite, reject democracy and religion, and espouse communal childrearing. Cultural engineering, particularly reinforcers, accounts for behavioral control and a strict adherence to a code of conduct (Rozycki 1999).

By contrast, contemporary CB approaches to social work practice are built on numerous replication studies. This research indicates that the approach is applicable to diverse client groups, offers many proven intervention techniques, and can be appreciated for its empirical base (see Chapter 10). In addition, the research shows that approach provides a means of assessing client change or outcomes (Thyer 1994).

Behavioral techniques are increasingly being associated with behavioral health and wellness, providing a means of combating smoking, overeating, and overdrinking (Corey 2001). As can be seen in the following case example, because CB interventions focus on specific meaning in life events, they can offer a plan of action that changes behavior.

## Case Example

From an observer's perspective, April Shriver had an enviable life. By her early forties she was married to her college sweetheart, and they had two healthy, well-adjusted sons. Both April and her husband had good jobs and there were no financial problems in the household. In fact, the children went to exclusive private schools, and April was the president of the parent–teacher association.

In spite of this, April felt depressed and anxious. Although she had a good job, she was being groomed to step into a demanding administrative role in her company. This change would necessitate a more intensive work schedule and supervisory tasks. Although there would also be an increase in her salary, April did not enjoy the administrative responsibilities that would accompany this promotion.

In addition, she felt pressure in her home life. Although she loved her husband Cal, he did very little around the house and worked long hours as an attorney. After coming home from her own job, she had the responsibility of picking up her sons from soccer or basketball practice, fixing dinner, and taking care of other household tasks. In addition, her seventy-five-year-old mother, who lived across town, was starting to experience some significant health problems and was becoming increasingly dependent on April, the only family member who lived in the same city.

One day on her drive to work, April pulled over on the side of the road and started to cry. She felt so bad that she turned around and drove back home, where she spent the rest of the day in bed. After calling her best friend in tears, April made an appointment with a psychotherapist who specialized in CBT.

During the course of the psychotherapy sessions, April examined some of her beliefs and behaviors. In particular, her belief that she had "no choice" in taking the promotion was causing her a great deal of stress and discomfort. With her therapist, she examined alternatives and the consequences of this new position for her and her family. When she made the decision to tell her company that she did not want to move into this new administrative role, she rehearsed the meeting with her boss. Although this encounter with her boss was not entirely easy, it did not end in the catastrophic outcomes (e.g., being fired) that April had initially feared.

During her sessions, April also explored areas of her life that felt burdensome and demanding. Although she loved her mother and sons, the level of responsibility that she assumed as the primary care provider in each of these roles was overwhelming her. She made some additional decisions about how to get support and help, including asking Cal to take more responsibility in the household and family life. A major breakthrough was the exploration of April's belief that she needed to "do it all": be the perfect wife, daughter, mother, and employee. Part of her therapy was analyzing and rethinking how she could establish limits within her family, volunteer, and work roles. The CB approach provided her with insight into her beliefs about herself and her behaviors and enabled her to learn new ways of interacting and coping in her relationships.

## References

Adler, A. 1959. *Understanding human nature.* New York: Premier Books.

Angelillo, J. C. 2001. Rational-emotive behavioral therapy in the treatment of pathological gambling. In *Innovations in clinical practice: A source book,* ed. T. L. Jackson and L. Vandecreek, 141–58. Sarasota, FL: Professional Resource Exchange.

Bandura, A. 1977. Self-efficacy: Toward a unifying theory of behavioral change. *Psychological Review* 84:191–215.

Bandura, A., D. Ross, and S. A. Ross. 1961. Transmission of aggression through imitation of aggressive models. *Journal of Abnormal and Social Psychology* 63:575–82.

Beck, A. 1976. *Cognitive therapy and emotional disorders.* New York: International Universities Press.

Beck, A. T., C. H. Ward, M. Mendelson, J. Mock, and J. Erbaugh. 1961. An inventory for measuring depression. *Archives of General Psychiatry* 4: 561–71.

Beck, J. 1995. *Cognitive therapy: Basics and beyond.* New York: Guilford Press.

Berlin, S. 1980. A cognitive-learning perspective for social work practice. *Social Service Review* 54:537–55.

____. 2001. *Clinical social work practice: A cognitive-integrative perspective.* New York: Oxford University Press.

Borsari, B., and K. Carey. 2006. How the quality of peer relationships influences college alcohol use. *Drug and Alcohol Review* 25:361–70.

Butler, A. C., J. E. Chapman, E. M. Forman, and A. T. Beck. 2005. The empirical status of cognitive-behavioral therapy: A review of meta-analyses. *Clinical Psychology Review* 26, no. 1:17–31.

Corey, G. 2001. *Theory and practice of counseling and psychotherapy.* Belmont, CA: Wadsworth/Thomson Learning.

Dobson, D. J. G., and K. S. Dobson. 2009. *Evidence-based practice of cognitive-behavioral therapy.* New York: Guilford Press.

Ellis, A. 1977. The basic theory of rational-emotive therapy. In *Handbook of rational-emotive therapy,* ed. A. Ellis and R. Grieger, 10–35. New York: Springer.

_____.1994. *Reason and emotion in psychotherapy.* New York: Birch Lane Press.

Ford, J. 2008. Social learning theory and nonmedical prescription drug use among adolescents. *Sociological Spectrum* 28:299–316.

Gandy, G. L. 1999. Rational-emotive behavior therapy (REBT): A cognitive-behavioral approach to acceptance and adjustment to disability. In *Counseling in the rehabilitation process,* ed. G. Gandy, E. D. Martin, and R. E. Hardy, 234–50. Springfield, IL: Charles C Thomas.

Garakani, A., S. Mathew, and D. Charney. 2006. Neurobiology of anxiety disorders and implications for treatment. *Mount Sinai Journal of Medicine* 73:941–49.

Garvin, C. 1991. Social learning and role theories. In *Human behavior and social work practice,* ed. R. R. Greene and P. H. Ephross, 151–76. Hawthorne, NY: Aldine de Gruyter.

Gough, D. L. 1990. Rational-emotive therapy: A cognitive-behavioral approach to working with hearing impaired clients. *Journal of the American Deafness and Rehabilitation Association* 23, no. 4:96–104.

Hudson, B., and G. Macdonald. 1986. *Behavioral social work: An introduction.* London: Macmillan.

Keefe, F. J., D. S. Caldwell, D. Baucom, A. Salley, and E. Robinson. 1999. Spouse-assisted coping skills training in the management of knee pain in osteoarthritis: Long-term follow-up results.*Arthritis Care and Research* 12, no. 2:101–11.

Kolko, D. 1996. Individual cognitive behavioral treatment and family treatment for physically abused children and their offending parents: A comparison of clinical outcomes. *Child Maltreatment* 1:322–42.

Kopec, A. M. 1995. Rational emotive behavioral therapy in a forensic setting: Practical issues. *Journal of Rational-Emotive & Cognitive Behavior Therapy* 13, no. 4:243–53.

Litz, B., S. Orsillo, D. Kaloupek, and F. Weathers. 2000. Emotional processing in posttraumatic stress disorder. *Journal of Abnormal Psychology* 109:26–39.

Meichenbaum, D. 1985. Cognitive-behavioral therapies. In *Contemporary psychotherapies: Models and methods,* ed. S.J.Lynn and J. P. Garske, 261–86. Columbus, OH: Bell & Howell.

Morrell, H., L. Cohen, and D. McChargue. 2010. Depression vulnerability predicts cigarette smoking among college students: Gender and negative reinforcement expectancies as contributing factors. *Addictive Behaviors* 35:607–11.

Pastorelli, C., G. Caprara, C. Barbaranelli, J. Rola, S. Rozsa, and A. Bandura. 2001. The structure of children's perceived self-efficacy: A cross-national study. *European Journal of Psychological Assessment* 17, no. 2:87–97.

Payne, M. 1997. *Modern social work theory.* 2nd ed. Chicago, IL: Lyceum.

Piaget, J. 1948. *Moral judgment of the child.* Glencoe, IL: Free Press.

Rimm, D. C., and H. M. Cunningham. 1985. Behavior therapies. In *Contemporary psychotherapies: Models and methods*, ed. S. J. Lynn and J. P. Ganske, 221–59. Columbus, OH: Merrill.

Rozycki, E. G. 1999. A critical review of B.F. Skinner's philosophy with focus on Walden Two. http://www.newfoundations.com/EGR/Walden.html (accessed November 9, 2009).

Sheldon, B. 1995. *Cognitive-behavioural therapy: Research, practice and philosophy.* London: Routledge.

Skinner, B. F. 1948. *Walden two.* Indianapolis, IN: Hackett.

____. 1953. *Science and human behavior.* New York: Free Press.

____. 1966. What is the experimental analysis of behavior? *Journal of the Experimental Analysis of Behavior* 9, no. 3:213–18.

____. 1974. *About behaviorism.* New York: Knopf.

____. 1985. Cognitive science and behaviorism. *British Journal of Psychology* 76:291–301.

____. 1988. The operant side of behavior therapy. *Journal of Behavior Therapy and Experimental Psychiatry* 19, no. 3:171–79.

Thyer, B. A. 1994. Social learning theory: Empirical applications to culturally diverse practice. In *Human behavior theory: A diversity framework*, ed. R. R. Greene, 133–46. Haworth, NY: Aldine de Gruyter.

Thyer, B., and L. Myers. 1997. Social learning theory: An empirically-based approach to understanding human behavior in the social environment. *Journal of Human Behavior in the Social Environment* 1, no. 1:33–52.

Watson, J. B. 1930. *Behaviorism.* Chicago, IL: University of Chicago Press.

Watson, J. B., and R. Rayner. 1920. Conditioned emotional reactions. *Journal of Experimental Psychology* 3:1–14.

# 7

# Older Adults: Life Transitions, Stress, and Resilience

*The idea that people can overcome stress successfully and continue to manage their own affairs speaks to their self-righting capacity or natural capacity to heal. This is accomplished through self-appraisal, an internal process that a person uses to evaluate his or her situation.*

—*Greene (2008b, 527)*

Older adulthood is a time of challenge and opportunity, as individuals modify their roles, adapt to their declining physical abilities, and meet demanding environmental challenges. Yet, older adults can continue to grow emotionally and mentally, contribute to their communities, and remain competent in everyday life (Diehl 1998).

Because older adults who seek help from a social worker may be frail or have limitations to their physical capacity, the social worker's major task is to assess the upper limit of their capacity to function in their environment or to determine the least restrictive environment in which they would want to function. If clients prefer to stay in their homes, can they? Do they need or want additional help (Greene, 1986; Greene et al. 2007)?

As with other junctures in the life course discussed in this text, no single theory explains competence and adaptability in late adulthood. This chapter expands on the concepts and models of the person–environment perspective presented in Chapter 1 to explain how life stressors are met by older adults, emphasizing older adults' self-efficacy and their mastery of the environment.

## Demographic Imperative

*The future population explosion does not necessarily mean that there will be an expanding number of stereotypically frail and dependent people. Neither should it be assumed that these older adults will want and require the same services as previous generations.*

*—Greene (2005, 109)*

The nation's rapidly expanding older population will demand a cadre of social workers well-equipped to deliver services, design suitable delivery systems, and formulate policy that supports the well-being of these older adults. By 2030 the U.S. population older than sixty-five years of age is projected to be double that in 2000—growing from the present 35 million to 71.5 million—and will represent 20 percent of the total U.S. population (Administration on Aging 2010). Because the number of older adults is expanding so rapidly, a human behavior theory base is needed to provide for an adequate *assessment* of life transitions, facilitating the match between a client's need for services and available care and resources. As the opening quote of this section suggestions, the emerging population of older adults is increasingly diverse in functional status and need for health and social welfare services. In the coming years, there will be an increased focus on how to promote positive aspects of aging and on how older adults can maintain their capacity to function well in their environment as they age.

A theory-based assessment would provide guidance on which older adults need which services and which can function more independently with the informal support of family and friends. This approach is known as *client triage*, a process that determines the most frail or physically and/or mentally challenged elderly clients who require the most intensive service (Greene 2005). In sum, the practitioner's ability to use theory to assess an older person's everyday competence—a necessity given the changes in society's age structure—allows for a proper evaluation of needs and services.

### Person-in-Environment

*Social work with the aged and their families reflects the profession's traditionally person-environment philosophy in which a middle ground is struck between interventions that address client's psychological development and those that address a client's social and environmental situation.*

*—Greene (2008c, 208)*

Social work assessment of older adults can best be carried out using the person–environment perspective, which facilitates a review of the multiple components composing competent functioning (Germain, 1994; Greene and Barnes, 1998). The theory base includes three major perspectives: (a) an ecological systems approach such as *environmental press*, which addresses the person's *goodness of fit* with his or her environment, or the match between a client's needs and the demands or quality of the environment; (b) a *risk and resilience* framework that emphasizes differences in response to stress; and (c) a *biopsychosocial spiritual life course* developmental framework, which reviews the person's behavior with respect to activities central to daily life.

Taken together, these perspectives afford a comprehensive picture of the older adult and his or her ability to function competently in the environment. These organizing constructs also provide a strengths-based perspective for a new gerontology based on a wellness approach to aging. The theorists discussed in this chapter include those who have addressed people's positive reactions to stress and their ability to maintain competence, particularly during times of rapid social change.

### Stress, Appraisal, and Coping: Lazarus and Lawton

*Our daily lives are filled with far less dramatic stressful experiences that arise from our roles in living. In our research we have referred to these as "daily hassles," the little things that can irritate and distress people, such as one's dog getting sick on the living room rug, dealing with an inconsiderate smoker, having too many responsibilities, feeling lonely, having an argument with a spouse, and so on.*

*—Lazarus and Folkman (1984, 13)*

### Stress

*Stress* may be acute (caused by a sudden event) or it may be chronic (the result of the wear and tear of everyday life). There are three components of a response to stress: (a) the *physical* response, such as fight or flight, which often involves an increase in heart rate and the release of extra adrenaline (Selye 1956); (b) the *emotional* response, which is characterized by fear, anxiety, and grief; and (c) the *behavioral* response, in which coping strategies and resources are used to deal with the stressor.

### Transactional View of Stress

Ecological theorists focus on a *transactional model* in which stress is the result of an imbalance between the person and the environment. Ecological theorists hold that the person and the environment are an inseparable unit of reciprocal influences. According to Lazarus (1980), there is a "fusion of person and environment into a unit, a relationship, a system" (38). This approach assesses cumulative person–environment exchanges and their effects over time.

How does the older adult function within his or her environment over time? Ecological theorists assume that *competence* reflects a person's history of successful transactions with the environment. However, such transactions may result in *stress*—"an imbalance between a person's perceived demands and his or her perceived capability to use resources to meet these demands" (Greene 2008a, 231). A social worker's major task is to evaluate these situations.

### Goodness of Fit

Assessing an older adult's person–environment exchanges over time allows the practitioner to determine *goodness of fit*, or the extent to which there is a nurturing or positive match between the individual's adaptive needs and the qualities of the environment. Goodness of fit provides an insight into the reasons for an older adult's sense of well-being or lack thereof. Interventions may be required for those older adults living in harsh or oppressive environments, such as those who live in poverty and/or who have inadequate health care.

### Appraisal

Whether an environment is nurturing must be seen from the client's vantage point. Lazarus (1980) argued that stress is not simply a matter of a person responding to negative environmental stimuli. Rather, when an adverse event occurs, people go through a subjective, cognitive process of appraising the resulting demands.

This *appraisal* involves how a person construes the event—What does he or she make of it? Lazarus viewed appraisal as an immediate, intuitive reaction to a *life stressor*, or something that triggers a person's perception that harm or loss may take place. "The meaning of the event shapes the emotional and behavioral response … Through cognitive appraisal processes the person evaluates the significance of what is happening for his or her well-being" (Lazarus and Folkman 1984, 52–53; see also Chapter 6).

People engage in *primary appraisal,* or an evaluation of the potential threat. What is the significance of the event? Is it controllable or challenging? The *secondary appraisal* involves thinking about the coping mechanisms and resources available to deal with the situation. At this point, the person decides what is at stake and what can be done. Lazarus and Folkman (1984) contended that the strength of a person's commitment to his or her goals in life can ward off threats and "impel" the person to cope with obstacles. A person's level of commitment may depend on what is important to him or her and can influence what is at stake. High levels of commitment (e.g., wanting to age in place in one's own home) can help sustain coping efforts.

Appraisal is also influenced by one's view of the purpose of life even under the most dire circumstances. For example, Lazarus and Folkman (1984) argued that traumatic events such as genocide can have no benefit or purpose and can appear senseless. Yet, although Nazi concentration camps were designed to remove any vestige of meaning, worth, autonomy, and control, almost all survivors reported finding purpose to their existence, which aided in their survival (Dimsdale 1974 ). For example, most concentration camp survivors found meaning or purpose in survival itself. This included living for the sake of family, bearing witness, and eventually seeking revenge (Benner, Roskies, and Lazarus 1980).

*Environmental Press*

The quality of an older adult's environment is critical to competent functioning, and delineating this quality is central to the assessment process. Environments may be understood in terms of how they affect the older adult's functional capacity (Greene et al. 2007). *Personal environments* may include significant others, such as the family or friends who engage in one-to-one personal relationships with the older adult. *Suprapersonal environments* are the "modal characteristics" of all of the people in physical proximity to the older person, including neighbors or the larger ethnic group (Lawton 1982, 40). Is the older adult living in ways consistent with his or her cultural beliefs? Does the older adult maintain friendships?

*Social environments* comprise the norms or values (such as the wish to live independently) and the institutions operating in the individual's culture, subgroup, or society. Do the social environment and its norms promote independence or interdependence? *Physical environments* refer to the nonpersonal, nonsocial aspects of the environment, such as space, noise, and pollution. For example, does the older adult live in a "neglected" neighborhood? In the environmental press model, the social worker's assessment is based on the client's behavioral outcome. It explores whether the older adult is able to balance his or her capabilities with the demands—or *press*—of his or her environment (Lawton and Nahemow 1973).

From the perspective of environmental press, *competence* is defined as the theoretical upper limit of the capacity of the individual to function in terms of

> *biological health*, or the absence of disease states that indicate the older adult may continue to function in the home;
>
> *sensory–perceptual capacity*, including of vision, audition, olfaction, gestation, somesthesis (body perception), and *kinesthesis* (the ability to sense the position, orientation, and movement of one's body), impairment of which makes movement within the home extremely difficult;
>
> *motor skills*, or the muscular strength and complex coordination that are necessary to perform on one's own;
>
> *cognitive capacity*, or the capacity to comprehend, process, and cope with the external world that is required to live alone; and
>
> *ego strength*, or the internal psychological strength that enhances independence (Lawton 1982, 37–38; see Figure 7.1).

## Coping

Coping involves the *appraisal*—or the mental process of viewing one's situation and how environmental demands affect functioning—sets the coping process into action. How will the individual manage stress in the environment? What behaviors are needed to ameliorate or master stress? Coping may require *personal resources* such as optimism and *environmental resources* such as social supports.

Coping may be emotion focused or problem focused. *Problem-focused coping* involves responding to a problem or stressful situation by formulating a plan or approach, changing the environment to make it more bearable, or managing or escaping from the problem. *Emotion-focused coping* involves reframing, denying, or distancing oneself from the problem or stressful situation. Knowing how a client attempts to manage his or her environment allows the practitioner to establish a mutual helping process.

**Figure 7.1 The Environmental Press–Competence Model**

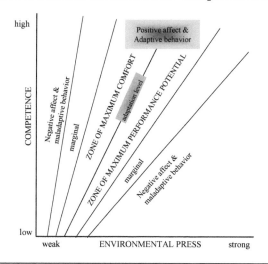

*Source:* From Lawton and Nahemow (1973, 619–74).

## Collective Stress, Appraisal, and Coping

The concepts of stress, appraisal, and coping have been applied to family situations as well. For example, the family adjustment and adaptation response model addresses a family's response to stress, emphasizing how a family uses coping behaviors to meet the stress of a crisis. When the demands are too great for the family, a crisis develops, causing a state of disequilibrium and the need for the *adjustment* of resources and coping strategies. As the perceptions of the crisis are sorted out, the meaning or the appraisal of the crisis affects how the family *adapts to* and meets the challenge (Patterson and Garwick 1998).

## Social Work Models of Stress

Social work theorists have developed working models to depict the effects of stress on how people function in their environment. For example, in their *life model of social work practice*, Gitterman and Germain (2008) argued that people have to meet the natural stresses of everyday life over the life course, including

> *difficult life transitions* involving developmental or social changes; *traumatic life events*, including grave losses or illness; and *environmental pressures*, encompassing poverty and violence.

## Figure 7.2 The Flow of Stress through the Family

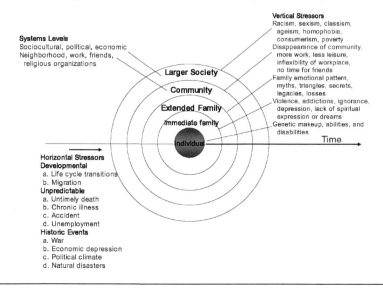

*Source:* From Lawton and Nahemow (1973, 619–74).

The purpose of the *life model* is to improve the fit between people's needs and capacities and their environmental supports and resources:

> By helping to change perceptions, cognitions, feelings, or behaviors, [people's] ability to manage a stressor is improved, or its adverse impact may be reduced. By effectively influencing environmental responsiveness, people gain access to desired support and resources and, in turn, develop greater control over their lives. (Gitterman 1996, 395)

Practitioners may also want to turn to a useful schema devised by Carter and McGoldrick (1999) that examines stress from the viewpoint of individuals and families within a larger cultural context. As can be seen in Figure 7.2, stressors on the horizontal axis include

> developmental events, such as life cycle transitions and migration; unpredictable events, such as untimely death, chronic illness, accident, or unemployment; and historical events, such as war, economic depression, the political climate, and natural disasters.

The stressors depicted along the vertical axis represent "cultural and societal histories, stereotypes, patterns of power, social hierarchies,

144

and beliefs" (Carter and McGoldrick 1999, 6). These stressors may affect the larger society as well as individuals. They are

racism, sexism, classism, ageism, consumerism, and poverty;

the disappearance of community, more work, less leisure, inflexibility of the workplace, and the absence of sufficient time for friends;

family emotional patterns, myths, triangles, secrets, legacies, and losses;

violence, addictions, ignorance, depression, and lack of spiritual expression or dreams; and

genetic makeup, abilities, and disabilities.

## Risk and Resilience

*The resilience-enhancing model (REM) ... developed new tenets of practice in aging for the present era and a philosophy for a new gerontology. Rather than an "aging as a problem" perspective of earlier gerontology and geriatric practice, resilience interventions are based on the self-direction and self-advocacy of older adults.*
                                    —*Damron-Rodriguez (2007, 5)*

Risk and resilience theory is linked to ecological thinking (Greene 2008b), incorporating many of its concepts (Gitterman and Germain 2008), such as its compatibility with stress theory, biopsychosocial spiritual development, concepts of adaptation, and cross-cultural applications (Fong and Greene 2009). According to the *Encyclopedia of Social Work*, *risk and resilience* is a multitheoretical framework for understanding how people maintain well-being despite adversity (Greene 2008a).

Risk and resilience theory holds that people have a natural capacity to rebound or self-right (Garmezy 1993, 129) following adverse events and that the practitioner may foster this through planned interventions. Risk and resilience theory has been applied in the fields of child welfare (Fraser 1997; Gilgun 1996), child abuse (Higgins 1994), substance abuse (Wolin and Wolin 1993), and family treatment (Walsh 1998). It has only recently been found useful for working with older adults (Greene et al. 2007; Lewis and Harrell 2002).

For example, Lewis and Harrell (2002) suggested that resilience among older adults is related to *safety and support*, including the stability and security of basic needs, and social relationships; *affiliation*, or one's connection to others; and *altruism*, which is manifested when

145

one exhibits socially responsible behavior on behalf of others.

## Terms

*Risk* includes "any influences that increase the probability of on-set, digression to a more serious state, or maintenance of a problem condition" (Kirby and Fraser 1997, 10–11). *Protective factors* are circumstances that safeguard or moderate risks or enhance adaptation. These may include temperament, a nurturing family, mentors, or humor (Garmezy 1991).

There are several definitions of resilience, suggesting that it is a broad concept and possibly more than a single phenomenon (Gordon and Song 1994). *Resilience* is the ability to recover quickly from illness, change, or misfortune.

The definitions of resilience most relevant for work with older adults include

> unpredicted or markedly successful adaptations to negative life events, trauma, stress, and other forms of risk (Fraser, Richman, and Galinsky 1999, 136);

> the ability to maintain continuity of one's personal narrative and a coherent sense of self following traumatic events (Borden 1992, 125);

> "a pattern over time, characterized by good eventual adaptation despite developmental risks, acute stressors, or chronic adversity" (Masten 1994, 5); and

> demonstrated competence following risk and the awareness of one's own competence (Masten 1994, 6).

If we as social workers can understand what helps some people to function well in the context of high adversity, we may be able to incorporate this knowledge into new practice strategies (Fraser, Richman, and Galinsky 1999, 136).

### Resilience and Stress

Although resilience is sometimes thought of as a trait, it should be understood primarily as a process that evolves over time as people successfully deal with stress in the environment (Werner and Smith 1977 ). According to Strumpfer (2002), the process of "resiling" starts when one perceives a challenge or threat that motivates the person to set goals and carry them out. In this sense, people do not have (ongoing) resilience but manifest it when appraising six demanding situations:

1. Exceptionally challenging experiences, for example, in a new challenging job
2. Developmental transitions, including the transition to parenthood
3. Individual adversity, for example, discrimination or persecution
4. Collective adversity, for example, the aftermath of natural disasters or war
5. Organizational change, including the use of technology
6. Large-scale sociopolitical change, such as Glasnost.

### Resilience and Biopsychosocial Spiritual Functioning

According to Greene (2002), resilience is a complex response to biopsychosocial and spiritual phenomena. A person's resilience is influenced by *biological functioning*, which involves genetic, health, physical, or vital life-limiting organ systems; *psychological functioning*, which involves affective, cognitive, and behavioral dimensions; and *social functioning*, or the individual's cultural, political, and economic life as a member of a group. *Spiritual functioning* refers to the client's "personal quest for meaning, mutually fulfilling relationships, and, for some, God" (Canda and Furman 1999, 243).

As Richardson's (2002) schema illustrates (see Figure 7.3), biopsychosocial spiritual functioning needs to be understood as a complementary element of competent functioning. His resiliency model suggests that daily stress may bombard an individual and disrupt his or her internal or external balance. This presents both challenges and opportunities for the older adult. Those people who grow and develop insight may be said to regroup or achieve what Richardson called *resilient reintegration*.

### Collective Resilience

Resilience is not simply a characteristic of individuals. It is a phenomenon that can be exhibited by families, groups, communities, and societies. For example, according to Walsh (1998), three properties are related to relational resilience in a family: its organizational and communication patterns and its belief system. *Belief systems* include values and attitudes about how one should act (in adverse situations), *organizational patterns* refer to expectations for behavior and structures for carrying out stressful tasks, and *communication patterns* encompass the exchange of information in the family. As families overcome an

## Figure 7.3 The Resiliency Model

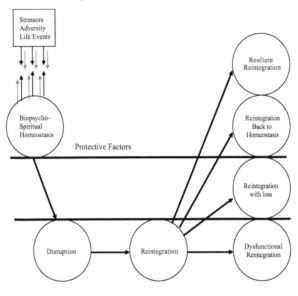

*Source:* From Richardson (2002, 308).

adverse event, they may grow and be transformed. Similarly, societies may attempt to heal following such adverse events as 9/11.

### A Resilience-Enhancing Model of Intervention

Social workers who use a resilience approach to helping believe that people have an innate resilience and an ability to make positive meaning out of adverse situations. They conduct an assessment to explore the client's balance between risk and resilience factors; examine the client's sources of stress; evaluate biopsychosocial and spiritual functioning in a cultural context; determine the goodness of fit between the individual, the family, and surrounding social systems; and evaluate client competence across the life course.

Greene and Armenta (2007) suggested that practitioners go through the following steps as they help a client overcome adversity (see also "Case Example" at the end of the chapter):

> Acknowledge client loss, vulnerability, and future
> Identify the source of and reaction to stress
> Stabilize or normalize the situation

Help clients take control

Provide resources for change

Promote self-efficacy

Collaborate in self-change

Strengthen problem-solving abilities

Address positive emotions

Achieve creative expressions

Listen to client stories

Make meaning of events

Find the benefits of adverse events

Attend to client spirituality
Transcend the immediate situation

## The Life Span: Hareven and Germain and Gitterman

*A stressful event does not occur in a vacuum, but in the context of the individual's life cycle and in relation to other events, be they distant, recent, or concurrent. These specific contextual properties define an event's timing.*

*—Lazarus and Folkman (1984, 108)*

The study of the life span is multidisciplinary, examining how people progress over their lifetime, providing a perspective on how people change over time. A *lifetime* is the number of years one has lived, and in most Western societies it is recorded in days and months (Merriam, Courtenay, and Reeves 2001). The passage of time may also be understood through a life stage or a life course approach, often exploring biopsychosocial and spiritual functioning.

### Life Stages

Developmental theorists present ideas about the ideal stages and tasks people must go through and accomplish at each stage of life (e.g., Atchley, 1999; Peck, 1968). An example is Erikson's view of the eight stages of the healthy personality a person must traverse (see Chapters 2 and 3). These stages are presumed to be fixed, sequential, and universal. The use of such an approach leads to the expectation that there is a "normal" life cycle with critical events (e.g., becoming a grandparent) occurring at certain times.

Erikson (1950) contended that older adults need to resolve the psychosocial crisis of *integrity versus despair*. He contended that this stage, which begins at age sixty and continues to the end of life, involves coming to terms with and appreciating the experiences of one's life. If, however, an individual is in despair, he or she may have little sense of world order or spiritual wholeness (Greene 2008c).

## *Life Course*

An alternative view of the life span stems from a person–environment concept called the *life course*. For example, Gitterman and Germain (2008) suggested that the life stage approach to development can be replaced with a life course perspective. The *life course perspective*, according to Hareven (1982, 1996), is a person-in-context view of how an individual goes through unique developmental pathways shaped by personal, historical, cultural, and environmental factors. The life course view of development is specific to the individual, incorporating diversity, emerging family forms, changing societal and community values and norms, and global and local environments (Gitterman and Germain 2008). Examining the life course thus becomes central to an ecological assessment of an older adult.

From a life course perspective, understanding human development involves examining three different concepts of time: (a) *historical time*, including the cohort or generation into which the person is born; (b) *individual time*, involving personal meanings, experiences, environmental factors over a lifetime; and (c) *social time*, referring to the way in which collective life experiences contribute to personal and group change or transformation. Social time, however, does not always follow a normal, expectable pattern, and critical events such as an illness or a grandparent returning to parenting, may be considered *off time*. A skilled practitioner's questions can reveal how clients' views of these three aspects of time define them as older adults.

## *Biopsychosocial Spiritual Functioning: Northern and Birren*

Similar to the environmental press framework already discussed, the life span may also be studied by exploring its biopsychosocial and spiritual elements. According to Northen (1995), the distinguishing feature of clinical social work is

> adequate appraisal of a person's biological, psychological, and social attributes, capacities, and resources as well as problems; the structure, and process of families and other groups; and the interconnectedness of people with their environments. Assessment

goes beyond diagnosis of a problem or illness to a broader appraisal of the interrelationships between physiological, emotional, and sociocultural factors and the external environmental conditions that influence well-being. (12)

Birren (1959) was one of the first gerontologists to address the issue of how to appraise an individual's level of functioning in a given environment, relative to others of his or her age. His interest in age-associated changes and their effect on a person's capacity to cope effectively with his or her living conditions led to his description of functional age as composed of three kinds of aging processes: biological, psychological, and social. He defined these ages in ways comparable with other theorists in the chapter. *Biological age* comprises the physiological age-related changes and the functional capacities of vital organ systems that contribute to life expectancy; *psychological age* reflects the adaptive capacities of the individual and his or her ability to adjust to environmental demands; and *social age* involves the roles and habits of individuals as they interact with other members of society. Understanding these "ages" can help guide assessment. Crowther et al.'s (2002) conceptualization of *positive spirituality* is also an important component of health and well-being.

*Social Work Interventions and the Life Span*

*Functional age model.* In 1986, Greene translated Birren's three types of functional aging into a model for clinical social work that addresses the functional age of the older adult in the context of family systems and their development. This model illustrates how several of the theoretical frameworks presented in the text can be synthesized and used to help older adults and their families (see Greene 2008c).

*Life review.* Life review takes advantage of the natural process of reminiscence by older adults. "In the course of remembering life out loud, an elder and a listener create a psychosocial legacy" (Kivnick 1996, 49). Older adults who share their stories with younger generations accept that they cannot alter the past but instead have a sense of overall integrity and hope for the future (Erikson, Erikson, and Kivnick 1986). Based on Eriksonian ideas of achieving integrity in old age, the process of reminiscence can be set in motion by the social worker going about the assessment of clients' current biopsychosocial spiritual functioning and can show how they have come to terms with their life experiences.

Psychotherapeutic work with older people involves the management of small deaths and intimations of mortality. Put succinctly, the psychotherapy of old age is the psychotherapy of grief and of accommodation, restitution, and resolution. "Coming to terms with", "bearing witness", reconciliation, atonement construction and reconstruction, integration, transcendence, creativity, realistic insight with modifications and substitutions, the introduction of meaning and of meaningful, useful, and contributory efforts: these are the terms that are pertinent to therapy with older people. (Butler 1968, 237)

*Narrative therapy.* Derived from constructionist theory, the *narrative approach* involves the practitioner exploring the client's critical life events on the personal level and the macrolevel. This contributes to a better understanding of a client's shared history, values, and beliefs (Webster 2002). In relating his or her narrative, the client becomes more aware of self and others, sets priorities, and finds meanings in behaviors. Social interactions and "reality" are created through stories and language.

During later life, older adults may experience a number of changes and transitions requiring new identities and roles. Unfortunately, many people experience these changes in the form of losses (e.g., the death of a spouse or life partner, declining health and functional ability, decreased independence). Losses that occur during this time of life can "rob" older adults of the meanings and stories that they have constructed about themselves. As an example of using a narrative approach to help an older client who is experiencing functional declines and role losses, Kropf and Tandy (1998) described deconstructing an older woman's initial narrative of frailty and worthlessness. By re-storying her life successes and achievements and applying them to current physical challenges, the client was able to recreate her own sense of resilience and competence. In the process, her narrative shifted from one of a "fragile old woman" to one of a "true survivor", instilling a sense of competence and reengagement in life tasks and social relationships.

## Critique: Diverse Elders

### *The Aging of the Baby Boomers*

Understanding the demographics of U.S. society helps social workers choose theories for practice that best suit a diverse aging population. For example, baby boomers, or those born after World War II between 1946 and 1964, are more likely than preceding generations to postpone marriage into their thirties, have smaller families, have more dual-career marriages, and have higher rates of divorce. They are also more likely to be single parents and to live in blended households (Maugans 1994). Consequently, baby boomers have a smaller pool of family members, which requires a reexamination of the distribution of caregiving as they age (Kiyak and Hooyman 1999).

Other patterns are emerging as the baby boom generation reaches later life. For example, although most people exit the workforce between ages fifty-five and seventy, research on employment and retirement patterns indicates that baby boomers are gradually transitioning from the workplace into retirement (Cahill, Giandrea, and Quinn 2006). This "step-down" approach can be beneficial to both the employer and the individual. The employer retains an experienced worker who can overlap with incoming employees, and the person retiring retains a valued social role while creating new, useful opportunities for the retirement years.

Although some retirees find leisure pursuits enjoyable, others find volunteer work and other civic-oriented experiences fulfilling. In fact, baby boomers are expected to volunteer in higher rates than past generations and in different venues. Religious organizations were once the primary outlets for volunteers, followed by civic or political organizations, but now educational, youth services, and environmental organizations are often selected, indicating baby boomers' shifting priorities (Corporation for National & Community Service 2007).

For some older adults, retirement may not be a viable option. Unmarried older women of color are at a particular risk for living in poverty during later life (Angel, Jimenez, and Angel 2007; Kiser and Kendal-Wilson 2002; Ozawa and Hong 2006). The triple jeopardy—being poor, female, and old—creates a cumulative disadvantage that leaves many in this category in dire financial straits. These women may have no viable option but to continue working in low-wage and physically demanding jobs to supplement insufficient Social Security and personal resources.

Many women face economic disadvantages because of caregiving responsibilities. Caregivers had to both expend their savings on caregiving and relinquish earnings by working fewer hours, exiting the labor force, and facing fewer better paying jobs (MetLife 1999). Longitudinal research on parents with and without children with disabilities supports these findings. By mid-life, those who had a child with a disability had significantly lower income levels than those who were raising children without disabilities (Parish et al. 2004). Being in a caregiving role clearly has a serious impact on financial status in later life, a fact that affects predominantly women.

### Diversity Within the Older Population

The aging population is not homogenous; in fact, older adults are less similar to one another than are members of younger cohorts. The demographics of the older population are changing in terms of race and ethnicity. In 2008, 80 percent of the older population was white non-Hispanic, 9 percent was African American, 7 percent was Hispanic, and 3 percent was Asian (Federal Interagency Forum on Aging-Related Statistics 2010). Methods of assessment and intervention, programs, and services will need to reflect these more diverse racial and ethnic backgrounds.

Family forms are also becoming more diverse. Life expectancy differs by gender, with women having longer predicted life spans; this implies growing differences in the family structures of older men and women. Men tend to live in a couple relationship, and if caregiving is needed, it is usually provided by the spouse or partner. Conversely, greater numbers of older women live alone, with adult children or other relatives, or in long-term care facilities (Federal Interagency Forum on Aging-Related Statistics 2010). In addition to being care providers for a spouse or partner, women may hold other caregiving roles in later life, such as continuing to care for younger generations (Dillenburger and McKerr 2009).

Gay, lesbian, bisexual, or transgender (GLBT) older adults are frequently an invisible segment of the population (Barranti and Cohen 2000). During their formative and early developmental years, few resources and positive role models were available to the current cohort of older GLBT adults, as being gay or lesbian was considered a psychiatric condition. Although some in this cohort have lived as GLBT individuals their entire lives, others realized or disclosed their sexual identity at later times in life. These individuals often coped by shrouding their sexual identity in secrecy or by engaging in self-denial. Many tried to "fit in" by having heterosexual relationships and/or getting married.

Even today, with more accepted and positive images of being GLBT, some older adults continue to feel uncomfortable with terms such as *gay* or *lesbian*. Others conceal their sexual identity to decrease the risk of rejection or alienation from caregivers, service providers, or other

154

residents in long-term care facilities. Jenkins et al. (2010) chronicled the complex strategies of identity management for an older lesbian while in a long-term care facility. Although previously an active member of the GLBT community, this woman did not divulge this part of her identity and experiences in the facility. The authors concluded that her decisions represent aspects of resilience in adapting in this environmental context. Other research concluded that older adults resist identifying as gay or lesbian because of perceived or experienced negative reactions of others (Cohen et al. 2008) and, for this reason, were concerned about the possibility of needing nursing home or assisted living care (Smith et al. 2010).

In sum, the developmental experience of acknowledging one's sexual identity may involve various pathways. As Fredriksen-Goldsen and Muraco (2010) stated, "Because many older LGB adults have spent a majority of their lives 'in the closet,' or masking their sexual orientation, their lives have remained largely silenced; thus, we are only beginning to understand the experiences and needs of these populations" (373).

Considering the experiences of diverse older adults requires alternative conceptualizations of competence. *Competence* has historically been defined by an individual's "attributes associated with a white middle-class type of success in school or society ... commonly involving the performance of a culturally specified task" (Ogbu 1985, 46). For some older adults, the experience of living in an oppressive social environment necessitates developing coping skills and increasing competence in dealing with difficult situations. For example, many GLBT individuals perceive that having to manage their sexual identity within a heterosexist environment has better prepared them to deal with the adjustments of later life (MetLife Mature Market Institute 2010).

The following case example illustrates the application of the functional-age model to assessing the difficulties faced by an older caregiver whose son has an intellectual disability. It also illustrates the lack of policy supports for family caregivers (cf. Dillenburger and McKerr 2009; Hayslip and Kaminski 2005).

## Case Example

Mrs. Hayes is an eighty-one-year-old widow who lives with her forty-two-year-old son, Joseph. Joseph has Down syndrome and attends a day activity program for adults with disabilities. Mrs. Hayes's husband died about six years ago after a brief illness. There are two other sons, both of whom live in other cities and see their mother and brother infrequently.

Although Joseph has Down syndrome, he is otherwise in good health, and Mrs. Hayes has been vigilant about keeping his weight within normal range. He is verbal, has a pleasing personality, and likes to be around others and to socialize. Mrs. Hayes has been fortunate that her friends have embraced Joseph and invited him to various social events. In addition, Mrs. Hayes and Joseph regularly attend services at the local Catholic church, of which they have been members for several years.

Although Mrs. Hayes is in relatively good health, she has experienced some adverse physical changes over the past year. Her stamina has decreased, and she is less able to manage some of the household responsibilities. Several months ago she fell, which was a frightening experience. Although she did not have major physical injuries, the experience reinforced the fact that some household changes needed to be made to allow Mrs. Hayes and Joseph to continue to live independently. In response, Joseph's case manager developed a plan with the family to teach Joseph some additional household tasks. Joseph was assigned a vocational therapist who did an assessment in the home. He was taught some basic household maintenance tasks that would take some of the physical demands off of Mrs. Hayes. These included carrying grocery bags from the car up the steps and into the home, unpacking the bags and shelving the groceries, vacuuming, and carrying out the trash, all of which had become difficult for Mrs. Hayes. With coaching, Joseph was able to master these chores without difficulty, and he enjoyed the additional responsibility of helping out around the house.

## References

Administration on Aging. 2010. *Aging statistics.* http://www.aoa.gov/AoARoot/Aging_Statistics/index.aspx accessed March 24, 2011.

Angel, J. L., M. A. Jimenez, and R. J. Angel. 2007. The economic consequences of widowhood for older minority women. *The Gerontologist* 47:224–34.

Atchley , R. C. 1999. *Continuity and adaptation in aging.* Baltimore: Johns Hopkins University Press.

Barranti, C., and H. Cohen. 2000. Lesbian and gay elders: An invisible minority. In *Gerontological social work: Knowledge, service settings and special populations,* ed. R. L. Schneider, N. P. Kropf, and A. Kisor, 2nd ed., 343–67. Belmont, CA: Wadsworth.

Benner, P., E. Roskies, and R. S. Lazarus. 1980. Stress and coping under extreme conditions. In *Survivors, victims, and perpetrators: Essays on the Nazi Holocaust,* ed. J. E. Dimsdale, 219–58. Washington, DC: Hemisphere.

Birren, J. E. 1959. Principles of research on aging. In *The handbook of aging and the individual*, ed. J. E. Birren, 3–42. Chicago, IL: University of Chicago Press.

Borden, W. 1992. Narrative perspectives in psychosocial intervention following adverse life events. *Social Work* 37:125–41.

Butler, R. N. 1968. Toward psychiatry of the life cycle: Implications of sociopsychologic studies of the aging process for the psychotherapeutic situation. In *Aging in modern society*, ed. A. Simon and L. Epstein, 233–48. Washington, DC: American Psychiatric Association.

Cahill, K. E., M. D. Giandrea, and J. F. Quinn. 2006. Retirement patterns from career employment. *The Gerontologist* 46:514–23.

Canda, E. R., and L. D. Furman. 1999. *Spiritual diversity in social work practice.* New York: Free Press.

Carter, B., and M. McGoldrick. 1999. *The expanded family life cycle: Individual, family, and social perspectives.* 3rd ed. Boston, MA: Allyn & Bacon.

Cohen, H., L. C. Curry, D. Jenkins, C. A. Walker, and M. O. Hogstel. 2008. Older lesbians and gay men: Long-term care issues. *Annals of Long-Term Care* 16, no. 2:33–38.

Corporation for National & Community Service. 2007, March. *Keeping baby boomers volunteering: A research brief on volunteer retention and turnover.* http://www.nationalservice.gov/pdf/07_0307_boomer_report.pdf (accessed June 2, 2007).

Crowther, M. R., M. W. Parker, W. A. Achenbaum, W. L. Larimore, and H. G. Koenig. 2002. Rowe and Kahn's model of successful aging revisited: Positive spirituality—The forgotten factor. *The Gerontologist* 42:613–20.

Damron-Rodriguez, J. 2007. Social work practice in aging: A competency-based approach for the 21st century. In *Foundations of social work practice in the field of aging*, ed. R. R. Greene, H. L. Cohen, C. Galambos, and N. P. Kropf, 1–16. Washington, DC: NASW Press.

Diehl, M. 1998. Everyday competence in later life: Current status and future directions. *The Gerontologist* 38:422–33.

Dillenburger, K., and L. McKerr. 2009. "40 years is an awful long time": Parents caring for adult sons and daughters with disabilities. *Behavior and Social Issues* 18, no. 1:1–20.

Dimsdale, J. E. 1974. The coping behavior of Nazi concentration camp survivors. *American Journal of Psychiatry* 131:792–97.

Erikson, E. 1950. *Childhood and society.* New York: W. W. Norton.

Erikson, E. H., J. M. Erikson, and H. Q. Kivnick. 1986. *Vital involvement in old age.* New York: W. W. Norton.

Federal Interagency Forum on Aging-Related Statistics. 2010. *Older Americans update 2006: Key indicators of well being.* http://www.agingstats.gov (accessed August 5, 2010).

Fong, R., and R. R. Greene. 2009. Risk, resilience, and resettlement. In *Human behavior theory: A diversity framework*, ed. R. R. Greene and N. Kropf, 147–66. New Brunswick, NJ: Aldine Transaction Press.

Fraser, M. 1997. *Risk and resilience in childhood.* Washington, DC: NASW Press.

Fraser, M., J. Richman, and M. Galinsky. 1999. Risk, protection, and resilience: Toward a conceptual framework for social work practice. *Social Work Research* 23, no. 3:131–44.

Fredriksen-Goldsen, K. I., and A. Muraco. 2010. Aging and sexual orientation: A 25-year review of the literature. *Research on Aging* 32:372–413.

Garmezy, N. 1991. Resiliency and vulnerability to adverse developmental outcomes associated with poverty. *American Behavioral Scientist* 34:416–30.

____. 1993. Children in poverty: Resilience despite risk. *Psychiatry—Interpersonal and Biological Processes* 56, no. 1:127–36.

Germain, C. B. 1994. Human behavior in the social environment. In *The foundation of social work knowledge,* ed. F. G. Reamer, 88–121. New York: Columbia University Press.

Gilgun, J. F. 1996. Human development and adversity in ecological perspective, Part 1: A conceptual framework. *Families in Society* 77:395–402.

Gitterman, A. 1996. Advances in the life model of social work practice. In *Social work treatment: Interlocking theoretical approaches,* ed. F. Turner, 389–408. New York: Free Press.

Gitterman, A., and C. Germain. 2008. *The life model of social work practice: Advances in theory and practice.* 3rd ed. New York: Columbia University Press.

Gordon, E. W., and L. D. Song. 1994. Variations in the experience of resilience. In *Educational resilience in inner-city America: Challenges and prospects,* ed. M. C. Wang and E. W. Gordon, 27–44. Hillsdale, NJ: Erlbaum.

Greene, R. R. 1986. *Social work with the aged and their families.* Hawthorne, NY: Aldine de Gruyter.

____. 2002. *Resiliency: An integrated approach to practice, policy, and research.* Washington, DC: NASW Press.

____. 2005. The changing family of later years and social work practice. In *Productive aging,* ed. L. Kaye, 107–122. Washington, DC: NASW Press.

____. 2008a. *Human behavior theory and social work practice.* New York: Aldine de Gruyter.

____. 2008b. Resilience. In *Encyclopedia of social work,* ed. T. Mizrahi and L. E. Davis (Eds.-in-Chief), vol. 3, 20th ed., 526–31. Washington, DC: NASW Press; New York: Oxford University Press.

____. 2008c. *Social work with the aged and their families.* New Brunswick, NJ: Aldine Transaction Press.

Greene, R. R., and K. Armenta. 2007. The REM model: Phase II—Practice strategies. In *Social work practice: A risk and resilience perspective,* ed. R. R. Greene, 67–90. Monterey, CA: Brooks/Cole.

Greene, R. R., and G. Barnes. 1998. The ecological perspective and social work practice. In *Serving diverse constituencies: Applying the ecological perspective,* ed. R. R. Greene and M. Watkins, 63–96. New York: Aldine de Gruyter.

Greene, R. R., H. L. Cohen, C. Galambos, and N. P. Kropf. 2007. *Foundations of social work practice in the field of aging.* Washington, DC: NASW Press.

Hareven, T. K. 1982. The life course and aging in historical perspective. In *Aging and life course transitions: An interdisciplinary perspective,* ed. T. K. Hareven and K. J. Adams, 1–26. New York: Guilford Press.

____. 1996. *Aging and generational relations over the life course: An historical and cross-cultural perspective.* Hawthorne, NY: Aldine de Gruyter.

Hayslip, B., and P. L. Kaminski. 2005. Grandparents raising their grandchildren: A review of the literature and suggestions for practice. *The Gerontologist* 45:262–69.

Higgins, G. O. 1994. *Resilient adults: Overcoming a cruel past.* San Francisco, CA: Jossey-Bass.

Jenkins, D., C. Walker, H. Cohen, and L. Curry. 2010. A lesbian older adult managing disclosure: A case study. *Journal of Gerontological Social Work* 53:402–20.

Kirby, L. D., and M. W. Fraser. 1997. Risk and resilience in childhood. In *Risk and resilience in childhood*, ed. M. W. Fraser, 10–33. Washington, DC: NASW Press.

Kiser, A. J., and L. Kendal-Wilson. 2002. Older homeless women: Reframing the stereotype of the bag lady. *Affilia* 17:354–70.

Kivnick, H. Q. 1996. Remembering and being remembered: The reciprocity of psychosocial legacy. *Generations* 20, no. 3:49–53.

Kiyak, N., and N. Hooyman. 1999. Aging in the twenty-first century. *Hallym International Journal of Aging* 1:56–66.

Kropf, N. P., and C. Tandy. 1998. Narrative therapy with older clients. *Clinical Gerontologist* 18, no. 4:3–16.

Lawton, M. P. 1982. Competence, environmental press, and the adaptation of older people. In *Aging and the environment: Theoretical approaches*, ed. M. P. Lawton, P. G. Windley, and T. O. Byerts, 33–59. New York: Springer.

Lawton, M. P., and L. Nahemow. 1973. Ecology and the aging process. In *The psychology of adult development and aging*, ed. C. Eisdorfer and M. P. Lawton, 619–74. Washington, DC: American Psychological Association.

Lazarus, R. S. 1980. The stress and coping paradigm. In *Competence and coping during adulthood*, ed. L. A. Bond and J. C. Rosen, 28–74. Hanover, NH: University of New England Press.

Lazarus, R. S., and S. Folkman. 1984. *Stress, appraisal, and coping.* New York: Springer.

Lewis, J., and E. B. Harrell. 2002. Resilience and the older adult. In *Resiliency: An integrated approach to practice, policy, and research*, ed. R. R. Greene, 277–92. Washington, DC: NASW Press.

Masten, A. 1994. Resilience in individual development: Successful adaptation despite risk and adversity. In *Educational resilience in inner-city America: Challenges and prospects*, ed. M. C. Wang and E. Gordon, 3–25. Hillsdale, NJ: Erlbaum.

Maugans, J. E. 1994. *Aging parents, ambivalent baby boomers: A critical approach to gerontology.* Dix Hills, NY: General Hall.

Merriam, S., B. Courtenay, and P. Reeves. 2001. Time and its relationship to development in the life course: Some reflections from a study of HIV-positive adults. *Journal of Adult Development* 8, no. 3:173–82.

MetLife. 1999. *The MetLife juggling act study: Balancing caregiving with work and the costs involved.* http://www.seniorcareconcepts.com/Insurance_Guides/Metlife%20Juggling%20Act%20Study.pdf (accessed June 13, 2007).

MetLife Mature Market Institute. 2010. *Still out, still aging: The MetLife Study of Gay, Lesbian, Bisexual, and Transgender Baby Boomers.* http://www.metlife. com/assets/cao/mmi/publications/studies/2010/mmi-still-out-still-aging.pdf (accessed September 1, 2010).

Northen, H. 1995. *Clinical social work.* New York: Columbia University Press.

Ogbu, J. U. 1985. A cultural ecology of competence among inner-city blacks. In *The beginnings: The social and affective development of black children,* ed. M. B. Spenser, G. K. Brookins, and W. R. Allen, 45–66. Hillsdale, NJ: Erlbaum.

Ozawa, M. N., and B. E. Hong. 2006. Postretirement earnings relative to preretirement earnings: Gender and racial differences. *Journal of Gerontological Social Work* 47, no. 3/4:63–82.

Parish, S. L., M. M. Seltzer, J. S. Greenberg, and F. Floyd. 2004. Economic implications of caregiving at midlife: Comparing parents with and without children who have developmental disabilities. *Mental Retardation* 42:413–26.

Patterson, J., and W. Garwick. 1998. *Stress, coping, and health in families.* Thousand Oaks, CA: Sage.

Peck , R. 1968. Psychological developments in the second half of life. In *Middle age and aging,* ed. B. Neugarten, 88–92. Chicago, IL: University of Chicago Press.

Richardson, G. E. 2002. The metatheory of resilience and resiliency. *Journal of Clinical Psychology* 58:307–21.

Selye, H. 1956. *The stress of life.* New York: McGraw-Hill.

Smith, L. A., R. McCaslin, J. Chang, P. Martinez, and P. McGrew. 2010. Assessing the needs of older gay, lesbian, bisexual and transgender people: A service-learning and agency partnership. *Journal of Gerontological Social Work* 53:387–401.

Strumpfer, D. J. W. 2002, September. *A different way of viewing adult resilience.* Paper presented at the 34th International Congress on Military Medicine, Sun City, North West Province, South Africa.

Walsh, F. 1998. *Strengthening family resilience.* New York: Guilford Press.

Webster, J. 2002. Reminiscence function in adulthood: Age, race, and family dynamics correlates. In *Critical advances in reminiscence work,* ed. J. D. Webster and B. K. Haight, 140–52. New York: Springer.

Werner, E. E., and R. S. Smith. 1977. *Kauai's children come of age.* Honolulu: University of Hawaii Press.

Wolin, S. J., and S. Wolin. 1993. *The resilient self.* New York: Willard.

# 8

# Effective Group Dynamics

*Studies on human bonding ... show that human beings—each in his or her individuated (but not individual) way—are components as members of groups. One's singularity is componential in relation to that of others.*

*—Falck (1984, 157)*

Because all of us are born into a family system of some sort, social membership begins at birth. Although families differ across cultures and social eras, everyone has biological and social ties to a family unit. As a child develops, the number of social memberships increases as he or she moves from the nuclear family into a social network of friends, peers, nonfamily adults (e.g., teachers, coaches, parents of friends), and other relationships. Concepts of dependence, independence, and interdependence are critical to understanding the individual within the context of his or her social and physical environments throughout the life course (Greene 2008b). In fact, some theorists have argued that individuals can *only* be understood within the context of their social relationships (Falck 1988). Within social work practice, groups provide individuals with the opportunity to develop skills and to function in relation to others. They also provide an environment in which an individual can work through stressors with others who may be having similar experiences.

Groupwork was one of the earliest forms of social work practice. Jane Addams, one of the pioneers of the profession, used various group approaches at Hull House. In her book *Twenty Years at Hull House*, Addams (1910/1990) described the "coffee clubs" that were some of the first initiatives to bring newly arriving immigrants together in mutual aid groups to support one another, including social clubs for adolescents and young adults, and arts and music groups to help children and young adults integrate into their new neighborhoods and become "new Americans."

Alissi (2009) traced some of the major developments in groupwork based on Addams' early work. During the 1920s and 1930s, large numbers of social work agencies incorporated educational and rec-reational activity and other forms of groupwork into their programs. The premise was that the group could provide a forum for mutual aid and support to increase members' abilities and skills. In the 1940s, groupwork began to have a more overt therapeutic focus. It was thought that the relationships and dynamics of the group could assist in increasing the competencies of its individual members. In the 1960s and 1970s, groupwork became more refined, with facilitators assisting members to achieve their social goals, develop mutual aid, and pursue more social interactions (e.g., Schwartz 1961, 1971), therefore helping to bring about positive changes in behavior (e.g., Vinter 1967).

Groupwork is still a part of the practice repertoire of many social workers. However, social welfare agencies now rarely rely solely on groupwork as a means of intervention. Besides facilitating client-oriented groups, social workers are often members of task groups themselves. Therefore, social workers need to have a solid understanding of group development, dynamics, and leadership as part of their professional education. This, in turn, can lead to an understanding of how people should behave to be effective members of groups and competent group leaders in educational and work settings.

## Common Dimensions of Groups

### Group Dynamics

Some basic characteristics are common to all groups. The concept of "group" implies the involvement of multiple individuals at a level sufficient to sustain interactions among them. Smaller groups typically produce higher levels of member satisfaction, but larger groups tend to have higher levels of productivity in completing more complex tasks (Zastrow 2001). Memberships of therapeutic groups tend to be smaller to permit greater interaction. In these groups, outcomes are focused on the group process and interactions of members with one another and with the facilitator. A critical outcome is that members become more competent in social functioning, achieving greater insight into the particular issues they bring to the group setting. The membership of task-oriented groups (e.g., committees, treatment teams) tends to be somewhat larger to provide more member resources and greater aggregate problem-solving skills. Within these groups, the combined expertise of the members produces the synergy needed to achieve outcomes that are beyond those that individuals can achieve alone.

Boundaries delineate group members and norms. Members develop roles, including formal and informal leadership, and patterns of relating (e.g., scapegoating, caregiving). Because of the nature of group settings, boundaries define *membership*, or who is inside and who is outside the group. In this way, the group setting becomes a "safe space" to discuss and process members' issues. This safety provides members the opportunity to bring up personal, troubling, or complicated issues in the presence of others. The process of mutual assistance promotes the competent functioning of group members.

Issues of group boundaries are particularly important in certain group settings, especially residential or institutional settings. Groups that take place in prisons, residential facilities for juveniles, shelters, long-term-care settings, and similar environments need to set expectations around how group members behave inside and outside the group setting. When there are preexisting and continuing relationships among members, it is crucial to clarify how the group will be established.

Some groups have open boundaries, and group members can join and leave freely. Many support groups function this way, with people affiliating as they need the experience of the group to help solve a difficulty in social functioning. Typically, such groups operate according to a more open-ended structure. In other groups, however, there are set expectations about participation. Membership in these groups is more strictly defined, and new members typically do not join after the beginning of the group cycle. These types of groups typically have a set time limit after which additional members are added or the group experience ends.

All groups have some type of leadership, although the role and expectations of the leader vary considerably depending on the theoretical orientation. In a *person-centered approach*, the group facilitator is a trained professional who maintains a leadership role. This leader is less directive than in a *behavior-oriented group*, which is more highly structured and has a more prominent leader. In *feminist groups*, indigenous leadership tends to develop from within the group, and one of the participants often takes a prominent role as the "formal" leader. Following the theoretical premises of feminism, degrees of power tend to be shared among members which means that leadership shifts among members depending on the content and issue under attention. In this way, the group tends to have a less hierarchical structure.

A group's leadership structure helps determine its competent functioning. More directive leadership promotes the process of moving through group dynamics in a way that is aligned with the theoretical orientation of the group. For example, the person-centered facilitator assists the group in moving through various phases competently (e.g., conflict, termination). The experiences and their resolution provide group members with learning that they can take beyond the group into other roles and relationships.

## Phases of Development

Just as with individuals, groups go through various stages of development. Depending on the theory of group process, this involves different experiences for the members, tasks for the facilitator, and outcomes or resolutions. Garland, Jones, and Kolodny (1965) proposed the *Boston model*, a basic five-stage model of group development describing how members enter the group relationship, navigate the experience of group membership, complete tasks, and finally separate from the group. Although there is some debate about the applicability of the model to short-term or open-ended groups (Schaefer 1999; Yalom 1995), the Boston model continues to hold a prime place in the theory of groupwork practice (Bartolomeo 2009).

*Pre-affiliation* is the first phase. The group is at first a collection of individuals who have not yet established a shared identity or purpose. Garland, Jones, and Kolodny (1965) described the conditions during this phase as approach-avoidance. Although there is anticipation and expectation about the group experience, there are also questions and uncertainty. The group that is forming is characterized by anxiety (What will happen?), ambivalence (Why am I here?), and superficiality ("cocktail talk"). During this stage, the function of the group facilitator is to enable the *individuals* to progress into being a *group*. Thus, the group members first learn how to join a group more comfortably no matter what its setting or purpose.

In this early stage, members develop competence in several areas. Through a common experience, members sort out ways to create and enter into relationships with one another. In addition, they explore how to take the risks of disclosure and sharing information about themselves with others.

In the second phase, known as *power and control*, the group begins to establish basic trust. According to Erikson's theory of development, establishing trust during infancy is a crucial developmental task.

Individuals who have difficulty developing trusting relationships can have experiences within the group that promote a sense of trust in self and others. During this stage, the group challenges the authority of the facilitator in various ways. Members exhibit limit-testing behaviors, such as nonparticipation and rebelliousness. The successful outcome of this stage involves a realignment of power within the group and the establishment of a system of member mutual aid. This mutual aid can be highly beneficial, such as when confronted with natural disasters and emergencies or even stress within the parent–teacher association.

Whereas the second stage is one of disruption and disharmony, the third stage or *intimacy stage* is characterized by affinity and cohesion. During this stage, the group develops deeper relationships and works to accomplish its goals. Members typically express themselves and share more private aspects of the self. As a result, the climate within the group changes to a sense of "we-ness." As a result of this intimacy, members can begin to share life experiences and histories with others in the group. During this stage, competence is developed both by risking intimacy with others and by promoting caring and concern toward others.

During the fourth phase, *differentiation*, group members distinguish between the group as a whole and the individuals who compose the group. As a result, there is interdependence, when differences in individual characteristics between members tend to be tolerated. There is then shared and flexible leadership, with attention paid to both the tasks of the group and the socioemotional life within the group. Group members develop competence in holding onto multiple forms of membership (being part of a group, but being an individual). More sophisticated boundary exploration develops. For example, subsystems may develop, for instance, connections that form among certain individuals within the group become deeper. As these multiple relationships evolve, members straddle their individual experiences within the group, their feelings of deeper affiliation and connection to certain members, and their overall sense of being part of the whole group.

The final stage, *separation*, is the process of group termination. The group has completed its tasks and goals, and individuals then face separation from one another and the group. A range of experiences and emotions exist, often including experiences of reflecting, reminiscing, and evaluating the group experience.

Numerous theories have been applied to groups, and different theoretical lenses are appropriate for groups focused on different issues. This chapter highlights three major theoretical perspectives on groups: person or client centered, behavioral, and feminist. Although there are other theoretical perspectives (e.g., psychoanalytic, Gestalt), the theories presented here illuminate the nature of group interaction, the role of the group leader or facilitator, and the types of issues that are typically addressed in groups.

The three theoretical approaches to groups presented in this chapter collectively represent various epistemological perspectives, and competence is conceptualized differently in each of these approaches. In the person-centered approach, competence is viewed as continued growth and development across the life course that leads to self-actualization. Within groups, the mechanisms for achieving a greater sense of competence are through interactions with an empathetic and unconditional leader. Over time, the members of the group begin to incorporate these dynamics within themselves, providing additional support and growth opportunities to one another. In the behavioral approach, competence is conceptualized as effective functioning in the here-and-now. From a group orientation, members assist one another in identifying those barriers (or stimuli) that create problems in functioning, such as phobias or anxieties. In addition, members learn from one another through modeling and practicing social interactions within the group. In feminist group work, members assist one another in raising awareness of oppressive conditions that negatively impact functioning. Through interactions, group members gain a sense of empowerment and agency within their lives, which increases their level of competence. In order to show how groups operate from each of these three perspectives, we provide a case vignette for each one.

### The Person-Centered Approach to Groupwork

*In a person centered group, a climate is established to help the members bring about change. This atmosphere is based on caring, genuineness, empathic understanding, warmth, and acceptance.*
—*Rogers (1970, 283)*

Carl Rogers is credited with being the father of person-centered, or client-centered, practice (Rogers 1951, 1961). (For additional content on a person-centered approach, see Chapter 5.) From his perspective, there is an inherent tendency for individuals to grow and develop—in essence, to become *self-actualized*. This process is the primary impetus for development across the life course. His perspective is hopeful, as the individual is viewed as striving for higher forms of functioning and development (Greene , 2008a). Even given this tendency toward self-actualization, the person must experience nurturing conditions in the environment that facilitate development.

*Major Principles*

Person-centered groupwork promotes an environment in which individuals have the resources and opportunity to increase self-understanding. In fact, one of Rogers' primary assumptions relates to how competent people are able to develop and grow. As members become safer and more comfortable within the group, trust develops and individuals are able to use the safety and the resources of the group process to gain additional insight into themselves. Their attitude becomes, "I trust the group, given a reasonably facilitating climate, to develop its own potential and that of its members" (Rogers 1970, 47). The central principle of the Rogerian approach to groupwork is that within the group, members themselves become the resources to support additional self-understanding and changing behaviors, attitudes, and self-impressions (Zastrow 2001).

The group facilitator takes a lead in developing a group environment in which individuals can gain insight into their abilities. Consistent with person-centered principles, the group facilitator must demonstrate *three therapeutic conditions*: genuineness, unconditional positive regard, and empathy. Being *genuine* means being aware of and open to the feelings being experienced by group members in the moment. Rogers stated that "personal growth is facilitated when the counselor is what he [sic] is ... without 'front' or facade" (Rogers 1962, 417, emphasis in the original). This process, termed *congruence*, promotes a person–person interaction in which the individual group members are able to connect with one another.

The experience of sharing genuineness is crucial even when the accompanying feelings are not positive. When a group member states "I'm bored," the process of exploring his or her feeling of boredom becomes central: For example, What about *my experience* in the group feels boring? In such situations, the group facilitator can demonstrate *unconditional positive regard*, or "caring for [the] client in a non-possessive way, as a person with potentialities" (Rogers 1962, 420).

When group members feel cared about by others, regardless of their actual behavior, the outcome is a sense of belonging and connectedness that enhances their self-concept.

*Empathy* is another aspect of the therapeutic relationship that the facilitator must demonstrate. Rogers (1962) described empathy as "[sensing] the client's inner world of private personal meanings as if it were your own, but without ever losing the 'as if' quality, that is empathy, and this seems essential to a growth-promoting relationship" (419). Empathy is a crucial component of human relationships and is practiced in the group setting by actively listening and reflecting. Group experiences and interactions with a skilled facilitator provide clients with the opportunity to connect and understand other members of the group in a deeper, more meaningful way, hopefully translating this experience to other aspects of life.

The primary goal of person-centered groupwork is for individuals to become more aware of their feelings. The focus is more on the individual than on the particular problem brought to the group. Rogers (1967) stated that significant personality change can only happen in a relationship. The relationships developed among and between the group facilitator and group members are conceptualized as a shared journey, one whose outcome is greater insight and awareness of their own growth and independence. Thus, the group relationship is a therapeutic bond that becomes a personal capacity.

In the Rogerian framework, the group facilitator does not have a specific role, unlike that in some other forms of groupwork. He or she does not prescribe the course of group interaction but instead provides an opportunity for reflection and self-exploration (Fatout 1992). However, group facilitators can ask themselves the questions such as the following (Kirschenbaum and Henderson 1989):

- How can I be perceived by others as trustworthy and dependable?
- How can I communicate unambiguously?
- Can I let myself experience positive attitudes toward the person?
- Can I be strong enough to be separate from the other?
- Am I secure enough to permit separateness?
- Can I let myself enter fully into the world of the client's feelings and personal meaning?
- Can I be accepting of each facet of the other person?
- Can I act with sufficient sensitivity in the relationship so that my behavior will not be a threat?
- Can I free the person from the threat of external evaluation?
- Can I meet this individual as a person in the process of becoming?

*Group Stages*

Rogers (1970) believed that as trust develops within the group, observable events take place that demonstrate the members' progress. During the initial stage, the members tend to "mill around" (Fatout 1992) and engage in superficial conversation. Despite the "swirling nature" of this phase, the person-centered facilitator does not take a directive role or attempt to move the group in a particular direction. One of the initial primary tasks is for the group members to dissolve mistrust and undertake risks, revealing themselves to one another (Rogers 1987).

Certain conditions are common during the early phases of the group. The experience of revealing personal information creates ambivalence. Although this process moves the group to a deeper level, there may also be resistance to breaking through more superficial experiences. Some of the early emotional experiences that are shared may also be negative; for example, feeling like there is no direction to the group, or wondering how the group experience will lead to an outcome. In addition, expressions tend to be "past oriented," such as talking about feelings and experiences members bring to the group. These negative feelings must be overcome for group members to build their own sense of self-efficacy that can be expressed in other interpersonal situations.

As trust builds within the group, the capacity for healing begins to develop. The interaction of members takes on a more "here-and-now" quality rather than focusing on past experiences. As Fatout (1992) stated, there is a cracking of members' facades and an expectation that members will be genuine with one another. Sometimes this expectation allows members to confront and give feedback to other members. A sense of personal competence increases during this phase. "Members begin to develop feelings of greater realness and authenticity as they accept themselves as they are with their strengths and weakness. This acceptance of the real self is the beginning of the change process" (Fatout 1992, 44).

In the mature group individuals relate to one another with a sense of genuineness and acceptance. Some of the indicators of this maturity can be heard in members' tones of voice as they address one another, the degree of spontaneity in the group, the amount and degree of caring that is part of the group experience, and expressions of closeness. In Rogers' (1967) description of the person-centered approach, there is no discussion of subgroupings or interventions that change the dynamics of the group. He believed that the role of the facilitator is to provide a fertile climate for the group to develop its own healing and therapeutic dimensions. As a result, members gain deeper insight into themselves and relate to others in a deeper, more genuine way. This can result in more positive and more connected relationships both within and outside of the group experience.

### Case Example

Allison Mitchell is a licensed clinical social worker in private practice. She works primarily with clients who have had experiences of trauma and loss. In addition to working with individual clients, she runs groups within her practice—one for adolescents and another for adults.

Her adult group has six members who have been together for several weeks. They are two men and four women with an average age of forty-seven. When the group first started, there were vague discussions about why members chose to join the group. Members said everything from "I tried individual therapy—I didn't like having to talk the entire hour" to "It sounded interesting."

During the initial sessions, one man continually brought up the question about what would happen within the group. He became annoyed when Allison would not provide him with measurable outcomes of the group process. One of the women was also adamant about having clarity about the group process and outcome, stating, "I'm not paying my money to come to something that I don't know where it will lead." Allison would respond with statements such as "I hear you saying that you are questioning where our group will go. That is a valid question to have and bring up." And to the whole group she posed the question, "Where would you like this group to go?"

Allison's invitation to the other members to discuss their ideas about the group was initially met with silence. However, one of the women finally responded that she would like to get some clarity about "who she is" in relationships. She shared some past experiences of having been in unsuccessful romantic relationships and said that she had just had a "nasty breakup" before entering the group. This statement precipitated a dialogue with some of the other members about issues that had brought them into the group, including lack of satisfaction with a job, a divorce, feeling like a bad parent, and anxiety. At the end of this potent session, Allison reflected that the members had shared some powerful stories with one another. She stated, "It takes courage to come to this group and admit that there are aspects of your life that feel wounded, hollow, and unfilled. I'm glad that you are here and that you chose this group to be the place to attend to those issues."

After this breakthrough, the group started to have different types of interactions. For example, Daniel "came out" to the group and described the pain that he was experiencing as he was deciding how he was going to tell his wife the news. With tears streaming down his face, he described what it was like knowing inside that "I'm gay, but I'm married and I care deeply about my wife. I don't want to hurt her.... but I can't live this way anymore." Hearing this story, several of the group members also started to cry. One of the women told Daniel how difficult it must be to live a life that is so "ungenuine." Another told him how courageous he was and how she has come to value him and his friendship within the group. In the most poignant display of caring, the other man in the group, Jay, walked over to Daniel and gave him a hug. Jay then stated, "At the beginning of this group, I didn't know what would happen, why I was here, and it made me angry. But being part of this process with you, Daniel, means more to me than I can tell you."

## Behavioral Approaches to Group Practice

*In behavioral approaches to groupwork, "change is the result of acquiring new behavior or of modifying existing behavior and as this happens, emotions and attitudes are also shifted."*

*—Fatout (1992, 53)*

Several theories fall under the umbrella of "behavioral approaches" or "behavioral theories." A major similarity among them is the perspective that problematic conditions (e.g., thoughts, feelings, and/or behaviors) are *learned*. However, from a strengths perspective, a related assumption is that new conditions can be learned to change these problems into better functioning. The following list summarizes commonalities in behavioral small-group approaches regardless of their specific orientation:

> The focus of the approach is on problematic or maladaptive behavior that needs to be changed.

There needs to be attention to the conditions in the environment that promote and maintain problematic behaviors.

Various methods are used to change these patterns, such as desensitization to the conditions, replacement of reinforcers, and modeling of alternative behaviors.

Once new behaviors are established, attention needs to be paid to generalizability (e.g., Does this happen outside the group session?) and sustainability (e.g., Will this new behavior continue over time?).

Assessment of behavioral changes is empirical and quantifiable. (Berkowitz 1982; Zastrow 2001)

### Major Types of Behavioral Group Approaches

Fatout (1992) organized behavioral groups into two major types. The first is organized around principles of reinforcement management. *Counterconditioning* principles (Wolpe 1958) are used to decrease anxiety, as with phobic conditions, whereas *operant conditioning* principles (Skinner 1976) examine contingencies that surround problematic behaviors such as compulsions. In these types of behavioral groups, the environmental aspects that create and maintain problematic social functioning are examined.

The second type of behavioral group uses the cognitive–behavioral approach that places a greater emphasis on the cognitive process that accompanies difficulties in functioning. In rational emotive therapy (Ellis and Grieger 1977), for example, thoughts that include "should" or "ought" are brought out to see how these irrational belief systems relate to problematic behaviors. There is an emphasis within these types of groups on group members' views and beliefs about their experiences.

In *reinforcement management groups* the facilitator leads the members in establishing a baseline for behavioral change. In the first part of the group process, members define their problems from their own perspectives. Problems tend to be specific, such as managing a child's difficult behaviors; stopping smoking or overeating; or conquering a specific fear, such as that of elevators. The purpose is for group members to recognize when the onset of the problem occurred and to identify and analyze antecedent and co-occurring conditions. Group members then determine how often the problematic condition occurs and determine situations in which it does and does not occur.

Questions are posed to determine the frequency and magnitude of the behavior (e.g., "How often does [the behavior] occur within a specific timeframe [hour, day, or week]?") and to contextualize the behavior (e.g., "Does [the behavior] happen [at home, at school, in the car, all of those places]?"). Finally, a historical analysis is made by asking questions such as "Has [this behavior] always occurred? When did it begin? Do you remember the first time it occurred?" By specifying their problems, group members work to establish goals, such as decreasing or increasing a behavior by a given amount (e.g., for a college student who is afraid of public speaking, speaking aloud in class five times per week). Whatever the situation, the assumption is that the condition decreases the competence and functioning of the group member.

Several interventions within the group can help members develop greater levels of social competence. *Desensitization* exposes group members to the situations that are troubling them most. Being in a group assists the individuals in feeling a degree of support and validation. In a group for people who were experiencing problems related to obsessive–compulsive behaviors, group members "reported that seeing others with similar symptoms expose themselves to the feared stimulus made it possible to challenge their own conviction" (Van Noppen et al. 1998, 276). These authors reported that other group members would sit on the floor or touch faucets along with those members who had a germ phobia. As trust developed, members were able to take additional risks within the safety of the group situation.

The group process may also involve modeling by the facilitator or other group members. According to social learning theory, imitative behavior begins in infancy as children take on behaviors they see in others (Bandura 1969). An example comes from a stress management group for police officers (Patterson 2008). As part of the group experience, members identified various coping strategies they used and modeled them, sharing these with other members of the group.

Reinforcement is also used in behavioral-oriented groups. *Positive reinforcers* may be smiles, praise, food, or other positive experiences. In addiction groups, for example, members may be rewarded with chips that note the length of their sobriety. Positive reinforcers are frequently given at the beginning period of sobriety, such as at a week, month, or year. As the process continues, reinforcement decreases so that there are longer periods between the rewards. *Negative reinforcement* involves avoiding unpleasant circumstances. This is routinely seen in college classrooms, where latecomers are forced to sit in the front of the room (where they can be called on more frequently by the professor). Arriving on time removes this unpleasantness.

*Cognitive–behavioral groups.* Cognitive–behavioral groups are a common type of therapeutic group. The hallmarks of these groups are the following:

> Identifying specific target thoughts and behaviors;
>
> Setting precise, measurable goals to evaluate change;
>
> Intervening to change the antecedents and consequences of problematic thoughts; and
>
> Helping generalize changes to other thoughts, behaviors, and settings. (Magen 2009)

The focus of cognitive–behavioral approaches is on current faulty processes, but attention is also given to times when more productive or capable processes are occurring. This translates the group experience to everyday activities.

As in other types of groups, the first part of the group process involves contextualizing the problematic experiences of group members. *Rational emotive therapy is* one type of cognitive–behavioral therapy. This involves identifying irrational thoughts and establishing goals for changing them. The person most closely associated with this approach, Albert Ellis, categorized most irrational beliefs into three forms of "musterbations" (Ellis and Grieger 1977). Fatout (1992) condensed these into three irrational thought systems:

> I *must* do well and be approved by *significant* others. If I do not, something is rotten about me.
>
> Others *must, ought, should* treat me fairly, considerately, or specially. If they do not, they should be punished for all eternity!
>
> My living conditions *must* be arranged so I get everything I want, and nothing that I do not want. This *should* occur comfortably, easily, and quickly. (68, emphasis in the original)

These irrational beliefs about the way that things should or ought to be create problems such as anger and depression and create barriers to social relationships and functioning. The resolution of these negative feelings may contribute to feelings of self-mastery.

Various techniques are used in cognitive–behavioral groups to question (and subsequently change) irrational thought patterns. Sheldon Rose (1977), a major social work group theorist, proposed a stage model of groupwork based on the relational aspects of group membership that focuses largely on fostering quality relationships between

174

members and the group facilitator and, during the early phases of the group, building group cohesion. In addition, these groups also draw on the dynamics of the relationships among members, for example, by using the buddy system (Rose 1977; Rose and Edleson 1987), to practice the development of new skills and to serve as a potential support system after groupwork is complete.

*Case Example*

Eric Hiller is a social worker at a community agency for older adults. Many of the older adults who use these services are physically frail and live with family members. In addition to providing older adults with meals and opportunities for socialization, the agency runs a group for care providers. Currently, ten attend this group on a regular basis.

Although the group can be generally classified as a "support group," some cognitive–behavioral elements are integrated into the group structure as well. An important issue brought to the group is caregiver stress, or the feeling of role overload by caregivers who also hold down their own jobs and have other family and community responsibilities.

An issue the group recently faced was difficulty in making decisions. This arose because one of the group members was having trouble deciding whether her mother needed to move into a nursing home. This decision is one of the most difficult caregivers face. Eric was aware that caregivers often have irrational thoughts, such as "I should always be able to take care of my mother" or "I am a bad daughter if my mother needs to enter a nursing home."

In the discussion, Eric gently probed the caregiver's thinking about her mother. When he asked whether there would ever be a time when the mother would need the care of a nursing facility, the caregiver stated, "She stayed by my side when I had mumps, measles, and strep throat. I should be able to care for her now when she is ill." In response, some of the other group members also gently entered the conversation. One woman said, "But your mother doesn't have the measles or mumps—she has Alzheimer's disease. Her condition is not going to get better next week or next month." One of the men in the group added, "I've been coming to this group for about 1½ years. During that time, I have heard you describe the loving and constant care that you have provided to your mother. You have been, and still are, a good daughter."

Although this did not provide the caregiver with a solid answer about what was best for her mother, it did provide her with insight into areas where her irrational thinking about her caregiving role and responsibilities got her "stuck." As a result of the group's process in challenging her beliefs about what she *should have been able to do*, this woman was able to own the fact that she had been a good caregiver for her mother and that she continues to have her mother's best interest at the forefront of her priorities.

## Feminist Groupwork

*There is a discernible pattern within feminist work which addresses the invisibility of women's experience ... [and] isolation and distance [are] at the heart of group member's experience.*
—Butler and Wintram (1991, 6)

Feminism is another theoretical orientation that can be used to guide the groupwork process. *Feminism* can be described as "certain ways of thinking and of acting that are designed to achieve women's liberation by eliminating the oppression of women in society" (Freeman 1990, 74). Like behavioral theories, feminism encompasses several variations and perspectives. Hyde (2009) outlined three common themes across different definitions and approaches to feminism:

1. Women collectively have been denied power, privilege, and status because of societal gender-based norms, values, and roles.
2. Structural inequalities constrain women's experiences. Therefore, many of the issues faced by women are not individual or personal problems but are created by power inequities.
3. Feminists take an activist approach, with the goal of realigning women's disadvantaged positions within society.

As Saulnier (2000) stated, "Feminist theories, unlike more familiar traditions, explain the structure and dynamics of women's experiences within sociopolitical and interpersonal sexual hierarchies and draw attention to the ways which everyday actions can shore up discriminatory social structures" (6).

From a social work perspective, a primary goal of feminist approaches is to reconfigure power within social relationships (Greene 2009). Bricker-Jenkins and Hooyman (1986) discussed empowerment as the central tenet of feminist social work practice. As an intervention approach, groupwork is a useful method for assisting clients with these tasks. Because of the primacy of relationships for women, group approaches draw on the collective strength, insight, and mutual aid of women participants. The goal is to help women understand how the inequality of certain societal structures, such as in terms of unfair promotions in the workplace, affects their lives negatively. The power of the group may enable members to find solutions.

*Overview of Feminist Theories*

In spite of the commonalities just described, various forms of feminism have evolved. Saulnier (2000) provided a succinct summary of various branches of feminist theory that may be useful for social groupwork approaches (see Table 8.1).

*Liberal feminism* emphasizes the way the characteristics of individual women may limit access to resources, power, and privilege. Jaggar (1983) underscored the point that these inequities are exacerbated when women are treated collectively instead of being judged on their individual merits and qualities. Another major premise is that public resources are allocated based on collective assumptions about women and that this decreases women's access to social goods and opportunities. One example of a structural inequality that illustrates the unequal distribution of goods and resources is the continued wage differential by gender.

Difficulties that women face are usually conceptualized as maladaptive coping mechanisms when inequity may be at the heart of the matter. Group approaches that are based on a liberal feminist perspective help women gain additional competence to deal with the oppressive conditions they may face (e.g., low-wage jobs, violent relationships). In addition, liberal feminist groups can help women become more assertive and increase their self-esteem. Collectively, this can help women reposition themselves within their social environment with more functional methods and social relationships.

*Cultural feminism* is another branch of feminist theory. Cultural feminism assumes that the characteristics, traits, and experiences identified with men are *privileged* or more valued over those identified with women and that women's experiences are devalued as a result. This can make women feel invisible, depressed, or isolated (Butler and Wintram 1991). One example is the different social value placed on aging and gender. Older men are often labeled as "distinguished" or "experienced," whereas older women are often described in negative terms, such as "frumpy" or "outdated." Traits assigned according to gender, such as women as nurturing and men as competitive and goal oriented, also track individuals into different gender-based roles

**Table 8.1 Overview of Feminist Groups: Summary
of Theoretical Approaches**

| Theoretical approach | Goals of the theory | Processes used | Goals of the group |
|---|---|---|---|
| Liberal | • Equal rights<br>• Equal access<br>• Control over<br>• privacy | • Psychoeducation<br>• Counseling | • Assertiveness<br>• Increased self-esteem<br>• Increased competence |
| Cultural | • Develop women's culture<br>• Restructure society<br>• Increase the valuation of women | • Consciousness-raising<br>• Support<br>• Self-help | • Political analysis<br>• Discovery of the essence of "womanness"<br>• Celebrating womanhood |
| Womanist | • Social action/ social change<br>• Articulation of a racial consciousness<br>• Self-healing<br>• Resistance of systems of oppression | • Consciousness-raising<br>• Support<br>• Community organizing | • Self-empowerment<br>• Community building<br>• Articulation of a racial consciousness |
| Radical | • Draw connections between the personal and political<br>• Eliminate male privilege in public and private spheres<br>• Heal internalized sexism<br>• Protect women from forms of male violence<br>• Restructure society | • Consciousness-raising<br>• Support<br>• Skill development<br>• Developing a plan for social action | • Healing the injuries of patriarchal society<br>• Challenging patriarchal indoctrination<br>• Empowering women to activism<br>• Social change |

*Source:* Adapted from Saulnier (2000).

(e.g., women should stay home and raise children while men earn a living). Cultural feminists seek to change societal stereotypes by un-covering these patriarchal assumptions and celebrating the "'feminist principle' in women" (Saulnier 2000, 11). Understanding patriarchal assumptions allows women to decide when and where they want to address them.

Cultural feminist group approaches provide an opportunity for women to develop and create their own culture. Instead of adhering to norms and approaches that set up false dichotomies (e.g., men are strong and women are weak), these groups provide a space for women to re-story their experiences, leading to additional self-discoveries. In addition, these groups help raise the consciousness of women, giv-ing them an insight into the insidious ways that language and culture create artificial divisions based on gender.

*Womanist feminism* is a community-building orientation. Based heavily on the work of African American feminists, this perspective highlights the intersectionality of various components of identity, including gender, race/ethnicity, sexual identity, disability status, and class. The womanist orientation holds that there is no "one woman." Rather, the experiences of women are diverse and reflect various po-sitions of privilege. For example, the gerontology literature describes the concept of "triple jeopardy" (i.e., being an older woman of color). Social oppressions by gender and race, combined with ageism, can interact to marginalize older women and severely affect their quality of life. For example, Wu (2007) analyzed poverty rates in the older population by gender and race/ethnicity. The overall poverty rate for all older adults was 10.1 percent, but it was 12.3 percent for older women. However, poverty rates were twice as high for older Hispanic (22.4%) and African American (25.4%) women, supporting the triple jeopardy argument.

Group approaches based on a womanist perspective have a strong foundation in social action. Goals of social work action include work-ing to build communities to unify strengths and concentrate political and social capital. *Social capital* refers to the societal norms and values that contribute to the stratification process that allows certain groups to have relatively more or less benefits and resources. A collective of women workers may gain access to more skills, qualifications, and economic resources (Dominguez and Watkins 2003).

In womanist feminist groups, women are encouraged to tell their own stories emphasizing their unique identity. An example of this type of group is the "I Am Woman Too" group structured for women with disabilities (Berwald and Houtstra 2002). In the group sessions, the participants are encouraged to talk about the experience of being a woman living with a disability. Several women describe the experience of overprotection by their parents and sexuality issues. In addition, a social action component works to increase the availability of transportation for people with disabilities. The process of integrating people with disabilities into the community increases both personal and community competence.

*Radical feminism* views society as dominated by patriarchal norms and standards. Echols (1989) has suggested that women are damaged by structures that incorporate and internalize patriarchal belief systems. Because society restricts women's opportunities, their social roles are more limited than those of men, and their primary responsibility is viewed as providing services to the patriarchy (Millett 1969). Radical feminists argue that violence against women is a political method of dominating and controlling women.

The answer of radical feminists is to overhaul social systems totally rather than focus on incremental change. For example, instead of concentrating on increasing women's pay to make it comparable to that of men, radical feminists argue that the current division of work and family life is fundamentally flawed. They suggest that child care and eldercare are fundamental rights that need to be readily available so that women can be in the labor force. In addition, they argue that because the current Social Security system favors a male model of wage earning, it needs to be totally realigned to account for different patterns of women's employment.

Radical feminist groupwork integrates intervention approaches similar to those as applied in other feminist groups, including raising consciousness, using support and mutual aid, and working to promote social action. The overarching goal, however, is to heal the wounds that women experience from living in a patriarchal society. Such wounds may come from violence, sexual exploitation, or other emotionally damaging experiences. Particular situations that might be addressed in these types of groups are concerns about weight and body image, incest or sexual assault, or domestic violence.

Research on the effectiveness of feminism as compared to other practice orientations has shown that feminist interventions are more effective (Gorey et al. 2002). Moreover, the analysis has found that radical feminist interventions are more effective than those of other feminist orientations. Radical feminism supports mutual client and practitioner strategies that have a multilevel impact. In addition to promoting enhanced functioning for the client, these groups pay attention to and set goals for changing the larger oppressive systems. This macropractice focus provides women with the sense of additional efficacy and competent functioning within their social environments.

*Feminist Group Processes*

Regardless of the particular theoretical perspective, other significant concepts influence feminist groupwork (Gottlieb et al. 1983). One is the redistribution of power within the group. In person-centered and behavioral groups, the facilitator assumes a qualitatively distinct role within the group. In fact, one of the stages of the group is built on challenging and testing the boundaries of authority between members of the group and the facilitator. In feminist groups, cooperation between facilitators and participants is used to "provide women participants with a living example of what working together co-operatively can entail" (Butler and Wintram 1991, 39). Feminist groups often use co-facilitators to diffuse the perspective that one person holds the authority. This level of cooperation among group members aims at building a system of mutual aid and reducing the sense of isolation that can exist in the "real world."

As the examples presented here have shown, consciousness raising is a typical element of feminist groupwork. Similar to other social oppression, gender-based discrimination and stereotyping is stitched into this country's social fabric. Because women experience it regularly, it becomes difficult for them to un-entrench themselves and question the larger social structures. Within groups, women can assist one another in identifying oppressive social conditions. With such insights, women can begin to make changes as well as wage battles against harmful social conditions. An example is the Take Back the Night rallies held regularly to raise awareness of sexual violence. These events deconstruct beliefs that women should not have the same access to their communities as men. The following type of statement is frequently heard at these rallies as a means of questioning the social narrative about violence against women: "I will not continue to reflect on whether my clothes cover enough of my body when I leave my house. Or that there will be enough light for my safety. Instead, I will reflect on why men never have to question these or related topics." By deconstructing oppressive assumptions, women can begin to move past the restrictive choices and opportunities that they feel are available. As a result, they are able to reclaim and rebalance their perception of power within their relationships and society.

Although feminist groupwork has been applied to men (e.g., Orme, Dominelli, and Mullender 2000), groups are typically gender specific. Being in a women-only group provides women with the space and opportunity for their female voices to be heard without the alteration or the interference of a man's perspective. This structure increases a sense of safety and allows for discussion of possibly painful narratives within a safe group context in situations in which trauma has occurred.

## Case Example

Myra Bolton is a clinical social worker at the Women's Health Initiative currently working with a group of six overweight women. All of these women have major medical conditions (e.g., hypertension, mobility limitations) and are struggling with their health. The group meets biweekly.

Using a feminist approach, Myra encouraged the women to tell the story of their weight. Several described the humiliation they feel when dealing with medical professionals, who dehumanize them in various ways because of their weight. In addition, the women described how they feel "non-gendered," as women's clothes and products privilege slender bodies that are vastly different from their own. As one woman stated, "I'll never fit into a size six dress. I figure, why should I even try? If I lose weight, people will still see me as overweight."

As part of the group experience, the women described their frustration with shopping for groceries. Some had difficulty shopping, and all but one of the women did not work, so money was an issue. As one woman stated, "Everything that is good for you costs so much more.... I simply can't afford to buy everything fresh!"

Using consciousness-raising approaches, Myra encouraged the women to identify images of women who were not the "typical" symbols of beauty. One of the women stated that she wished that she could look like a certain movie star: "She can sing, act, and be on the cover of beauty magazines. And she is not little—she carries some weight on her." As the women began to embrace alternative images of women, they began to consider other ways to define attractiveness. As part of this process, they started to identify those qualities within themselves that are beautiful at their current weight. One of the participants said, "We are all here because we weigh too much, and as a result we are not healthy. But we can't hate ourselves, because that will not get us to be healthier. We have to accept ourselves now." As the women started to accept their own bodies, they began to take better care of themselves.

In addition, the group also started to look for ways to be healthier. They started to save coupons and swap them at the meetings. In addition, they e-mailed about sales at their local grocery stores, and for each session someone would volunteer to bring a healthy snack. Everyone started an exercise program (walking, riding a stationary bike), and they supported one another with new goals. As a result of being in this group, many of the women started to lose weight. More significantly, the women started to feel more comfortable living in their own bodies regardless of their size.

## Critique

Each of the theoretical approaches discussed in this chapter addresses relational issues, and each has a different perspective on how members within the group form bonds, experience conflict, and deal with issues of power. The literature on diversity in group settings explores these aspects in more depth and can aid in understanding how various cultural conditions influence the group experience.

This chapter has explored conflict through a cultural lens. As Martin and Nakayama (2000) posited, conflict occurs when there is a real or perceived incompatibility of values, interests, or goals between members or subgroups within the group setting. There is ample evidence that homogenous groups provide an optimal atmosphere for work when safety or exploration, such as in issues related to gender or race, is a primary goal (Brown and Mistry 2005). This is because in groups of people who are the same gender or the same ethnicity, experiences of oppression and discrimination are less than in mixed-member groups.

However, there are questions about what constitutes a homogenous group. A case study involving a Latino group revealed that members and the facilitator (a Latina herself) experienced conflicts during the group process (Camacho 2002). In deconstructing the source of the issues, the researcher found that several subgroups based on gender, sexual orientation, and ethnicity (various cultural traditions that constitute the larger Latino/a culture) were represented in the group experience. Although on the surface the members of the group appeared more similar than different, numerous backgrounds and cultures were actually represented. As Camacho (2002) summarized, "Latino groups need to be viewed as diverse, given the heterogeneity of this population. Conflict around issues of diversity should be expected in such groups" (151).

In addition to assumptions about dynamics of and conflict within groups, evaluations of group process and outcomes take various forms. In particular, evaluation goals differ based on the theoretical orientation of the group. In behavioral groups, for example, outcome analysis may be the primary indicator of success. For example, is someone who joined a group because of a particular phobia able to tolerate certain experiences better? Some outcomes can be quantified easily. For example, the length of time someone with claustrophobia can be in a closed elevator can be a way of measuring progress.

In other groups, however, a process orientation may be more important. In person-centered groups, evaluation of the group experience is central. How is the group as a whole changing? How does this affect the experience of the individual members of the group? In a feminist-oriented group, evaluations may focus on both outcome and process. In a group of women with disabilities, standardized outcome measures were used along with a more subjective measure of participants' experiences with the group (Berwald and Houtstra 2002). Groups that are run according to other theoretical orientations should include evaluation components consistent with those theories.

In this chapter, three common theoretical approaches to groupwork were presented. These three approaches vary considerably in their assumptions about the nature of interpersonal dynamics, the phases of group development, the role of the social worker, and the tasks and experiences of the participants. Regardless of its particular theoretical perspective, there is an assumption that involvement in a group will help members function more effectively, enhance well-being, and increase competence.

## References

Addams, J. 1990. *Twenty years at Hull House.* Urbana: University of Illinois Press. (Original work published 1910.)

Alissi, A. S. 2009. Group work history: United States. In *Encyclopedia of social work with groups,* ed. A. Gitterman and R. Salmon, 6–13. London: Routledge.

Bandura, A. 1969. *Principles of behavior modification.* New York: Holt, Rinehart & Winston.

Bartolomeo, F. 2009. Group stages of development: Boston model. In *Encyclopedia of social work with groups*, ed. A. Gitterman and R. Salmon, 103–6. London: Routledge.

Berkowitz, S. 1982. Behavior therapy. In *The newer therapies: A sourcebook*, ed. L. E. Abt and I. R. Stuart. New York: Von Nostrand Reinhold .

Berwald, C., and T. Houtstra. 2002. Joining feminism and social group work practice: A women's disability group. *Social Work With Groups* 25, no. 4:71–83.

Bricker-Jenkins, M., and N. Hooyman. 1986. *Not for women only: Social work practice for a feminist future.* Silver Spring, MD: NASW Press.

Brown, A., and T. Mistry. 2005. Group work with "mixed membership" groups: Issues of race and gender. *Social Work With Groups* 28, no. 3/4:133–48.

Butler, S., and C. Wintram. 1991. *Feminist groupwork.* London: Sage.

Camacho, S. F. 2002. Addressing conflict rooted in diversity: The role of the facilitator. *Social Work With Groups* 24, no. 3/4:135–52.

Dominguez, S., and C. Watkins. 2003. Creating networks for survival and mobility: Social capital among African-American and Latin-American low-income mothers. *Social Problems* 50, no. 1:111–35.

Echols, A. 1989. *Daring to be bad: Radical feminism in America, 1967–1975.* Minneapolis: University of Minnesota Press.

Ellis, A., and R. Grieger, eds. 1977. *RET handbook of rational-emotive therapy.* New York: Springer.

Falck, H. 1984. The membership model of social work. *Social Work* 29, no. 2:155–60.

____. (1988). *Social work: The membership perspective.* New York: Springer.

Fatout, M. F. 1992. *Models for change in social group work.* New York: Aldine de Gruyter.

Freeman, M. L. 1990. Beyond women's issues: Feminism and social work. *Affilia* 5, no. 2:72–89.

Garland, J. A., H. E. Jones, and R. L. Kolodny. 1965. A model for stages of development in social work groups. In *Explorations in group work: Essays in theory and practice*, ed. S. Bernstein, 251–94. Boston, MA: Boston University School of Social Work.

Gorey, K. M., C. Daly, N. L. Richter, D. R. Gleason, and M. J. A. McCallum. 2002. The effectiveness of feminist social work methods: An integrative review. *Journal of Social Service Research* 29, no. 1:37–55.

Gottlieb, N., D. Burden, R. McCormick, and G. Nicarthy. 1983. The distinctive attributes of feminist groups. *Social Work With Groups* 6, no. 3/4: 81–93.

Greene , R. R. 2008a. Carl Rogers and the person-centered approach. In *Human behavior theory and social work practice*, ed. R. R. Greene, 113–31. New Brunswick, NJ: Aldine Transaction.

____. 2008b. *Social work with the aged and their families.* 3rd ed. New Brunswick, NJ: Aldine Transaction.

____. 2009. Power factors in social work practice. In *Human behavior theory: A diversity framework*, ed. R. R. Greene and N. P. Kropf, 2nd ed., 251–74. New Brunswick, NJ: Aldine Transaction.

Hyde, C. 2009. Feminist social work practice. In *Encyclopedia of social work*, ed. T. Mizrahi and L. E. Davis, 20th ed., vol. 2, 216–20. New York: National Association of Social Workers and Oxford University Press.

Jaggar, A. 1983. *Feminist politics and human nature.* Totowa, NJ: Rowman & Allanheld.

Kirschenbaum, H., and V. L. Henderson, eds. 1989. *Carl Rogers: Dialogues.* Boston, MA: Houghton Mifflin.

Magen, R. 2009. Cognitive-behavioral model. In *Encyclopedia of social work with groups*, ed. A. Gitterman and R. Salmon, 45–47. London: Taylor & Francis.

Martin, J. N., and T. K. Nakayama. 2000. Culture, communication, and conflict. In *Intercultural communication in contexts*, ed. J. N. Martin and T. K. Nakayama, 287–315. Mountain View, CA: Mayfield.

Millett, K. 1969. *Sexual politics.* New York: Ballantine Books.

Orme, J., L. Dominelli, and A. Mullender. 2000. Working with violent men from a feminist social work perspective. *International Social Work* 43, no. 1:89–105.

Patterson, G. T. 2008. A framework for facilitating stress management educational groups for police officers. *Social Work With Groups* 31, no. 1:53–70.

Rogers, C. 1951. *Client centered therapy.* Boston, MA: Houghton Mifflin

——. 1961. *On becoming a person.* Boston, MA: Houghton Mifflin.

——. 1962. The interpersonal relationship: The core of guidance. *Harvard Educational Review* 32:416–29.

——. 1967. The process of the basic encounter group. In *Challenges of humanistic psychology*, ed. J. F. Baental, 261–76. New York: McGraw-Hill.

——. 1970. *Carl Rogers on encounter groups.* New York: Harper & Row.

——. 1987. The underlying theory: Drawn from experience with individuals and groups. *Counseling and Values* 32, no. 1:38–45.

Rose, S. D. 1977. *Group therapy: A behavioral approach.* Englewood Cliffs, NJ: Prentice Hall.

Rose, S., and J. Edleson. 1987. *Working with children and adolescents in groups.* San Francisco, CA: Jossey Bass.

Saulnier, C. F. 2000. Incorporating feminist theory into social work practice: Group work examples. *Social Work With Groups* 23, no. 1:5–29.

Schaefer, C. E., ed. 1999. *Short term psychotherapy groups for children: Adapting group processes for specific problems.* Northvale, NJ: Jason Aronson.

Schwartz, W. 1961. The social worker in the group. In *Social welfare forum*, ed. A. Allisi, 146–77. New York: Columbia University Press.

——. 1971. On the use of groups in social work practice. In *The practice of groupwork*, ed. W. Schwartz and S. Zalba, 3–24. New York: Columbia University Press.

Skinner, B. F. 1976. *About behaviorism.* New York: Random House.

Van Noppen, B. L., M. T. Pato, R. Marsland, and S. A. Rasmussen. 1998. A time limited behavioral group for treatment of obsessive-compulsive disorder. *Journal of Psychotherapy Practice and Research* 7:272–80.

Vinter, R., ed. 1967. *Readings in groupwork practice.* Ann Arbor, MI: Campus Publishing.

Wolpe, J. 1958. *Psychotherapy by reciprocal inhibition.* Stanford, CA: Stanford University Press.

Wu, K. B. 2007. Sources of income for women age 65 and older. *PPI Data Digest* 161:1–4.

Yalom, I. D. 1995. *The theory and practice of group psychotherapy.* 4th ed. New York: Basic Books.

Zastrow, C. 2001. *Social work with groups.* 5th ed. Pacific Grove, CA: Brooks/Cole.

# 9

# Communities and Neighborhoods

*The meaning of community varies with each new generation, each distinct geographic location, and each community of interest.*
*—Gamble and Weil (2010, 1)*

Although social work theory and practice are based upon the person-in-environment paradigm, much greater attention has been focused upon the "person" (McKinnon 2008). In this chapter, we focus on the structural and human elements of community, or the spaces and places that provide the context in which individuals and families should be able to function competently.

A multidimensional framework is used to examine competence at the community level, exploring physical and structural elements and human connections that contribute to social capital. The chapter concludes with a case study that addresses community conflict between groups of families who reside in the same neighborhood. Using a restorative justice approach, we discuss community-level interventions to reduce conflict and create opportunities for individuals and families to live in a more harmonious, competent community.

Communities are composed of several components that are both natural and constructed by members. Hart (1999) developed a Community Capital Triangle similar to Maslow's (1968) conception of the conditions necessary for human functioning (see Chapter 5) that illustrates these three layers of resources that represent natural, human, and constructed capital (see Figure 9.1).

1.  The base of Hart's Community Capital Triangle is *Natural Capital*, which is composed of natural resources (e.g., food, water, energy); ecosystem services (e.g., water filtration, fisheries), the use of which enhances available resources; and the beauty of nature (e.g., mountains, seashore, forests), which enhances quality of life.

## Figure 9.1. Hart's Community Capital Triangle

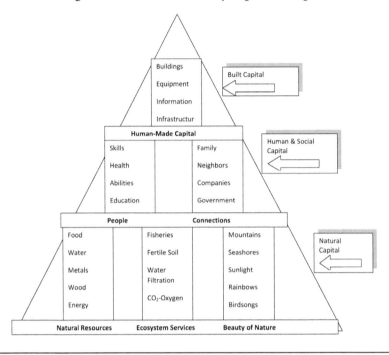

*Source*: From Guide to Sustainable Community Indicators, second edition (p. 16), by M. Hart, (1999, 16). North Andover: MA: Hart Environmental Data. Available from Sustainable Measures (www.sustainablemeasures.com)

2.  The middle stratum is *Human and Social Capital*, which includes factors related to the people of the community (e.g., their skills, their ability, resources such as income) and their social connections (e.g., families, businesses and organizations, neighbors).

3.  At the top of the pyramid is *Built Capital*, or the human-made, created environment. Human-made environments rest on the other blocks of the pyramid and include infrastructure and the production of goods and services such as roads, sewerage, information systems, and government.

The Community Capital Triangle thus depicts the relationship between the resources available to communities and the way in which these are strengthened or preserved within the community structure (Gamble & Weil, 2010).

## The Natural and Built Environment

*Architecture has the capacity to connect to the self, and our inter-pretation of places and things often reflect who we are or what we would like to project about ourselves to others.*
*—Smith and Bugni (2006, 129)*

Hart's Community Capital Triangle depicts the two dimensions of the community—natural elements and constructed (or built) ele-ments—that form the environment.

### Natural Capital

What Hart (1999) termed *Natural Capital* are the natural resources found in a particular geographic area that can be used to enhance community life. These bring a community the physical, economic, and social resources that eventuate in jobs and income, improving and enhancing the quality of life in a geographic area.

However, there is the risk that global conditions can change, creat-ing precarious situations that may reduce employment and income. For example, in the past several years, social workers have been in-volved in providing relief and assistance for recovery to communities affected by disasters such as hurricanes, typhoons, and earthquakes (Mathbor 2007).

Although social workers have been involved in the recovery ef-forts of natural disasters, there has been only limited discussion of environmental factors affecting local communities.

However, some researchers have examined issues social justice relat-ed to environmental disasters and their impact on the social conditions in communities (Rogge 1998) and the implications of the changing ecology on social work practice (Besthorn 2001; Hoff and McNutt 1994). McKinnon (2008) discussed the environmental implications for social work practice, arguing that additional attention needs to be paid to the environment during the present era of global change:

> Thus far there has not been a substantial debate about environ-mental issues in the social work literature as we struggle to elicit the implications of the environmental crisis for social work theory and practice. Such a debate would go to the very heart of the way social work, as a profession, is defined and the boundaries of its professional domain. (257)

## Constructed or Built Capital

*Constructed or built* elements are an important dimension of the physical environment. They affect the way communities are configured, including divisions based on natural boundaries (e.g., rivers, mountains) or built capital that defines communities (e.g., roadways, city limits, zip codes). Not everyone in the same geographic location holds the same definition of what constitutes his or her community. For example, research indicates that one's sense of community may differ by race and economic status. A study of a mixed-race and - income area found differences in place attachment among black and white respondents (Long and Perkins 2007). Regardless of income, black respondents had a greater sense of community and attachment to their neighborhood; only more affluent white respondents felt this way (lower income white respondents had a lower sense of attachment and community). The researchers concluded that a shared sense of identity accounted for community cohesiveness among black residents. The lack of a shared racial identity among white residents and disparities in income and resource levels appeared to detract from the sense of community. In fact, poorer whites reported a sense of isolation and alienation from their neighbors, perhaps decreasing their overall sense of community.

## The Meaning of Built Capital

*Architecture* is another aspect of the physical, built environment that affects the way in which space is created. According to Smith and Bugni (2006),

> Architecture include[s] forms designed and built by specialists. This includes buildings (e.g., houses, churches, hospitals, prisons, factories, office buildings, and recreational and sports complexes), bounded spaces (e.g., streets, plazas, communities, and office spaces), objects (e.g., monuments, shrines, landmarks, and furniture), and the many elements that are part of architectural design (e.g., shapes, size, location, openness, designed landscapes, boundaries, lighting, color, textures, and materials used). (124)

These also contribute to the ways in which people define their communities, and their sense of connection and attachment.

The environment can assert a significant influence on an individual's sense of self and the meanings attached to certain structures. Herbert Blumer's (1969) definition of *symbolic interaction* (see Chapter 3) describes three types of objects from which individuals derive meaning: *social objects* (e.g., parents, soldiers, physicians), which have certain meanings attached to them; *abstractions* (e.g., loyalty, bravery, intelligence), which elicit certain emotions; and *physical objects* (e.g., buildings and open spaces), which are related to the environment. Others have developed the physical object realm in greater detail. Milligan (1998, 2003) argued that one's attachment to place is based upon prior experiences that have been attached to similar physical settings. Positive perceptions translate into beliefs that there will be additional positive experiences in the future.

Others may attach different meanings to similar spaces; this creates dissonance at the community level. An example is the planning process for the World Trade Center Memorial, which is being constructed to commemorate those who lost their lives on September 11, 2001 (see National September 11 Memorial & Museum, http://www.national911memorial.org). The planning process has involved a significant amount of time and emotion, and almost a decade after the events of September 11 the memorial is still not complete.

Sorkin (2003) discussed the various perceptions of the multiple communities that have been involved. The non-place community of families who lost loved ones at the site have particular perspectives about how the space, which likely still contains trace remains of those lost, should be portrayed. However, local residents and businesses have called for a larger public space, voicing a lack of connection to the memorial design and a fear that there will be a negative impact as a result of increased traffic in the area. Although there is little dispute about the idea that the loss of life at this site should be commemorated, how and where the memorial should be constructed and the meaning it holds for the various communities remains a topic of emotional debate.

### Human and Social Capital

*[Community] is a feeling, a perception of connectedness.*
—*McCold and Wachtel (1998, 294)*

Human and social capital is the middle level proposed by Hart (1999). It includes the resources associated with individuals of the community, such as their level of education, income, health, and skills/abilities. In addition, this capital is based on the bonds and connections between members in the community and with entities external to the community. Like their members, communities can be "resilient," meaning that they build upon the resources and talents of their members. In addition, there is a growing awareness that the resilience of communities and residents is intrinsically linked and can enhance or inhibit competent functioning (Cohen and Greene 2005).

Unlike the physical environment, which has received only limited attention in the field of social work, the human and social capital of communities has received significant attention. In this section, we examine social capital and the cohesiveness of relationships within communities. We also review the idea of collective efficacy, an extension of Bandura's (1995) concept of self-efficacy (see Chapter 6) to the community context. Finally, we discuss empowerment and relate it to community functioning. Collectively, these various theoretical approaches focus on the human aspects within community levels.

*Social Capital*

In 2000, Robert Putnam, a Harvard University faculty member, published the groundbreaking book on social capital *Bowling Alone: The Collapse and Revival of American Community*. He used a historical perspective to examine social ties within communities and the ways in which Americans are less connected socially now than in the past. Most of the trends Putnam examined indicated that social ties, including knowing one's neighbors, volunteering patterns, civic participation (e.g., voting), and religious participation, are eroding. Putnam attributed these changing patterns to several factors. These included greater time and monetary pressures that resulted in priority being given to non-paid social roles, mobility and transitory lifestyles that include frequent relocation, and the impact of technology (which lets one "bowl alone" on the computer instead of joining a league with others). Clearly, the trends identified in this comprehensive analysis indicate that the quantity and quality of social cohesion has changed over generations.

There are several definitions of *social capital*. An initial definition moved social capital out of a more economic focus and now includes more social components (Bourdieu 1985). This more comprehensive definition notes that social capital is "the aggregate of the actual or potential resources which are linked to the possession of durable network of more or less institutionalized relationships of mutual acquaintance or recognition" (248). Later definitions refined and contextualized the concept. Loeffler et al. (2004) defined social capital as trusting relationships, mutual understanding, and shared actions that connect individuals, communities, and institutions. Other definitions are more specific, including, for instance, competence in raising children effectively, providing services to low-income individuals or families, or caring for older adults. An example of a more focused definition was provided by Coleman's (1988) studies of community public and parochial schools. He defined social capital as "the norms, the social networks, and the relationships between adults and children that are of value for the child's growing up" (36). A final definition expresses both the reciprocity inherent in the concept and the motivation for individuals to engage with others:

> Social capital is the network of trusting relationships that exist in a community that creates benefits for community members. A central element of social capital theory is the basic idea that people invest in social relationships with the expectation of some return. (Brisson and Usher, 2005, 644)

As Brisson and Usher's definition indicates, investment in the community comes with expectations that involvement will enhance quality of life in various ways (Lin 2001), such as increased access to information, community resources, social standing and credibility within the community, and support. As social entities, communities are dynamic and changing and need to be able adapt to new conditions and opportunities. The concept of *community capacity* addresses the ways in which communities are able to navigate both internal and external change.

Chaskin et al. (2001) defined community capacity as "the interaction of human capital, organizational resources, and social capital existing within a given community that can be leveraged to solve collective problems and improve or maintain the well-being of that community" (7). Chaskin (2001) proposed a multidimensional model that depicts community capacity as consisting of six interrelated parts (see Figure 9.2). This framework highlights various levels of intervention to enhance community capacity and competence. These include the connection of community members; skills and resources that can be mobilized for social change; and the sense of community that can produce higher levels of goods, services, and other positive outcomes.

The dimensions of social capital include various types of linkages and connections between community members (Brisson 2009;

## Figure 9.2. Model of Community Capacity

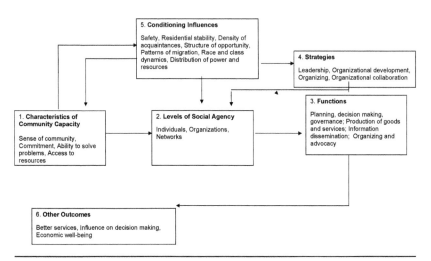

*Source*: From "Building Community Capacity: A Definitional Framework and Case Studies From a Comprehensive Community Initiative," by R. J. Chaskin, (2001, 296). Urban Affairs Review, 36, p. 296. Reprinted with permission.

Brisson and Usher 2005; Woolley et al. 2008). The linkages that exist between members within the community are called *bonding capital*. These linkages exist in the form of trusting relationships between community members or feelings of social cohesion in neighborhoods. Examples of positive linkages are watching over a neighbor's property or being able to send a child to stay next door if his or her parent has an emergency. *Bridging capital* includes ties that exist between a community or neighborhood and outside entities, such as other communities or neighborhoods. An example is the relationship a particular neighborhood has with the city council, school board, or other governmental entity.

Although communities require economic resources to function effectively, social relations are also necessary. As Weil (2005) stated, "A range of scholars ... now identify the development of social and human capital and community capacity as essential elements of community health or competence" (225). The relationship between economic and human factors has been explored in research on low-income communities and in social connections. Low-income communities and the relationship between social capital and various outcomes for individuals and families have been one focus of research. School achievement has been a focus in both social work and education research. Studies suggest that increased levels of neighborhood bonding have a positive impact on students' school performance and their cognitive abilities (Caughy and O'Campo 2006; Woolley et al. 2008). Children in neighborhoods with more interaction between families and educational systems performed more competently than children in communities with looser social connections.

Research has focused on community-level factors and the experience of older adults as well. In one study, health, community characteristics, and happiness of young, middle-aged, and older adults were compared (Payne et al. 2010). Community disorganization as indicated by factors, such as vandalism, unsupervised youth, and public drinking, were significant in decreasing the happiness of the older adult group. This finding suggests that feeling secure and attached within one's community is especially important for well-being in later life.

In addition to decreasing happiness in later life, neighborhoods with more limited social capital are associated with the older population's lower health and mental health status. Data from the English Longitudinal Study of Ageing were used to study the relationship between urban neighborhood disorganization (e.g., crime, barriers to adequate living conditions) and cognitive functioning (Lang et al. 2008). Regardless of socioeconomic status and level of education, older adults who lived in neighborhoods with higher levels of social disorganization had lower rates of cognitive functioning. This is consistent with research that reported higher rates of depression in older adults who live in urban areas with higher rates of disorganization and deprivation (Aneshensel et al. 2007; Cagney, Browning, and Wen 2005).

*Collective Efficacy*

Efficacy, a concept attributed to Bandura (1982; see Chapter 6 on cognitive behavioral theory), is an individual's self-appraisal or -judgment about his or her capability to take action to accomplish specific tasks or goals. The concept of efficacy has also been used to describe attributes that relate to larger systems, such as neighborhoods and communities. *Collective efficacy* is defined as "social cohesion among neighbors combined with their willingness to intervene on behalf of the common good" (Sampson and Raudenbush 1997, 918). Applied to the neighborhood level, collective efficacy implies that residents have a shared willingness to be involved in their community for the common good. In addition, there is a sense of mutual trust and belief that investment will produce positive outcomes for the community as a whole (Ohmer and Beck 2006).

Although collective efficacy relates to social capital, the two terms are not synonymous. "The notion of collective efficacy emphasizes residents' sense of active engagement that is not well captured by the term social capital" (Sampson, Morenoff, and Earls 1999, 635). Whereas social capital focuses on one's perception of the social environment, collective efficacy emphasizes more the behavior or action that results from this perception. Sampson et al. further specified that collective efficacy involves the process of converting social connections to achieve desired results within a community. An example is when an individual believes that violating a community norm may be viewed negatively by a neighbor and thus abstains from doing so. Examples of actions that may violate community norms are littering, playing loud music, letting dogs roam the neighborhood, and other behaviors that disrupt the lives of other neighborhood residents. When neighbors have a sense of their own power and collective abilities, they are more apt to exert influence to address problems that are complex and difficult to solve (Ohmer and Beck 2006).

Research indicates that high levels of collective efficacy result in positive outcomes for neighborhoods and communities. Cagney, Browning, and Wen (2005) studied the self-rated health of African American and white older adults. Their findings indicated that regardless of race, poorer people had lower levels of self-reported health. Further analyses at the neighborhood level, however, resulted in some interesting findings. Using the emphasis of collective efficacy theory on the availability of resources within the community (i.e., beyond the individual level), the researchers found that neighborhood factors had a significant positive impact on health for lower income residents. The researchers hypothesized that residents benefited from the more socially and economically advantaged neighbors who had the capacity to mobilize to enhance health and well-being for all.

However, there is also some indication that collective efficacy and competence are enhanced by migration and exchange to bring new energy, ideas, and resources to community life. Yet Cagney, Browning, and Wen's (2005) research produced a counterintuitive result: that residential stability was associated with poorer health. This finding suggests that neighborhoods that experience little change or internal movement may suffer from economic disadvantage and social isolation. A study of community efficacy and community policing reported similar findings (Wells et al. 2006). In this research, the relationship between neighborhood problems and citizen reactions was investigated. Low levels of involvement with police were reported, even in areas where significant crime occurred. The explanation of the researchers was that residents in communities where there is significant disadvantage or high levels of stability may become tolerant of or desensitized to ongoing problems. As a result, they may fail to contact or work with police to resolve these issues.

*Community Empowerment*

Just as the concept of self-efficacy has been applied at the community level, the idea of empowerment has also been considered at this level of practice. Parsons (2008) emphasized multiple levels of empowerment and how empowerment enhances a sense of competence:

> Empowerment outcomes include personal empowerment—self efficacy and perception of the ability to resolve and influence one's own issues; interpersonal knowledge and skill acquisition attained through interactions with others that facilitate overcoming barriers; and sociopolitical actions influencing societal institutions that can facilitate or impede self-help and mutual aid efforts. These interacting concepts influence one another, but act as parts of a whole dynamic of perceived competency and liberation. (123)

Emerging from the original works of Solomon (1976), the concept of empowerment works at the community level to promote relationships between community members. A major emphasis is on the resulting action to eradicate community-level social problems that hinder competent functioning.

Similar to Putnam (2000), who argued the erosion of social capital, Cox (2001) discussed the fact that community-level changes necessitate additional social work efforts to enhance communal ties. A declining sense of community and the increasing isolation inherent in people's lives today lead to an overall sense of helplessness. Such feelings can create perceptions of personal inefficacy that diminish motivation to take action within one's community (Pecukonis and Wencur 1994). Especially with members of disenfranchised communities who face multiple oppressions (e.g., racism, poverty), perceptions of hopelessness or helplessness may need to be the target of intervention prior to addressing other challenging issues.

Empowerment in the context of community development focuses on issues of economic growth and sustainability. Within this context, *empowerment* is "the creation of sustainable structures, processes, and mechanisms, over which local communities have an increased degree of control, and from which they have a measurable impact on public and social policies affecting these communities" (Craig 2002, 125–126). Practitioners can carry out various roles that can empower communities (Toomey 2009). However, some of the roles that have been advocated in the past, such as doing tasks "for" a community instead of using a development-oriented approach, may have the consequence of decreasing community competence. As Cox (2001) reminded social work professionals, "Future community practice ... will have the opportunity to increase its effectiveness as a critical component of social change, and an effective partner in developing communities" (53).

Increased citizen participation, especially of the more marginalized populations of communities (e.g., individuals with mental illness or low income), is a form of empowerment as well. *Citizen participation* has been defined as "the active, voluntary involvement of individuals and groups in changing problematic conditions in communities and influencing the policies and programs that affect the quality of their lives and the lives of other residents" (Ohmer 2007, 109). Interventions that help empower these individuals build self-advocacy skills, raise political awareness, promote a sense of competence through increased problem solving, and reduce a sense of alienation (Chaskin et al. 2001; Ohmer and Beck 2006; Ohmer 2007). Furthermore, citizen participation can facilitate neighborhood collective efficacy by establishing trusting bonds and relationships to promote competency and shared community expectations (Ohmer 2010).

## Research and Practice Issues

*It is important for social workers to understand the underlying theory and research that informs strategies to engage and empower residents to improve their lives and the lives of other residents.*
—Ohmer (2010, 13)

Although the community is the foundation for the competent functioning of individuals and families, practice and research is much more developed in other areas of social work. As Coulton (2005) argued, knowledge of and theory about community-level functioning would be enhanced by advancing research through hypothesis testing of the factors that promote individual and family functioning. In addition, research and practice models of communities need to be developed to determine the factors that enhance community-level competence. However, Coulton (2005) identified several challenges to community-level research such as defining the boundaries of the community, developing appropriate community measures, and utilizing appropriate statistical methods for analysis. These challenges point to the need to develop additional community content at the theoretical, empirical, and practice levels.

Ohmer and Korr (2006) analyzed the literature on outcomes of community-level interventions. However, they found relatively few intervention studies that targeted communities. Nevertheless, three major areas did emerge in community-level intervention research. They were (a) the impact of the interventions on psychosocial aspects of communities, such as the level of citizen participation and consequences for residents; (b) the impact of the intervention on physical, social, and economic conditions; and (c) contextual factors that facilitate interventions, such as characteristics of residents related to increased involvement in communities. As in the case of evidence-based approaches with other systems, this type of analysis helps practitioners determine the interventions that promote certain types of changes within community contexts.

Besides interventions that have a demonstrated level of efficacy, emerging community practice approaches promote additional competence that fosters enhanced relationships and functioning. The Naturally Occurring Retirement Community (NORC) model is a community-level program focused on older adults. A NORC, a community with a large population of older adults within a geographic area, includes both urban and rural sites (Hunt and Ross 1990; Marshall and Hunt 1999). Older adults within these communities are supported to remain in their homes and in familiar surroundings. Although a significant body of literature is developing about the positive impact of NORCs on older adults' health, mental health, and functioning (Black 2008; Pickard and Tang 2009), attention has also been paid to the community-level factors that increase their competence. Research on community-level factors of NORCs indicates that the ability to foster a sense of community among the residents and to promote strategic community partnerships increases the effectiveness of this program model for older adults (Ivery and Akstein-Kahan2010; Ivery, Akstein-Kahan, and Murphy 2010).

Another approach within communities focuses on mediating conflicts and dealing with the ruptures that are part of community life. Community conferencing is a restorative justice approach that brings together community factions involved in some type of conflict situation. *Restorative justice*, which is different from punitive processes (e.g., legal or civil action), is based on the philosophy that communities are places in which problems can be resolved (Abramson and Beck 2010). The community conference has the goal of addressing common concerns by bringing together groups that have experienced conflict. As a result, participants in a community conference typically form a shared understanding about the causes and consequences of conflict and can move toward a plan of action (Abramson and Moore 2001). This approach seeks to address three basic questions: (a) What happened? (b) Who has been affected and how? and (c) What can be done to repair the harm and make things better in the future? This approach has the potential to shift discourse and decision making from a "perpetrator–victim" paradigm to one in which community members approach the problem from multiple perspectives and seek ways to function more harmoniously and competently in the future.

## Case Example

This case example shows how a community-level restorative justice approaches can build community competence. It examines the tensions in a transitional community in which families from different racial/ethnic backgrounds experience conflict over how to share resources. Strategies to promote understanding and build capacity were developed as a result of a community conference.

Miguel Garrido was a social worker and community activist in the Latino community of South River, a medium-size southern city. Together Miguel and an African American social worker, Lila Forest, organized a community conference to ease rising tensions they observed in town. A number of Latinos had moved to South River over the past few years because there were employment opportunities in agriculture. Although several smaller incidents had erupted over the years, about two weeks ago a major fight involving several adolescents had broken out at the school. As a result, simmering tensions had grown to a rolling boil. Miguel and Lila, proponents of mediation and dialogue, got together and planned a community conference before additional confrontations developed.

The conference was scheduled for a Sunday afternoon, and several methods were used to invite members of the community to attend. Because both Miguel and Lila had strong connections within the community, they personally invited individuals and families by phone and posted flyers in strategic locations around the community. The event was planned for the local Boys and Girls Club, which supported the event.

About forty people, ranging from children to older adults, showed up at the conference. Because both English and Spanish were spoken, Miguel had arranged for a translator who agreed to volunteer her time because of the importance of the event. It was evident that tensions existed, as the room was divided by race/ethnicity: Latinos on one side and African Americans on the other.

Using the three-question outline (i.e., What happened? Who has been affected and how? and What can be done to repair the harm and make things better in the future?), Miguel and Lila began the conference by asking participants to describe the nature of the problem. From their stories, it was clear to Miguel and Lila that several issues were being experienced differently by the different groups in the room. Miguel and Lila started the conversation by asking about the incident on the playground. Some of the boys described what had taken place. A fight had broken out because African American boys were playing basketball on the school playground while some Latino boys were constructing a makeshift soccer field. The soccer ball would occasionally drift into the basketball court and disrupt play. This led to the fight. One Latino mother stated in Spanish, "Where are my children supposed to play? Do they want them to play *fútbol* in the street so they get hit by a car?" Clearly, concerns were about more than the ballgame, as parents were concerned about safety issues as well.

One of the older African American men stood up and stated that regardless of race, the children in the neighborhood were destroying the property. He said, "I don't care about their skin color, they all run wild through the neighborhood. I try to keep them out of my yard but they trample my grass and my shrubs. When I talk to them, they sass back at me and use awful language. Something must be done about the kids."

An African American mother had a different perspective. She stood up and said, "It's the men that bother me—not the kids.

My 12-year-old daughter walks to school by the Mexican men who watch her and say things to each other in Spanish. They are standing there in the morning, waiting for a ride to work at the same time that kids are walking to school. My daughter is afraid—she doesn't know what they are saying and it makes her feel bad."

Other statements were about experiences that had resulted from transitions within the neighborhood. These included loud music, litter accumulating, and public drinking. Some themes were emerging that cut across segments of the community, although there was still obvious stress in the room.

In the next step, Miguel and Lila summarized the problems articulated and the people they affected. These included children who did not have adequate space to play in and as a result had to play in unsafe conditions. Another affected group was the parents, who worried about the safety of their children. Other residents had concerns about their property and the declining appearance of the neighborhood. Themes emerged from the stories of community residents that went beyond race and ethnicity.

Although the residents did not the end community strife at this meeting, they did begin putting together a plan for action. Holding the community accountable for problems is a way that moves past these tensions to a more functional and competent way of being—an important component of restorative justice practice. Miguel and Lila asked for ideas and volunteers to deal with some of the problems. A retired African American man volunteered to pick up the trash that had accumulated near a small convenience store. Miguel asked whether anyone would join him, and a few hands went up. Because Lila knew the store owner, she volunteered to talk with him about setting up trash receptacles so that litter would not pile up. One of the bilingual Latina mothers volunteered to walk the children to school and confront several disrespectful Latino men. The African American woman who raised this issue also volunteered to walk children to school, creating a shared solution to this problem.

The major issue that precipitated the conference—the schoolyard fight—was addressed by the Boys and Girls Club. They offered their land as a soccer field so that children would not have to play on the blacktop at the school. This was a good beginning, as it created a safe place for the boys to play.

These beginnings grew into other initiatives aimed at bringing the members of the community together. After hearing about these steps, the clergy in the African American church reached out to the Latino clergy to find out how the faith communities could be involved. They organized a joint prayer service and picnic for members in the congregations. Miguel and Lila were invited as well and helped the members of the different congregations find mutual and intersecting solutions.

Although other areas remained to be addressed, the conference and subsequent actions brought disparate sections of the community together. The relations with the community organizations that were established also provided support and accountability. Overall, these steps provided a way for the community to deal with perceived differences and conflict more competently.

# References

Abramson, L., and E. Beck. 2010. Using conflict to build community: Community conferencing. In *Social work and restorative justice: Skills for dialogue, peacemaking, and reconciliation*, ed. E. Beck, N. P. Kropf, and P. B. Leonard, 149–74. Oxford: Oxford University Press.

Abramson, L., and D. B. Moore 2001. Transforming conflict in the inner city community: Conferencing in Baltimore. *Contemporary Justice Review* 4, no. 3–4:321–40.

Aneshensel, C. S., R. G. Wight, D. Miller-Martinez, A. L. Botticello, A. Karlamangla, and T. E. Seeman 2007. Urban neighborhoods and depressive symptoms among older adults. *Journal of Gerontology: Social Sciences* 62B: S52–69.

Bandura, A. 1982. Self efficacy mechanism in human agency. *American Psychologist* 37: 122–147.

_____. ed. 1995. *Self efficacy in changing societies.* Cambridge: Cambridge University Press.

Besthorn, F. H. 2001. Is it time for a new ecological approach to social work: What is the environment telling us? *Spirituality and Social Work Forum* 9:2–5.

Black, K. 2008. Health and aging in place: Implications for community practice. *Journal of Community Practice* 16:79–95.

Blumer, H. 1969. *Symbolic interactionism: Perspective and method.* Englewood Cliffs, NJ: Prentice Hall.

Bourdieu, P. 1985. The forms of capital. In *Handbook of theory and research for the sociology of education*, ed. J. G. Richardson, 241–58. New York: Greenwood.

Brisson, D. 2009. Testing the relationship of formal bonding, informal bonding, and formal bridging social capital on key outcomes for families in low-income neighborhoods. *Journal of Sociology and Social Welfare* 36, no.1:167–83.

Brisson, D. S., and C. L. Usher. 2005. Bonding social capital in low-income neighborhoods. *Family Relations* 54:644–53.

Cagney, K. A., C. R. Browning, and M. Wen. 2005. Racial disparities in self-rated health at older ages: What difference does the neighborhood make? *Journal of Gerontology: Social Sciences* 60B:S181–90.

Caughy, M. O., and P. J. O'Campo. 2006. Neighborhood poverty, social capital, and the cognitive development of African American preschoolers. *American Journal of Community Psychology* 37, no. 1/2:141–54.

Chaskin, R. J. 2001. Building community capacity: A definitional framework and case studies from a comprehensive community initiative. *Urban Affairs Review* 36:291–323.

Chaskin, R. J., P. Brown, S. Venkatesh, and A. Vidal. 2001. *Building community capacity*. New York: Aldine de Gruyter.

Cohen, H., and R. R. Greene. 2005. Older adults who overcame oppression. *Families in Society* 87, no.1:1–8.

Coleman, J. A. 1988. Families and schools. *Educational Researcher* 16, no. 6:32–38.

Coulton, C. 2005. The place of community in social work practice research: Conceptual and methodological developments. *Social Work Research* 29, no.2:73–86.

Cox, E. O. 2001. Community-practice issues in the 21st century: Questions and challenges for empowerment-oriented practitioners. *Journal of Community Practice* 9, no.1:37–55.

Craig, G. 2002. Towards measurement of empowerment: The evaluation of community development. *Journal of Community Development Society* 33, no.1:124–146.

Gamble, D. N., and M. Weil. 2010. *Community practice skills: Local to global perspectives*. New York: Columbia University Press.

Hart, M. 1999. *Guide to sustainable community indicators*. 2nd ed. North Andover: MA: Hart Environmental Data.

Hoff, M., and J. G. McNutt, eds. 1994. *The global environmental crisis: Implications for social welfare and social work*. Brookfield, VT: Ashgate.

Hunt, M. E., and L. E. Ross. 1990. Naturally occurring retirement communities: A multiattribute examination of desirability factors. *The Gerontologist* 30:667–73.

Ivery, J. M., and D. Akstein-Kahan. (2010). Naturally occurring retirement communities (NORC): Developing and managing collaborative partnerships to support older adults. *Administration in Social Work*. , 34, 329–343.

Ivery, J. M., D. Akstein-Kahan, and K. Murphy. 2010. NORC supportive services model implementation and community capacity. *Journal of Gerontological Social Work* 51:21–42.

Lang, I. A., D. J. Llewellyn, K. M. Langa, R. B. Wallace, F. A. Huppert, and D. Melzer. 2008. Neighborhood deprivation, individual socioeconomic status, and cognitive function in older people: Analyses from the English Longitudinal Study of Ageing. *Journal of the American Geriatrics Society* 56:191–98.

Lin, N. 2001. *Social capital: A theory of social structure and action*. Cambridge: Cambridge University Press.

Loeffler, D. N., D. C. Christiansen, M. B. Tracey, M. C. Secret, R. L. Ersing, S. R. Fairchild, & Sutphen R. 2004. Social capital for social work: Toward a definition and conceptual framework. *Social Development Issues* 26, no. 2/3:22–38.

Long, D. A., and D. D. Perkins. 2007. Community social and place predictors of sense of community: A multilevel and longitudinal analysis. *Journal of Community Psychology* 35:563–81.

Marshall, L. J., and M. E. Hunt. 1999. Rural naturally occurring retirement communities: A community assessment procedure. *Journal of Housing for the Elderly* 13:19–34.

Maslow, A. J. 1968. *Toward a psychology of being*. New York: Van Nostrand Reinhold.

Mathbor, G. M. 2007. Enhancement of community preparedness for natural disasters: The role of social work in building social capital for sustainable disaster relief and management. *International Social Work* 50:357–69.

McCold, P., and B. Wachtel. 1998. *Restorative policing experiment: The Bethlehem Pennsylvania police family group conferencing project*. Washington, DC: U.S. Government Printing Office.

McKinnon, J. 2008. Exploring the nexus between social work and the environment. *Australian Social Work* 61:256–68.

Milligan, M. J. 1998. Interactional past and potential: The social construction of place attachment. *Symbolic Interaction* 21:1–33.

_____. 2003. Displacement and identity discontinuity: The role of nostalgia in establishing new identity categories. *Symbolic Interaction* 26:381–403.

Ohmer, M. 2007. Citizen participation in neighborhood organizations and its relationship to volunteers' self- and collective efficacy and sense of community. *Social Work Research*, 31, no. 2:109–20.

_____. 2010. How theory and research inform citizen participation in poor communities: The ecological perspective and theories on self-and collective efficacy and sense of community. *Journal of Human Behavior in the Social Environment* 20:1–19.

Ohmer, M., and E. Beck. 2006. Citizen participation in neighborhood organizations in poor communities and its relationship to neighborhood and organizational collective efficacy. *Journal of Sociology and Social Welfare* 33, no.1:179–201.

Ohmer, M. L., and W. S. Korr. 2006. The effectiveness of community practice interventions: A review of the literature. *Research on Social Work Practice* 16, no. 2:132–45.

Parsons, R. J. 2008. Empowerment practice. In *Encyclopedia of social work*, ed. T. Mizrahi and L. E. Davis, 20th ed., vol. 2, 123–26. New York: NASW Press & Oxford University Press.

Payne, B. K., E. Monk-Turner, N. P. Kropf, and C. Turner. 2010. The influence of aging, health and community characteristics on happiness. *International Public Health Journal* 2, no. 2:1–11.

Pecukonis, E. V., and S. Wencur. 1994. Perceptions of self and collective efficacy in community organization theory and practice. *Journal of Community Practice* 1, no. 2:5–21.

Pickard, J. G., and F. Y. Tang. 2009. Older adults seeking mental health counseling in a NORC. *Research on Aging* 31:638–60.

Putnam, R. 2000. *Bowling alone: The collapse and revival of American community*. New York: Simon & Schuster.

Rogge, M. E. 1998. Toxic risk, resilience and justice in Chattanooga. In *Sustainable community development: Studies in economic, environmental, and cultural revitalization*, ed. M. D. Hoff, 105–22. New York: Lewis.

Sampson, R. J., J. D. Morenoff, and F. Earls. 1999. Beyond social capital: Spatial dynamics of collective efficacy for children. *American Sociological Review* 64:633–60.

Sampson, R. J., and S. W. Raudenbush. 1997, August 15. Neighborhoods and violent crime: A multilevel study of collective efficacy. *Science* 277:918–25.

Smith, R. W., V. Bugni. 2006. Symbolic interaction theory and architecture. *Symbolic Interaction* 29:123–55.

Solomon, B. 1976. *Black empowerment: Social work in oppressed communities.* New York: Columbia University Press.

Sorkin, M. 2003. *Starting from zero: Reconstructing downtown New York.* New York: Routledge.

Toomey, A. 2009. Empowerment and disempowerment in community development practice: Eight roles practitioners play. *Community Development Journal.* doi:10.1093/cdj/bsp060

Weil, M., ed. 2005. *The handbook of community practice.* Thousand Oaks, CA: Sage.

Wells, W., J. A. Schafer, S. P. Varano, and T. S. Bynum. 2006. Neighborhood residents' production of order: The effects of collective efficacy on responses to neighborhood problems. *Crime & Delinquency,* 52:523–50.

Woolley, M. E., A. Grogan-Kalyor, A., J. E. Gilster, R. A. Karb, L. M. Gant, T. M. Reischl, et al. Alaimo, K . 2008. Neighborhood social capital, poor physical conditions, and school achievement. *Children & Schools* 30, no. 3:133–45.

# 10

## Evaluating Effectiveness

*An important attribute of a profession is the systematic study of its practices, to continually advance its service modalities. Since the inception of the social work profession more than a century ago, research on interventions, social problems, and social policy have been important to its purpose and function.*

—*Zlotnik (2008, 521)*

Competence has been reviewed and described in this book using several theoretical approaches. Case studies have provided examples of social work practice from a number of theory bases. Basic principles of evaluation and measurement are described in this final chapter. In addition, the ways in which people exhibit competence, and the associated concepts of resilience and healthy functioning, are summarized.

*Social work research* uses scientific methods to produce knowledge pertinent to social work practice (Rubin and Babbie 2005; Tripodi and Potocky-Tripodi 2007). Social work research tends to focus on everyday problems social workers are called on to assist in resolving, including mental health disturbances, substance abuse, and poverty (Tripodi and Lalayants 2008). This research may be qualitative and/ or quantitative. *Qualitative* research uses data derived from words, pictures, or objects and might be considered subjective; *quantitative* research uses statistical data and is generally thought of as more objective in design (Miles and Huberman 1994).

In the early years of the profession, practitioners were trained by social scientists and master practitioners. They studied theories that were current in the fields of sociology and economics. Classes were held at field agencies, and the practice approach to research was combined with the social sciences of the day. The *practice-based approach to research*, reemphasized during the 1980s and 1990s, often uses knowledge derived from master practitioners; it assumes that these masters are exemplars at reflecting on and interpreting complex situations (Laird 1993; Schon 1983).

From this perspective, knowledge involves a process in which social workers learn from "lived experience" (Weick 1993, 12). The practitioner's goal, called *knowing-in-action*, is to make sense of "an uncertain situation that initially makes no sense" (Schon 1983, 40). The emphasis is on the ability to think critically within the larger sociopolitical context and engage in lifelong learning (Greene 2005).

During the 1980s, practitioners generally used single-subject research designs to learn more about client outcomes. *Single-subject designs* involve the collection of time series data before and after an intervention (Tripodi and Lalayants 2008). Although the role of the practitioner acting as a researcher in an agency has been limited, it can contribute to creating partnerships among researchers/practitioners, universities, and communities (Zlotnik 2008).

Recently there has been interest in evidence-based social work practice. In *evidence-based practice*, the social worker identifies the best evidence available related to his or her case. According to Jenson and Howard (2008), the five steps in the evidence-based practice process are designed to "select, deliver, and evaluate individual and social interventions aimed at preventing or ameliorating client problems and social conditions" (158). These steps are

1. Converting practice information into answerable questions, including client-oriented practical information
2. Locating evidence that could help in answering questions, for example by obtaining books, journals, reviews, and so forth
3. Appraising and applying available evidence to practice and policy decisions
4. Using research designs to practice situations and decide on the utility of information
5. Evaluating the process, which requires a knowledge of the literature and the ability to conduct searches. (159–61)

This chapter provides knowledge and skills to help to evaluate effectiveness of various theoretical approaches to competence outlined within this book.

### Research in Human Behavior

*At the very least we ought to know what concepts we are utilizing and where the concepts come from, and the state of their verification.*
*—Firestone (1962, 312)*

A *theory* is a set of interrelated ideas composed of assumptions, hypotheses, and predictions. The purpose of a theory critique is to evaluate the efficacy of the theory selected for use in social work practice. Is the theory accurate? Are the interventions derived from the theory's assumptions effective with clients? In order to test a theory, the researcher needs to operationalize it by translating its ideas into observable and measurable concepts. Theories can then be tested by systematic observation and experimentation. The results may be analyzed statistically; based on this analysis, the theory can be supported revised, or rejected or a new theory may be hypothesized (Newman and Newman 2005).

> No single theory to date has been able to provide the organizing principles to meet the challenge of understanding fully the person as well as the systems with which he or she interacts. The dual goals of [social work in terms of] improving societal institutions and assisting clients within their social and cultural milieu have led to the mining of concepts from different disciplines. Each concept or theory attempts to explain the complex interplay of physical, psychological, cognitive, social, and cultural variables that shape human behavior. As a result, the profession's theoretical base has come to incorporate a number of theories, each with its own constellation of values, purposes, assumptions, and prescriptions for interventive behavior. (Greene 2005, 50)

## Scientific Methods

The study of human behavior uses scientific methods to gain knowledge about the development of people and the social systems that make up their environments. Most research methods used to develop human behavior theories require theorists to garner a complete, detailed description of the subject matter (Miles and Huberman 1994) using one or more of the following methods:

> Direct observation. The researcher's approach is objective, repeatable, and systematic.

> Naturalistic observation. The research takes place in the environment in which the behavior occurs.

> Clinical studies. The researcher engages in a face-to-face gathering of clinical data.

> Participant observation. The researcher is active with the individual or in the group under study.

Case studies. The researcher provides an in-depth account of a single individual, family, or group. He or she may document the lives of famous individuals (e.g., as Erik Erikson did in his studies of Martin Luther and Mahatma Gandhi).

Interviews. The researcher collects interviews in which individuals are asked to tell their stories, often emphasizing particular critical events. For example, Greene et al. (2010) interviewed Holocaust survivors to learn about resiliency and survivorship under severe stress.

Retrospective studies. The Holocaust study by Greene et al. (2010), which was retrospective in design, asked individuals to recall past experiences.

Ecological designs. The use of an ecological design, a sociocultural approach, requires that the researcher consider the full context in which development takes place, at all levels of systems (see Chapter 4). Bronfenbrenner's (1979) model of complex child development requires a research design that considers all of the important settings for children, including family, extended family, early education and care, health care agencies, and community learning centers such as libraries and playgrounds.

## Research: Erik Erikson's Healthy Personality

*The emphasis of [Erikson's] psychosocial theory on ego development and ego processes provides insight into the directions of healthy development throughout life. Concepts central to the theory such as trust, autonomy, identity achievement, generativity, coping, well-being, social support, and intergenerational interdependence have become thoroughly integrated into contemporary human development scholarship.*

*—Newman and Newman (2005, 52)*

Classic human behavior theorists used the science of the day to construct their theories. Although Piaget has been criticized for using small samples For example, he used systematic observation to construct his theory of cognition. Sigmund Freud, a trained physician, began his career as a medical neurologist, studying the nervous system of the eel. He also investigated the biological causes of cerebral palsy in humans (Prosek 2010). He aspired to eventually discover the biological basis for human behavior. When the Nazi regime forced Freud out of the university and his laboratory because he was Jewish, he shifted his research to developing theories of personality theory using interviews and case studies. Although most of his premises about personality were not testable as written, his hypotheses about the neurological bases of human attachment are now being revived by neurobiologists (Cozolino 2002; Schore 2002).

Erik Erikson used anthropological field studies to research identity formation among the Sioux Indians and the case study method to explore the personality of Mahatma Gandhi. He also used observations from his clinical practice with children to construct his theory of the healthy personality. Erikson's psychosocial theory provides a broad context, linking the process of child development to personality in later life and to the context of the broader society (Newman and Newman 2005).

Later researchers have operationalized and created measures to verify Eriksonian concepts. For example, Markstrom et al. (1997) developed the Psychosocial Inventory of Ego Strengths to examine Erikson's concept of ego strengths. Kowaz and Marcia (1991), who were interested in the relationship between perceived competence and the sense of industry, formulated and validated a measure of industry. Industry was operationalized by identifying three components: (a) the cognitive component, or the skills and knowledge relating to tools, symbols, and concepts based on culture; (b) the behavioral component, or the application of skills in a productive direction; and (c) the affective component, or the experience of pride in skill acquisition and application.

Kowaz and Marcia (1991) studied 187 pupils in Grades 4, 5, and 6 from three different schools. Sample surveys were conducted in ethnically diverse rural and urban environments. Children or their parents had the right to refuse to participate in the study. Teachers and parents observed the same variables. Correlations were obtained for measures of the children's industry and parents' and teachers' ratings of the children's industry. The correlations were all statistically significant, leading the researchers to believe that their instrument tapped the industry construct.

## Risk and Resilience Theory Research Approaches

*The repeated documentation of this "resiliency"—the ability to bounce back successfully despite exposure to severe risk—has clearly established the self-righting nature of human development.*
*—Benard (1993, 44)*

213

## Fostering Resilience

Depending on how the researcher envisions resiliency, he or she may focus on people's *assets*, or evidence of positive developmental outcomes; *resources*, or human, social, and material capital; or *protective factors*, or the qualities that predict better outcomes following adverse events.

## Masten and Reed: Resilience in Development

Masten and Reed (2002) outlined three research perspectives that have been used to study how resilience affects human development. In the *risk factor* approach, researchers identify individual traits and environmental characteristics of youth that might increase the probability of a problem in development. Masten and Reed believe the value of this approach is its use of large samples and multivariate statistical analysis and its usefulness for producing information about the protective factors that might produce resilient children and youth.

For example, Werner and Smith (1982, 1992) carried out a large longitudinal study involving a diverse group of 837 high-risk children for whom demographic, prenatal, and perinatal data were available and followed them through mid-life. They collected data from interviews with parents, clinical psychological evaluations, and the records of public agencies. This allowed them to identify early influences that differentiated resilient children from their less resilient peers (Barton 2002). Werner and Smith then concluded that a resilient subgroup of adults was identifiable by their employment, marriages, education, and military service.

In the *asset-focused approach*, researchers study the factors that predict what better developmental outcomes in the context in which they occur. This includes such factors as gender, ability, ethnicity, age, and sexual orientation. Researchers use an asset-focused approach to explore how quality of life can be improved by increasing the quantity or quality of resources available, including social capital. For example, assets might be increased by providing children with mentors and recreation centers and by improving parenting skills by having parents take parenting classes. Research findings can then be used to design intervention strategies. Researchers taking a *process-oriented approach* are interested in the activities and interventions that influence a person's everyday life. They focus on whether a sequence of successful mastery builds a sense of competence.

## Richardson: Three Waves of Resilience Research

Richardson (2002) identified three waves of resilience research findings that have led resilience-enhancing educational programs and therapeutic interventions. In the *first wave* of inquiry, researchers explored the traits and environmental characteristics enabling people to overcome adversity. This knowledge was then used to design interventions that promoted these positive attributes, including school programs that build self-esteem.

In the *second wave* of inquiry, researchers investigated the processes related to stress and coping. Interventions identified through this line of inquiry, such as treatment models, have been applied to families in crisis (Walsh 1998a, 1998b). In the current or *third wave* of inquiry, researchers have been examining less verifiable factors that affect resiliency, including how people grow and are transformed by adverse events. Interventions identified by this orientation have been developed to help clients self-actualize and tap client creativity and spirituality as sources of strength (Richardson 2002).

## Studies of Resilience

### Children Who Can

The International Resilience Project surveyed 589 children (approximately 48 percent girls and 52 percent boys) and their families in 30 countries. Grotberg (1995, 1997), the principal investigator, defined resilience as a universal capacity of individuals, groups, and communities. This reflected her belief that people can be taught to overcome adversity. She concluded that "every country in the study is drawing on a common set of resilience factors to promote resilience in their children" (1995, 3). Findings from the International Resilience Project suggested that resilient children often receive social support, have the opportunity for educational attainment and success, participate in activities and hobbies, and connect with competent adults. Based on these findings, Grotberg designed a practice and reflection series to improve the lives of young children living in disadvantaged circumstances.

### Unique Pathways to Resilience

Ungar et al. (2007) explored the cross-cultural aspects of resilience in another international project. They hypothesized that "resilience is not only an individual's capacity to overcome adversity, but the capacity of the individual's environment to provide access to health-enhancing resources in culturally relevant ways" (288). They carried out a fourteen-site study in eleven countries (in North America, Asia, Africa, South America, and the Middle East), interviewing eighty-nine youth ages twelve to twenty-three using face-to-face and electronic discussions. They wanted to know

1. How is resilience defined by different culture groups or disadvantaged communities?
2. Are there global and/or culturally specific aspects of resilience? and
3. What unique processes and outcomes are associated with resilience in specific cultures and contexts? (292)

The researchers asked the youth

1. What would I need to know to grow up well here?
2. How would you describe people who grow up well here, despite the many problems they face?
3. What does it mean to you, to your family, and to your community when bad things happen?
4. What kinds of things are most challenging for you growing up here?
5. What do you do when you face difficulties in your life?
6. What does being healthy mean to you and others in your family and community?
7. What do you do, and others you know, do to keep healthy mentally, physically, emotionally, spiritually?
8. Can you share a story with me about another child who grew up well in this community despite facing many challenges?
9. Can you share a story about how you have managed to overcome challenges you personally have faced in your family or outside your home in your community?

Ungar et al. (2007) identified seven tensions involved in the formation of resilience and recognized the value of interpreting distress and resilience from a culturally specific point of view (Shoeb, Weinstein, and Mollica 2007). These are:

| | |
|---|---|
| 1. Access to material resources | Availability of financial, educational, medical, and employment opportunities, as well as food, clothing, and shelter |
| 2. Relationships | Relationships with significant others, peers, and adults in the community |

| | |
|---|---|
| 3. Identity | Personal and collective sense of purpose, self-appraisal of strengths and weaknesses; beliefs and values, including spiritual and religious identification |
| 4. Power and control | Experience of caring for oneself and others; the ability to effect change and to access resources |
| 5. Cultural adherence | Adherence to one's own local and/or global cultural practices, values, and beliefs |
| 6. Social justice | Experience related to finding a meaningful role and social equality |
| 7. Cohesion | Balancing one's personal interest and sense of responsibility |

### Bosnian Women Come to the United States

Sossou et al. (2008) conducted qualitative research on seven female Bosnian refugees ranging in age from thirty-two to forty-seven years who resettled in the southeastern United States. The *purposive sample*—data sources that met a specific criteria—included refugees who had escaped war-torn Bosnia between 1992 and 1995. During the war, the women and their families were affected by multiple traumatic events, including bombings, torture, rape, and genocide. In addition, like most refugees, the women faced the stress of immigrating to the United States, adapting to a new culture, and integrating into a new society (Fong and Greene 2009).

The researchers wanted to explore in-depth the factors that contributed to the women's resilience by examining their personal narratives for major themes. They used a *phenomenological approach*—a method of inquiry based on subjective experience or a first-person account—to understand the meaning of events. Four areas were examined: (a) What was the women's general well-being before their flight from Bosnia? (b) How would they describe their families', their children's, and their own well-being? (c) Did they engage in a spiritual or religious life? and (d) What were the challenges of resettling in a new country?

They found that the seven women had had good and stable family lives before the war; they had had good jobs, homes, and so forth. Most engaged in a spiritual life, but one that did not involve organized religion. The researchers concluded that the major barriers to resettle-ment were learning a new language; the absence of adequate public transportation; inadequate educational opportunities; and miscon-ceptions about accessing mental health services, including prejudices against medication. The well-being and safety of their families was a primary concern. The women felt that family and community social supports were the major factors contributing to resilience (Sossou et al. 2008).

## Studies Based on Cognitive and Behavioral Theory

*The adoption of interventions whose effectiveness has been demon-strated by clinical and social services research can serve to enhance the quality of service delivery and, thereby, improve the lives of many individuals.*

—*Cummings and Kropf (2009, 2)*

Cognitive and behavioral theories have influenced a number of intervention approaches (see Chapters 6 and 8). Because of the focus on observable and quantitative outcomes, an extensive literature ex-ists for evaluation of clinical approaches based upon cognitive and behavioral theories. Depending on the particular treatment issue(s) being addressed, cognitive–behavioral interventions are structured to promote greater competence by changing individuals' distorted thoughts and consequent behaviors that result in difficulties in func-tioning.

Evaluation of cognitive–behavioral therapy (CBT) has been under-taken with numerous client populations and contexts. In fact, *meta-analyses*, which go beyond individual studies to determine the strength of findings for similar intervention approaches, have been performed in many areas. These studies have shown that CBT interventions are effective in several areas of social work practice.

### Depression and Anxiety

CBT interventions are effective at decreasing depression and anxi-ety across the life course. Gregory (2010) analyzed CBT interventions with clients who were experiencing bipolar disorder (a disorder in which a person experiences mood swings from mania to depression). The meta-analysis included four studies that had assigned clients to randomized groups. Gregory concluded that CBT has a small but significant effect on the depression that is part of bipolar disorder.

However, he also noted the lack of studies in this area that included diverse populations. Research on bipolar disorder has found that African Americans with this psychiatric diagnosis have a greater risk for suicide or attempted suicide than Caucasians (Kupfer et al. 2005). Unfortunately, none of the studies in the meta-analysis specifically addressed bipolar disorder in African Americans.

Meta-analyses that have synthesized and combined a number of independent but related studies have addressed CBT interventions in later life. Depression and anxiety are the most common mental health problems among older adults. Estimates indicate that from 8 percent to 20 percent of older adults in the community (American Association of Geriatric Psychiatry 2005, Depression section) and up to 50 percent of those residing in long-term-care settings (Adamek 2003) suffer from these conditions. Sadly, many older adults suffering from untreated depression become suicidal. Many suicides among older adults can be attributed to untreated depression (National Institute of Mental Health 2006).

Adamek and Slater (2009) reviewed the literature on the treatment of depressed and/or anxious older adults. They found fourteen meta-analyses on these conditions, twelve of which evaluated CBT. The various reviews found that CBT treatments were clearly associated with improved functioning with older clients, and better outcomes were achieved in CBT groups as compared to control groups. In addition, several of the studies compared CBT with other types of interventions (e.g., reminiscence, relaxation), with results indicating higher degrees of effectiveness associated with CBT protocols. In light of these findings, Adamek and Slater suggested that psychosocial interventions (especially CBT) can be effective in treating late-life depression and anxiety, and should be considered as an alternative to pharmacological interventions. In fact, one meta-analysis of CBT for anxiety concluded that CBT should be considered the first-line treatment in late-life anxiety interventions (Alwahhabi 2003).

*Health Conditions*

CBT interventions have been used to help individuals, spouses, and families cope with various health conditions. Often, the identification of health problems can stress or compromise the functioning of individuals and their families. Several studies on coping with cancer have reported that CBT protocols help patients live more successfully with this diagnosis. Antoni et al. (2001) studied one hundred women with breast cancer who were assigned to a CBT group or a control group. After ten weeks, the CBT group had significantly reduced depression and increased optimism about the future.

CBT interventions have also been used to decrease depression after cardiac events such as heart attacks. In a very large multisite study, the ENRICHD Investigators (2003, 2004a, 2004b) examined a diverse sample in terms of gender, race/ethnicity, and age. Included in the research were 73 hospitals that used a standard CBT protocol for about 2,500 cardiac patients. The treatment group received an average of eleven sessions of CBT during a six-month period and group therapy when feasible. Patients with clinically significant depression scores were also prescribed antidepressant medications. Twelve weekly two-hour group sessions complemented individual sessions, allowing patients to learn new skills, increase their social support networks, and validate the changes that they were experiencing as a result of their health condition. The ENRICHD intervention improved psychosocial outcomes in the treatment group, including decreased depression and reduced social isolation.

CBT interventions have been found to be effective in decreasing the pain and discomfort of arthritis that can severely compromise functioning. Rhee et al. (2000) implemented a stress management intervention using CBT principles. Participants who completed the stress management course had lower levels of pain and depression as compared to those treated with usual rheumatological approaches. Similarly, Keefe et al. (1999) implemented a CBT approach that integrated spouses and partners into pain management protocols. This approach was also successful in helping patients cope with arthritis conditions.

*Behavioral Changes*

In addition to physical and mental health diagnoses, research on CBT interventions has provided evidence about their effectiveness in creating behavioral change. Lipsey, Landenberger, and Wilson (2007) performed a meta-analysis of studies of CBT programs for criminal offenders. A total of fifty-eight studies were part of the meta-analysis, and they included programs on anger control, substance abuse, poor social skills, and improving moral reasoning. The authors concluded that CBT approaches have a positive impact on reducing recidivism among those who have committed criminal offenses.

CBT approaches have also been used with children. Blonk et al. (1996) ran a CBT group for children who had difficulty interacting socially with others. Their goal was to help these children become more competent in their interactions with peers, teachers and other authority figures, and their parents. At the end of the twenty sessions, the children were rated by others and by themselves as being less anxious, having a greater number of friendships, and behaving in more socially appropriate ways.

### Community: Measuring Efficacy and Integration

*There is something about the places and people with whom we surround ourselves that matters to our lives.*
*—Robert (2002, 579)*

Although much of the research on various aspects of social work practice has evaluated individual functioning, other levels of measurement are appropriate to use when measuring the impact of interventions on larger systems. A research question may address whether a particular program can enhance an individual's ability to function effectively, yet there are also ways to measure the competence of a community overall. If neighborhoods and communities have adequate human and social capital, residents will have more opportunities for a better quality of life.

The effectiveness of CBT interventions on communities is more limited than that on individuals and/or families (Ohmer and Korr 2006; Thyer 2001). Ross (1996) analyzed community development in New York across a seventeen-year time span. Community-level interventions addressed local problems (e.g., crime and safety) and programs that promoted affordable home ownership. The findings showed that over time these programs provided greater opportunities for families to own homes and as a side effect increased the quality of education in their community.

Other research has focused on interventions to promote citizen participation in community affairs. Typically, the goal of this type of intervention is to promote efficacy and to increase social action and leadership. Ohmer (2007) studied volunteerism in four socioeconomically depressed communities. Her findings indicated that persons who were more involved in their communities reported higher levels of self-efficacy, which in turn led to a positive impact on collective efficacy and community functioning.

Similarly, Knight (1997) studied leadership development in an economically depressed rural community. Participants who completed the leadership training program reported greater social involvement in community leadership and community political and educational life. Using the same data, Threadgill (1998) examined the leadership behavior of black and white citizens. These findings indicated that black citizens had higher overall community involvement.

The community context can also indicate whether members will avail themselves of resources and supports. Gainey, Payne, and Kropf (2010) studied maltreatment of older adults and rates of refusal of formal services in three communities. Their results indicated that caregivers of persons with Alzheimer's disease who lived in the most disadvantaged neighborhoods were the most likely to refuse services. If care providers perceive that becoming involved with services will add to their stress, they might not accept services that could potentially support them in carrying out their caregiving responsibilities.

## Summary

This chapter examined various theoretical perspectives of how competence is operationalized and measured. Although many studies have looked at outcomes for individuals, competence can also be explored in families, groups, and communities. The associated research suggests that there are various methods of evaluating competence, and they share certain common features. As the first sentence of this book states, "This text focuses on the lifelong process of achieving competence in social functioning as an individual and in families, groups, and communities." This final chapter has arrived at ways of promoting critical thinking about how competence can be conceptualized and has evaluated how it can be used in social work practice.

A competency-based approach to social work education requires that students think critically about theory, practice, research, and policy. Accreditation standards in social work education require that courses focus on ten competency areas, including multiple practice behaviors. Throughout this book, theory and practice have been summarized to highlight theories that reflected approaches to understanding how individuals, families, groups, and communities function in competent, functional, and productive ways. This approach provides a solid foundation upon which emerging social work practitioners can build an understanding of social functioning and human behavior.

# References

Adamek, M. 2003. Late-life depression in nursing home residents: Social work opportunities to prevent, educate, and alleviate. In *Social work and health care in an aging society: Education, policy, practice and research*, ed. B. Berkman and L. Harootyan, 15–47. New York: Springer.

Adamek, M., and G. Y. Slater. 2009. Depression and anxiety. In *Handbook of psychosocial interventions with older adults: Evidence-based approaches*, ed. S. M. Cummings and N. P. Kropf, 146–81. New York: Routledge.

Alwahhabi, F. 2003. Anxiety symptoms and generalized anxiety disorder in the elderly: A review. *Harvard Review of Psychiatry* 11, no. 4:180–93.

American Association of Geriatric Psychiatry. 2005. *Geriatrics and mental health: The facts.* http://www.aagponline.org/prof.facts_mh.asp (accessed October 30, 2005).

Antoni, M., J. Lehman, K. Kilbourn, A. Boyers, J. Culver, S. Alferi, Yount, S.E., McGregor, B. A., Arena, P. L., Harris, S. D. Price, A. A., Carver, C. S 2001. Cognitive-behavioral stress management intervention decreases the prevalence of depression and enhances benefit finding among women under treatment for early-stage breast cancer. *Health Psychology* 20, no. 1:20–32.

Barton, W. 2002. Methodological square pegs and theoretical black holes. In *Resiliency: An integrated approach to practice, policy, and research*, ed. R. R. Greene, 95–113. Washington, DC: NASW Press.

Benard, B. 1993. Fostering resiliency in kids. *Educational Leadership* 51, no. 3:44–48.

Blonk, R. W. B., P. M. Prins, J. A. Sergeant, J. Ringrose, and A. G. Brinkman. 1996. Cognitive-behavioral group therapy for socially incompetent children: Short-term and maintenance effects with a clinical sample. *Journal of Clinical Child & Adolescent Psychology* 25:215–24.

Bronfenbrenner, U. 1979. *The ecology of human development: Experiments by nature and design.* Cambridge, MA: Harvard University Press.

Cozolino, L. J. 2002. *The neuroscience of psychotherapy: Building and rebuilding the human brain.* New York: Norton.

Cummings, S. M., and N. P. Kropf. 2009. Evidence based psychosocial approaches with older adults: An overview. In *Handbook of psychosocial interventions with older adults: Evidence-based approaches*, ed. S. M. Cummings and N. P. Kropf, 1–10. New York: Routledge.

ENRICHD Investigators. 2003. Effects of treating depression and low perceived social support on clinical events after myocardial infarction: The Enhancing Recovery in Coronary Heart Disease Patients (ENRICHD) randomized trial. *Journal of the American Medical Association* 289:3106–16.

_____. 2004a. Depression and late mortality after myocardial infarction in the Enhancing Recovery in Coronary Heart Disease (ENRICHD) study. *Psychosomatic Medicine* 66:466–74.

_____. 2004b. Psychosocial treatment within sex by ethnicity subgroups in the Enhancing Recovery in Coronary Heart Disease clinical trial. *Psychosomatic Medicine* 66:475–83.

Firestone, S. 1962. The scientific component in the casework field curriculum. In *Social casework in the fifties*, ed. C. Kasius, 311–25. New York: Family Service Association of America.

Fong, R., and R. R. Greene. 2009. Risk, resilience, and resettlement. In *Human behavior theory: A diversity framework*, ed. R. R. Greene and N. P. Kropf, 147–66. New Brunswick, NJ: Aldine Transaction.

Gainey, R. R., B. K. Payne, and N. P. Kropf. 2010. Neighborhood disadvantage and refusal of formal services among cases reported to adult protective services. *Journal of Evidence Based Social Work* 7:348–60.

Greene, R. R. 2005. Redefining social work for the new millennium: Setting a context. *Journal of Human Behavior and the Social Environment* 10, no. 4:37–54.

Greene, R. R., M. Armour, S. Hantman, S. Graham, and A. Sharabi. 2010. Conceptualizing a Holocaust survivorship model. *Journal of Human Behavior and the Social Environment* 20:423–39.

Gregory, V. L., Jr. (2010). Cognitive-behavioral therapy for depression in bipolar disorder: A meta-analysis. *Journal of Evidence-Based Social Work*, 7:269–79.

Grotberg, E. H. 1995, September. *The International Resilience Project: Research, application and policy.* Paper presented at the Symposio Internacional Stress e Violencia, Lisbon, Portugal.

_____. 1997. *A guide to promoting resilience in children: Strengthening the human spirit.* The Hague, The Netherlands: Bernard van Leer Foundation.

Jenson, J. M., and M. O. Howard. 2008. Evidence-based practice. In *Encyclopedia of social work*, ed. T. Mizrahi and L. E. Davis (Eds.-in-Chief), 20th ed., vol. 3, 158–65. Washington, DC: NASW Press.

Keefe, F. J., D. S. Caldwell, D. Baucom, A. Salley, and E. Robinson. 1999. Spouse-assisted coping skills training in the management of knee pain in osteoarthritis: Long-term follow-up results. *Arthritis Care and Research* 12, no. 2: 101–11.

Knight, E. 1997. A description of the effectiveness of Promoting Rural Opportunity in Mississippi (PRO-MISS) leadership program over time. *Masters Abstracts International* 36, no. 03:660. (UMI No. 1388114.)

Kowaz, A. M., and J. E. Marcia. 1991. Development and validation of a measure of Eriksonian industry. *Journal of Personality and Social Psychology* 60:390–97.

Kupfer, D. J., E. Frank, V. J. Grochocinski, P. R. Houck, and C. Brown. 2005. African-American participants in a bipolar registry: Clinical and treatment characteristics. *Bipolar Disorders* 7:82–88.

Laird, J. 1993. *Revisioning social work education: A social construction approach.* New York: Haworth Press.

Lipsey, M. W., N. A. Landenberger, and S. J. Wilson. 2007. *Effects of cognitive-behavioral programs for criminal offenders.* http://www.campbellcollaboration.org/library.php (accessed September 28, 2010).

Markstrom, C., V. Sabino, B. J. Turner, and R. Berman. 1997. The Psychosocial Inventory of Ego Strengths: Development and validation of a new Eriksonian measure. *Journal of Youth and Adolescence* 26:705–32.

Masten, A. S., and M. Reed. 2002. Resilience in development. In *Handbook of positive psychology*, ed. C. R. Snyder and S. J. Lopez, 74–88. New York: Oxford University Press.

Miles, M. B., and M. Huberman. 1994. *Qualitative data analysis*. Thousand Oaks, CA: Sage.

National Institute of Mental Health. 2006. *Older adults: Depression and suicide facts*. http://www.nimh.nih.gov/publicat/elderlydepsuicide.cfm (accessed March 20, 2006).

Newman, B. M., and P. R. Newman. 2005. *Development through life: A psychosocial approach*. 9th ed. Belmont, CA: Wadsworth/Thomson.

Ohmer, M. 2007. Citizen participation in neighborhood organizations and its relationship to volunteers' self- and collective efficacy and sense of community. *Social Work Research* 31, no. 2:109–20.

Ohmer, M. L., and W. S. Korr. 2006. The effectiveness of community practice interventions: A review of the literature. *Research on Social Work Practice* 16, no. 2:132–45.

Prosek, J. 2010. Mystery travelers eels. *National Geographic* 218, no. 3:122–37.

Rhee, S. H., J. G. Parker, K. L. Smarr, G. F. Petroski, J. C. Johnson, J. E. Hewett, Wright, G.1, Multon, K.D, • Walker, S.E. 2000. Stress management in rheumatoid arthritis: What is the underlying mechanism? *Arthritis Care and Research* 13:435–42.

Richardson, G. E. 2002. The metatheory of resilience and resiliency. *Journal of Clinical Psychology* 58:307–21.

Robert, S. A. 2002. Community context and aging: Future research issues. *Research on Aging* 24:579–99.

Ross, T. 1996. The impact of community organizing on East Brooklyn, 1978–1995. *Dissertation Abstracts International* 58, no. 01:276A. (UMI No. 9719819.)

Rubin, A., and E. R. Babbie. 2005. *Research methods for social work*. 5th ed. Belmont, CA: Wadsworth/Thomson Learning.

Schon, D. A. 1983. *The reflective practitioner: How professionals think in action*. New York: Basic Books.

Schore, A. N. 2002. The right brain as the neurobiological substratum of Freud's dynamic unconscious. In *The psychoanalytic century: Freud's legacy for the future*, ed. D. Scharff, 61–88. New York: Other Press.

Shoeb, M., H. Weinstein, and R. Mollica. 2007. The Harvard Trauma Questionnaire: Adapting a cross-cultural instrument for measuring torture, trauma and posttraumatic stress disorder in Iraqi refugees. *International Journal of Social Psychiatry* 53:447–63.

Sossou, M., C. Craig, H. Ogren, and M. Schnak. 2008. A qualitative study of resilience factors of Bosnian refugee women resettled in the southern United States. *Journal of Ethnic & Cultural Diversity in Social Work* 17: 365–85.

Threadgill, P. I. 1998. A comparison of the levels of leadership activities of the Promoting Rural Opportunity in Mississippi Leadership Development Program between graduates and nonparticipants. *Dissertation Abstracts International* 59, no. 8:2821A. (UMI No. 9903526.)

Thyer, B. A. 2001. Evidence-based approaches to community practice. In *Social work practice: Treating common clients problems*, ed. H. Briggs and K Corcoran, 54–65. Chicago, IL: Lyceum.

Tripodi, T., and M. Lalayants. 2008. Research: Overview. In *Encyclopedia of social work*, ed. T. Mizrahi and L. E. Davis (Eds.-in- Chief), 20th ed., vol. 3, 512–20. Washington, DC: NASW Press.

Tripodi, T., and M. Potocky-Tripodi. 2007. *International social work research: Issues and prospects*. New York: Oxford University Press.

Ungar, M., M. Brown, L. Liebenberg, R. Othman, W. M. Kwong, M. Armstrong, et al. 2007. Unique pathways to resilience across cultures. *Adolescence* 20:187–310.

Walsh, F. 1998a. Beliefs, spirituality, and transcendence: Keys to family resilience. In *Re-visioning family therapy: Race, culture, and gender in clinical practice*, ed. M. McGoldrick, 62–77. New York: Guilford Press.

_____. 1998b. *Strengthening family resilience*. New York: Guilford Press.

Weick, A. 1993. Reconstructing social work education. In *Revisioning social work education: A social construction approach*, ed. J. Laird, 11–30. New York: Haworth Press.

Werner, E., and R. Smith. 1982. *Vulnerable, but invincible: A longitudinal study of resilient children and youth*. New York: McGraw-Hill.

_____. 1992. *Overcoming the odds: High risk children from birth to adulthood*. Ithaca, NY: Cornell University Press.

Zlotnik, J. 2008. Research: History of research. In *Encyclopedia of social work*, ed. T. Mizrahi and L. E. Davis (Eds.-in-Chief), 20th ed., vol. 3, 521–26. Washington, DC: NASW Press.

# Appendix

### Practice Behaviors

The following summary provides a listing of various practice behaviors that are associated with the ten chapters of the book. These lists will assist students with anchoring concepts and principles about the theories within their experiences as social workers and human service practitioners. At the conclusion of each chapter, students will be able to:

### Chapter 1 Practice Behaviors

*Social Work's Mission: Fostering Competence*

Become knowledgeable about competency-based education
Define the core competencies of social work education
Delineate the social worker's role in enhancing social competence
Articulate why practitioners take a person-in-environment, multisystem approach to social work practice
Explain clients' help-seeking behaviors in culturally sensitive terms
Adopt a repertoire of questions to use to critique the theories presented in the text

### Chapter 2 Practice Behaviors

*Infancy and Toddlerhood: The Foundations of Competency*

Explain why infancy is a critical time in the formation of competence
Critique and compare the four extensions of Freudian theory as they pertain to development in infancy
Make suggestions about how the theoretical concepts in the chapter relate to the client–social worker relationship
Debate whether the concept of object relations is culture-bound
Apply intervention strategies that relate object relations theory to the case provided in the chapter

## Chapter 3 Practice Behaviors

*Early Life Stages and Identity Formation*

Use a case from their field experience (or the one provided at the end of the chapter) to explain why the self emerges as a result of human interaction, the use of language or symbols, and role taking

Analyze the case and describe how the client must overcome a period of role experimentation and alternative choices to become a competent adult

Apply the dual perspective to assess the client's current situation

Construct interventions to enhance client competence

## Chapter 4 Practice Behaviors

*Living in Systems: Work and Love*

Debate the merits of the general systems approach

Analyze a family case and describe both the functional and dysfunctional family characteristics

Describe how role allocation in the family contributes to family competence

Devise interventions that foster or enhance family competence

## Chapter 5 Practice Behaviors

*Meaning Making: Self-Affirmation and Transcendence*

Develop a critique about the benefits of using transpersonal theory in social work practice

Analyze the case at the end of the chapter to explain why competence is related to meaning-making

Use their methods texts to research the efficacy of the Rogerian approach and its effect on social work practice

Describe how they use concepts of spirituality in assessment

## Chapter 6 Practice Behaviors

*Cognitive and Behavioral Approaches*

Contrast how various theoretical perspectives view behavior and functioning

Distinguish between reinforcement in different behavioral theories

Determine how experiences and events compromise individuals' ability to function competently

## Chapter 7 Practice Behaviors

*Older Adults: Life Transitions, Stress, and Resilience*

Describe the merits of using a person–environment approach to social work with older adults and their families

Distinguish the life stage approach from the life course perspective

Use a case to assess an older adult's biopsychosocial spiritual functioning and evaluate client competence in living independently

Assess a case using Carter and McGoldrick's schema, determining examples of events that are horizontal and vertical stressors

Choose intervention strategies to lessen stress and foster competence

## Chapter 8 Practice Behaviors

*Effective Group Dynamics*

Distinguish various theoretical perspectives on group dynamics, leadership, and functioning

Debate the benefits of various theories in fostering competence

Use the case examples provided in the chapter to distinguish different uses of the social worker group facilitator

## Chapter 9 Practice Behaviors

*Communities and Neighborhoods*

Understand community from a physical and social environmental perspective

Determine how competence is defined within a community context

Articulate how collective competence can be observed within a community

## Chapter 10 Practice Behaviors

*Evaluating Effectiveness*

Articulate the connection between human behavior theory, and evaluation and research

Summarize various studies that support the theoretical perspectives on competence and human functioning presented within this book

Articulate studies that have been conducted at the individual and family, group, and community levels

# Index

For Product Safety Concerns and Information please contact our EU representative GPSR@taylorandfrancis.com Taylor & Francis Verlag GmbH, Kaufingerstraße 24, 80331 München, Germany

**Batch number: 08158437**

Printed by Printforce, the Netherlands